CARPETS of CHINA
and Its Border Regions

CARPETS of CHINA
and
Its Border Regions

By

Virginia Dulany Hyman

and

William C. C. Hu

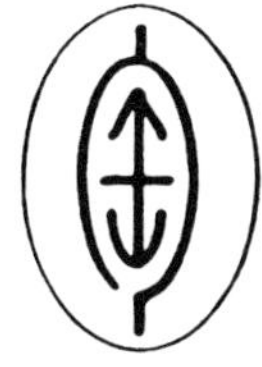

Ars Ceramica, Ltd.

Ann Arbor, Michigan
1982

Library of Congress Cataloging in Publication Data.

Hyman, Virginia Dulany. 1929-
     Carpets of China and Its Border Regions. by Virginia Dulany Hyman and William C. C. Hu.

     Bibliography: p.

1. Rugs, Chinese.   2. Rugs, Asia.   3. Rugs, Oriental
I. Hu, William Chao-chung.   II. Title.

NK 2882.A1H8'7   746.7

ISBN: 0-89344-030-2
LC: 82-82969

Manufactured in the United States of America

Ars Ceramica, Ltd.
P. O. Box 7500
Ann Arbor, Michigan 48107

TABLE OF CONTENTS

FOREWORD

The authors of this book, one of whom is my wife, have suggested that I assume an obligation totally unfamiliar to me -- that of writing a foreword to their work on Chinese domestic carpets. I presume that because I was exposed in part to their working endeavor which included their research, their discussions, their long hours of reconciling their different notions, they might have felt that I could make some small contribution by way of objectivity to their work. I must confess that not only does the art of China present the mystical and mysterious problems that generally are attributed to antiquity, but particularly with reference to the so-called Chinese domestic rugs, so little has been written that for literally centuries the entire tradition of Chinese domestic rugs has been virtually ignored. When I inquired of the authors why they undertook this monumental research task which may never give them fame or fortune, their answer was simply:

"that the previous endeavors had left the subject with many gaps, omissions, misconceptions and just plain errors. It would be intellectually dishonest to allow the subject to remain in its destitute state."

It was upon this premise that the authors launched what I perceive to be the most definitive discourse on the subject.

This book makes an attempt to present a historical survey of the history of the Chinese domestic rug. It illustrates some of the major themes running through centuries and highlights the distinctiveness of the Chinese tradition as applied to its domestic carpets.

It should be noted that when reference is made to rugs and/or carpets it is not necessarily intended to mean what our Western mind conceives as rugs -- floor coverings. Some were used exclusively for ceremonies, some for wall hangings, decorating the walls of tents, containers for transporting possessions, for saddle covers, etc. Basically they were utilitarian but, nevertheless, carried the Oriental tradition and symbolism that made up the everyday way of life and thinking process. They are decorative and boldly colored and reach out with their notions of naturalism and symbolism. The walk that my wife, Virginia Dulany Hyman, and William Hu, have taken through the historical process examining the roots of Chinese rugs, has been very exciting and informative and combines a blend of creative scholarship with appreciation and an in-depth understanding of the Oriental mind and culture. The experience of sharing this with them has given me a new respect and appreciation for the Chinese culture and I trust the reader will find the same rewarding and enriching experience that I have. It has been a wonderful experience to listen and share the expertise and knowledge coming from the writers as they speak of the Chinese historical roots on Chinese domestic carpets and the historical embryo from which they came.

J. Leonard Hyman
Hyman, Gurwin, Nachman, Friedman & Winkelman

Southfield, Michigan, 1982

ACKNOWLEDGMENTS

In producing this book the cooperation and devotion of many individuals and institutions were needed.

We are greatly indebted to the following institutions: The University of Michigan, Ann Arbor; Cornell University, Ithaca; Harvard University, Cambridge; University of Hawaii, Honolulu; New York Public Library, New York City; University of California, Berkeley; UCLA, Los Angeles; and The National Palace Museum, Peking.

We were extremely fortunate to have the use of the extensive library on Oriental Art of the Sung-yin-lu Collection.

We acknowledge the professional skills of the photographers, Rogér of Birmingham and Andy Oberdick.

We hope all those who aided us along the way will accept our apology, should specific mention inadvertently have been omitted. We owe thanks to everyone who gave us cooperation and support in the course of a difficult and lengthy undertaking, but to no one more than Marjorie E. Uren for her untiring efforts in seeing through all stages of the manuscript until we finished.

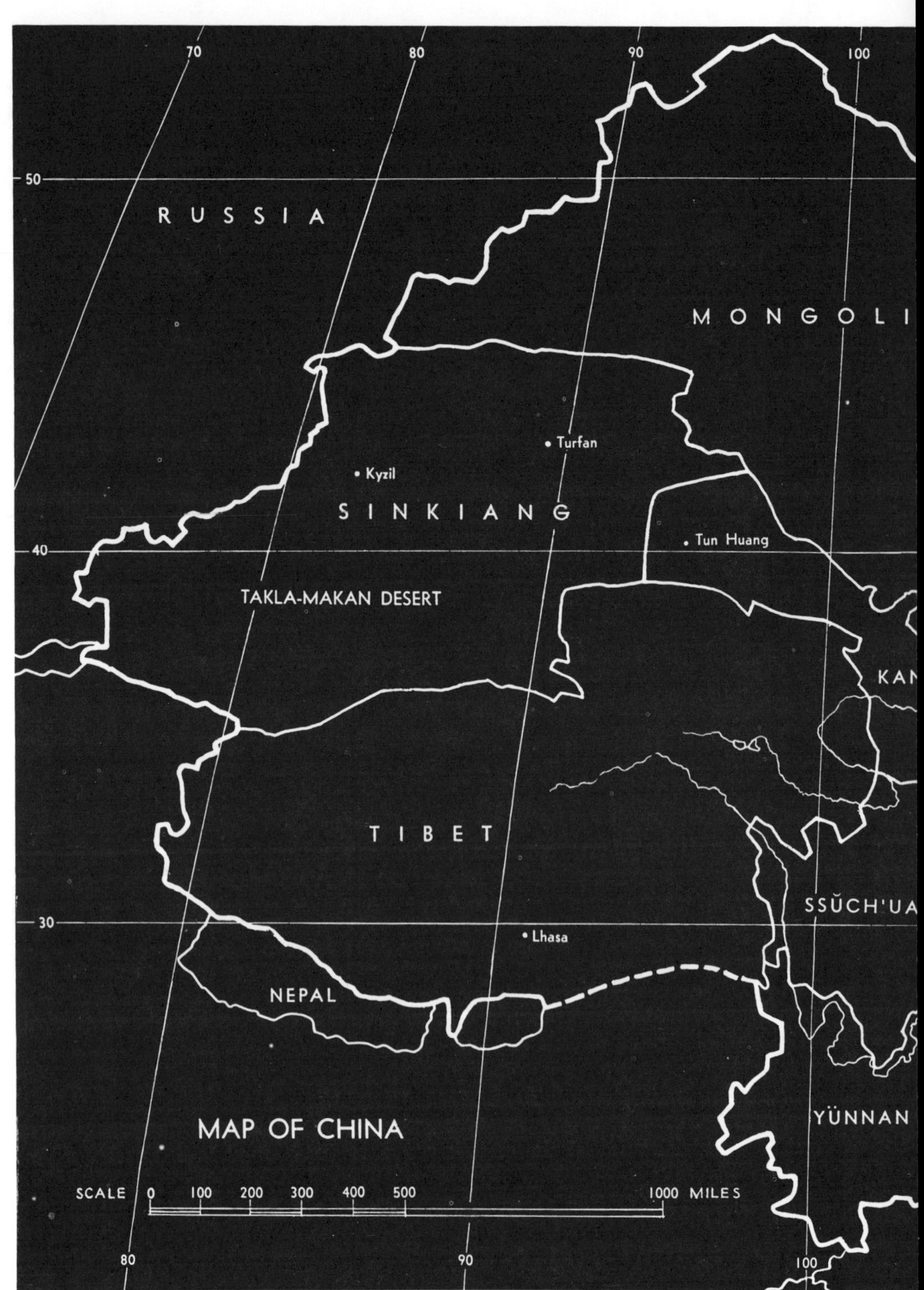
RUSSIA
MONGOLI
Turfan
Kyzil
SINKIANG
Tun Huang
40
TAKLA-MAKAN DESERT
KAN
TIBET
SSŬCH'UA
30
Lhasa
NEPAL
MAP OF CHINA
YÜNNAN
SCALE 0 100 200 300 400 500 1000 MILES
50
70 80 90 100
80 90 100

110
120
130
140
50
40
30
120
130
HOPEI
Ta-t'ung
Peking
I-chou
Wu T'ai Shan
Ting-chou
SHANSI
T'aiyüanfu
Ch'ing-ping-hsien
An-yang
Weihuifu
SHANTUNG
Sianfu
Lo-yang
Chêngchow
SHENSI
HONAN
ng-ho
g Hsien
Yang-tzŭ-chiang

A NOTE ON CHINESE PRONUNCIATION

This book uses the standard Wade-Giles system for the transliteration of Chinese sounds into English. The lettres of the alphabet according to this sytem sound as follows:

Vowels

a	*as in father*
ai	*like the i in ice*
ao	*like the ow in cow*
e	*like the u in up (except after i or y)*
i	*like the letter e (as in east)*
ih	*like the ir fir*
o	*as in old; but sometimes like o in soft*
ou	*like o in occur*
ŭ	*like the English oo; but very short after ss or tz*

Consonants

Aspirated consonants (i.e., those marked by a sharp expiration of air) are followed by an apostrophe, and generally resemble their English equivalents. Consonants not aspirated roughly resemble the corresponding voiced sounds in English, as follows:

ch'	*as in church*
ch	*like j*
k'	*as in kite*
k	*like the g in go*
p'	*as in pear*
p	*like b*
t'	*as in to*
t	*like the d in dog*
ts' & tz'	*like ts in hits*
ts & tz	*like dz*
Also: *hs*	*similar to the English sh*
j	*resembles English r; jen sounds something like run*
ss	*not distiguished from s*

Other consonants generally resemble their English equivalents.

Chinese place names follow the postal spelling established by the 1919 *Postal Atlas of China*. For example: Pei-ching is Peking; Kuang-chou is Canton; Fu-chien is Fukien, etc.

As with most systems of transliteration from one language into another, the equivalents are approximate, and only partially correspond to the actual Chinese sounds. Moreover, the same combination of English lettres may indicate several distinct sounds in the original Chinese.

HISTORY

Whenever Oriental rugs are discussed in the West, current West-European and American tastes tend to favour the Persian rug. The figurative decorated rugs, made in the sixteenth century in the workshops of Kashan and Tabriz have been admired for many decades while Turkish rugs have stood in the shadow and Chinese rugs have been almost totally ignored.

Artistically, the design, colour and overall concept in Chinese rugs and carpets are both powerful and subtle, reflecting a long and matured tradition of aesthetic expression. Their delicacy of colouration and balanced composition, although different from Near Eastern Islamic rugs, nevertheless, create a tremendous impact equal to other rugs.

Inasmuch as traditional Chinese rugs were not common place in the West, they were known and have appeared in personal property inventories as early as the seventeenth century. Among the possessions of Henry Howard, Earl of Northampton, who died in 1614, is "a China carpet of several colours, the ground white and weaved in with antiques of several colours, lined with watchett taffeta."[1] In the drawing room of the Countess of Warwick, about 1657, there were two little China carpets with coloured silks and gold.[2]

Aside from scattered inventories, it becomes evident that Chinese rugs were uncommon in the West, although examples of various other Chinese arts were very much the trapping of luxury and high taste. By the late eighteenth century, Lord George Macartney was sent to China in an attempt to broaden England's access to trade with China. The taste for things uniquely Chinese began to develop, resulting in a craze and vogue called "Chinoiserie". Not only in art and decoration was the impact of Chinoiserie felt, but also in literature, drama, and philosophy as reflected in the works of Leibnitz, Voltaire, Quesnay, Du Halde and Thomas Percy.

Leibnitz, the first European philosopher to recognize the great intellectual importance of China for the development of the West, declared in 1687 that he was immersed in the work of Confucius, and in 1697 published his *Novissima Sinica* in which he advocated an interchange of civilization between China and Europe. Later Voltaire converted Confucius into an eighteenth century rationalist and transformed China into a Gallic Utopia.

Francois Quesnay, whom his pupils dubbed "the Confucius of Europe", concocted a system of political economy after the Chinese pattern. In his *Le Despotisme de la Chine*, 1767, he considered China an examplar as "a state founded on science and the natural law, whose concrete development it represents."

Du Halde's encyclopaedic compilation, *Description geographique, historique, . . . de l'empire de la Chine*, Paris, 1735, created a vision of China which shone so brightly in the eyes of European artists, poets, architects and philosophers, that it brought the vogue and cult of things Chinese to a fever pitch.

At the height of Chinoiserie, Thomas Percy made serious attempts to study Chinese literature and translated a long episodic Chinese novel, *Hau Kiou Choaan* [Hao-chiao chüan]. He also translated a thirteenth Chinese drama [Chao-shih ku-erh] which he entitled "Little Orphan of the House of Chao".

By the mid-eighteenth century the Chinese rage had influenced England so completely that James Cawthorne, the satirist, lapsed into into reproachful and almost plangent terms to describe the abjectness of the surrender:

> *Of late, 'tis true, quite sick of Rome and Greece,*
> *We fetch our models from the wise Chinese,*
> *European artists are too cool and chaste,*
> *For Mand'rin only is the man of taste.*[3]

By the nineteenth century there was more considerable interest in Chinese art among cultivated and sophisticated Europeans. George IV has usually been given credit for the revival of Chinoiserie in late Georgian England. At Carlton House he commissioned a room which must be among the most exquisite examples of Chinoiserie decoration ever created, and in the pavilion at Brighton, he left a monument to the Regency

Plate I
Ladies seated on a rug while doing embroidery. The rug has a wide reddish outer border with a floral design. The central panel of the rug is decorated with five floral medallions -- each medallion framed by the same floral design as corners. A Sung painting by Chou Fang.

vogue for exoticism at its most feverish. In the music room at the north end of the pavilion, the floor was covered with a blue Axminster carpet which was decorated with dragons, serpents and vast flowers. Throughout the pavilion, every corner was crowded with a profusion of objects of Chinese virtu. In Sweden, the Chinese Pavilion at Dröttningholm, built first in 1753 and rebuilt a decade later, is one of the most remarkable "Chinoiseries" anywhere in the North of Europe. It is an extremely charming blend of the genuinely Chinese decor and Swedish Rococo, with touches of classicism, of French-inspired chinoiserie and 'Chinese' furnishings based on contemporary English prints.

Despite this earlier fascination with things Chinese, it was not until the closing of the nineteenth century that authentic Chinese rugs first began to be appreciated by the Western world. There were several events which stimulated the demand for Chinese rugs to unprecedented activity and vogue and which also resulted in the evolution of the Chinese rug.

German exporters were the first to see the value in Chinese rugs which were sent to Europe for trade. The instant acclaim which was accorded these rugs justified their efforts. One of the first exhibitions of Chinese carpets in the West is referred to by Stephen W. Bushell who describes a silk carpet sent from China to the International Inventions Exhibition in 1885. The eleven foot long carpet with an all-over floral design was described as having a blue ground with a red-orange border. Then, in 1903, at the St. Louis International Exposition, Chinese rugs were awarded First Prize.

Interest in Chinese rugs took hold in England and the United States as collectors such as H. O. Havemeyer started their collections during the 1890's.[4] Writers such as John Mumford[5] started to write about Chinese carpets and suggested that this interest had been stimulated by the architect Stanford White, who used them to decorate the William C. Whitney house. These rugs arouse considerable enthusiasm both at auction and retail sales, resulting in enormous prices even for small pieces. Tiffany & Co. issued several catalogues[6] which devoted large portions to Chinese rugs. In 1916 an auction of the collection of Frank Moore and J. K. Mumford[7] offered three hundred pieces. All these events ushered in an intense enthusiasm for Chinese rugs.

The greatest impetus to the Chinese rug and carpet trade, however, came from the closing of the Near Eastern sources of supply during and immediately following World War I. With much of the Middle East embroiled in conflict, the interruption of the flow of Turkish and Persian rugs opened a wider market for Chinese products. From the beginning of World War I to the end of the war, the number of Chinese rugs exported more than doubled, with the figures continuing to escalate dramatically throughout the 1920's.

The Chinese rug dealers, attempting to meet the sudden demand for their products, undertook great contracts which they had difficulty in fulfilling.

It is most unfortunate that at the time of the peak of the Western public's interest in and exposure to Chinese rugs, what came onto the vast market were products made to meet tastes of Western export markets. These rugs were intended as trade items and were chiefly products of large factories owned and operated by the firms of such foreigners as Fette, Nichol, Shoemaker, and E. A. Punnett, with Nichol's Manchu Rug Palace being the largest. These factories were carefully supervised by the foreign exporters who imposed their designs and tastes to create their concept of an exotic "Chinese" rug.

Although these rugs were made in China, by Chinese workers with disjointed fragments of Chinese designs, they were not traditional creations but a bland mixture of nineteenth and twentieth century Chinoiserie taste, empty and quite foreign to the Chinese artistic tradition and development. Unfortunately, these rugs have become known and associated as "Chinese", Peking or Tientsin rugs to the general public.

Fortunately however, a small body of earlier seventeenth, eighteenth and early nineteenth century traditional Chinese rugs, woven as indigenous works, have found their way into museums and private collections in the West. These rugs were mainly used in palaces and large estates for court ceremonies and on festive and religious occasions by both the literati and the peerage. Set along side the trade items, they become most startling in comparison and quite obviously superior in all aspects.

Early Finds

Although Chinese rugs have enjoyed much popularity, it seems ironic that not much has been written in depth about the subject. Of the books published on the general subject of Oriental rugs, Chinese rugs are either totally ignored or else treated with a pedestrian and casual overview. Earlier writers tend to dismiss Chinese rugs as mainly late-comers, claiming that there are none earlier than the nineteenth century and that the art of rug and carpet weaving was imported from the Near East. However, more recently as a result of archaeological discoveries and studies, Chinese rugs have been dated earlier. Many scholars and writers now accept the fact that knotted pile rugs were woven and used extensively in China in the seventh and eighth centuries A.D. More recent excavations in China of sites dating to the Han dynasty (206 B. C.-220 A. D.)[8] has produced archaeological fragments indicating a high technological development of dyeing and weaving suggesting even an earlier development. In addition mention in Chinese literature suggests the use of rugs could be traced to even earlier periods.

Moreover, a number of archaeological examples of carpets that predate anything similar from the Middle East, were discovered in what was traditional Chinese territory or areas culturally influenced by China. This includes what now constitutes the People's Republic of China, Sinkiang (which includes Eastern or Chinese Turkestan), Inner and Outer Mongolia (including parts of Southern Siberia), and Tibet. Despite these early archaeological discoveries, relatively little scholarly attention has been accorded to the subject of Chinese rugs.

The oldest pile rug was discovered in 1949 by the Russian archaeologist Sergei I. Rudenko of the mounds in the Pazyryk region in the Altai mountains near the present Russian frontier with Mongolia and China. These finds have been arbitrarily assigned by the Russians as the fourth and fifth century B. C.

Among the forty gravesite finds, the one which caused the most dispute at the time it was discovered (and remains the subject of controversy after more than thirty years) is what is commonly known as the Pazyryk carpet found in Kurgan V.

Kurgans are mounds which may be 20 metres high and 250 metres in circumference raised over the graves of Scythian chieftains. The graves themselves are dug deep into the ground and supported by wooden structures.

Despite the passage of approximately 2200 years the excellent state of preservation of the textiles found in the Kurgans was aided by grave robbers. Their breaking into these mounds enabled water to seep into the interior of the tomb where it froze into a preservative layer which in turn was protected by an insulation of stone slabs laid over the graves thus causing a state of permafrost. The seepage of water into the opened Tomb chamber, located in the layer of permafrost, caused the items to be frozen into protective ice until their discovery.

In Kurgan V, was found a woolen knotted pile carpet used as a saddle-cover, measuring 200 x 183 centimetres in size; with a composition of equestrian figures, elks, and lion-griffons. This rug is woven in Ghiordes knots at a density of 3,600 knots per square decimetre. A band with a row of four-rayed stars with a cross-shaped ornament of four flowers with a square in the centre divides the equestrian figures and the elks. The centre field consists of four-rayed stars with a cross-shaped ornament of four flowers with a square in the centre enclosed in square frames.

The discoverer, Rudenko considered this carpet to have been woven in the Achaemenid period (ca. 550 - 331 B. C.) and exported to the Altai region. Others have expressed various opinions as to other areas of Central Asia, while some scholars believe that it could not have been made in an area uninfluenced by an urban culture. The technique and decoration are rich and sophisticated which has led some scholars to believe that it could not have been made by equestrian, nomadic Turkish tribes like the peoples of the Steppes.

This argument ignores the long and unbroken tradition of carpet weaving practiced by the Turkish peoples of the Steppes in an area stretching from Mongolia and Eastern Turkestan westward to Central Asia.

Information derived from contemporary Chinese sources confirms that the tribes living to the East of the Altai were the Huns and Wu-huan, who worshipped the spirits and made sacrifice to Heaven, Earth, Sun, Moon and Stars, and their ancestors.[9] In addition, according to the *Hou-Han Shu*, Annals of the Latter Han dynasty, the Wu-huan women were capable of weaving woolen carpets called Lo-ho.[10] The Wu-huan tribe is also known as Tung-hu, Eastern barbarians, Su-shên, and Hsiu-hsun or commonly called Scythians.

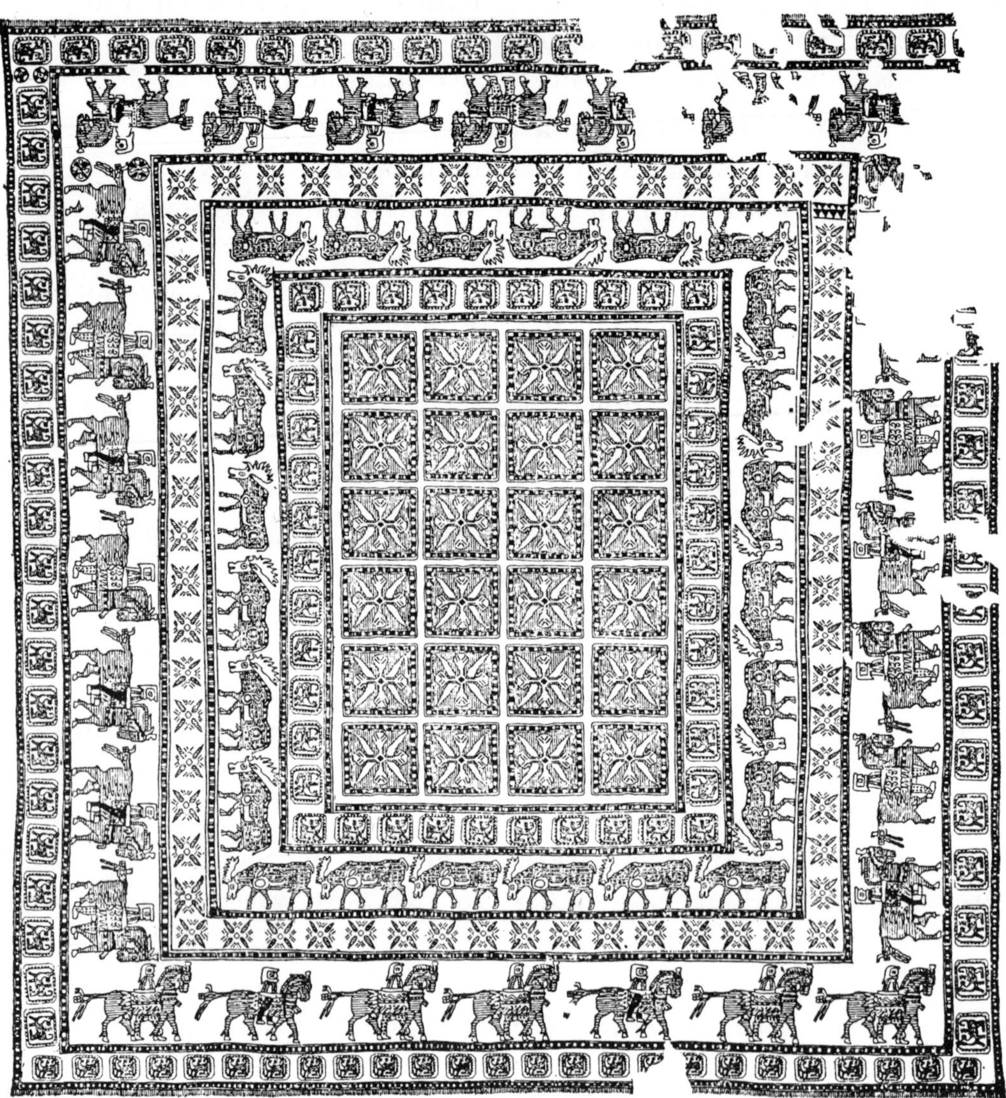

Figure 1
Drawing of the carpet found in Kurgan V in the Pazyryk Valley, Siberia

A number of references are made relating to Han dynasty trade with the Turkish peoples residing in these areas. The historian Pan Ku (32 - 92 A. D.), in several of his lettres to his brother General Pan Chao in the Western Regions, informs us that a certain Mr. Tou, presumably an imperial in-law, bought various kinds of luxuries from that area. One lettre noted that Mr. Tou had once sent there a sum of 800,000 cash with which more than ten rugs were purchased.[11] The large sum paid leads us to believe that these were knotted pile rugs.

The carpet fragments discovered by Sir Aurel Stein between 1906 and 1908 at Lou-lan, Tun-huang, Lop Nor and Niya.[12] showed that this area of Eastern Turkestan was an important weaving centre by at least the second or third century A. D. Niya was a settlement abandoned by the Chinese during the Latter Han dynasty (25 - 220 A. D.).[13] A great number of Chinese items were discovered in all of these sites. In the case of Tun-huang, a large number of written documents were uncovered. These finds indicate that there were social and cultural interchange as well as trading intercourse, between the peoples of these areas and China.

From 1910 to 1920 the excavations of Noin-ula in North Mongolia by the Russian archaeologist Colonel P. Koslov and studied by Sueji Umehara, brought out a woolen carpet called *t'a-têng*, with a bull's head design. These discoveries were dated as first century B. C. Moreover, a large number of items either from China or with Chinese influenced designs were excavated. Again, proof of contacts with China is provided.

We may conclude that there is little evidence to suppose that the Pazyryk carpet was a totally independent and unique work of art which had been imported from elsewhere. There is ample evidence to show that the Pazyryk carpet was woven locally by the peoples of the Steppes.

The Pazyryk Carpet

In the design of the Pazyryk carpet, the outer major border contains horsemen, both mounted and on foot, marching in single file. The tails of the horse are plaited and knotted and their manes trimmed as a sign of mourning. This is similar to depictions on funerary tiles of the Ch'in and Han periods.

Horsemen of North China in early times placed a felt blanket, with tassels on the edges, on the horse's back which absorbs the animal's sweat. Saddle cloths with hanging ornaments have been, and still are, in common use among many Turkish tribes. The Chinese also followed this practice.

The central design of four-rayed stars with a cross-shaped ornament of four flowers with a square in the centre and enclosed in square frames, is divided in a similar manner to those found on later Seljuk carpets; each square cuts the star motif into four and each quarter square contains three diagonal foliated elements. There is little doubt that the Pazyryk carpet, with its division into four by six squares represents the source of the main design composition of carpets woven by the Turkoman tribes such as the Oghuz. The same motif within the square could well be the basis for the octagonal Seljuk patterns and the "Gül" in modern Turkoman carpets. Similarly the carpets woven in Khotan and Kashgar in Eastern Turkestan contain the same basic division of the field as in the Pazyryk carpet. With slight changes the "Khotan gül" is similar to that of the Pazyryk carpet. Later, Chinese artists during the T'ang dynasty (618 - 907 A. D.) also used variations of the same design on the walls of the Lin-tê salon in the Royal Palace of Ch'ang-an in Shansi Province.

An even more convincing evidence that the Pazyryk carpet should be attributed to local weavers in Eastern Turkestan and not an Iranian import is in the design of the elk. The elk, *Alcas machlis*, a species of the reindeer, is native to Inner Asia and is found neither in Iran nor the Near East. These are the traditional designs of the area of Eastern Turkestan and Mongolia. The Pazyryk carpet contains motifs which could be found in many variations throughout their historical development within Turkish and Hun art and they all bear a strong resemblence to their proto-types. Many of the elements found on the Pazyryk carpet can be traced through later Turkish rugs.

In Kurgan II at Bash-Adar, Pazyryk found a piece of another woolen pile carpet, only small tatters of which survived, which was also used as a saddle cover. In spite of the small size of the piece, it was possible to establish that this carpet was very well woven with an average of 7,000 knots per decimetre, almost double that of the pile carpet from Kurgan V. Here it was discovered that another technique of knotting was utilized which is the Sennah knot or the so-called one and a half knot. It is important to note that the Sennah knot is open to the left, similar to that knotting practiced by the Chinese weavers. Although this small fragment is not as well known as the Pazyryk carpet, nevertheless, within the same vicinity and approximately within the same time period both the Ghiordes and Sennah knots have been found. Moreover, both flat-weaves and felt carpets and wall-hangings with appliques have also been discovered in these burial mounds. With this treasure-house of various weaves, it becomes evident that although there may have been an evolution and advancement of technique and technology in rug-making, all these different kinds of rugs could exist simultaneously according to their usage and purpose. Although one form of carpet making may have evolved from another technique, it did not necessarily totally eliminate its antecedent.

The art of the carpet developed as a functional necessity within the lives of the Turkic tribes of the Steppes and its scheme of decorative elements became the proto-type of a style which reflects their culture. The star motif truly reflected their religious beliefs. Although the rugs of the various Turkish communities in Eastern and Western Turkestan may be separated by considerable distances, they demonstrate a parallel design composition marked both by the division of the field into squares and by the filling of those squares with their various motifs. These are the focal points of the Turkish carpet and, indeed, of all Turkish decorative art.

Several scholars including Uhlemann[14] and Kurt Erdmann[15] have suggested that East Turkestan is the home of carpet weaving and as they have pointed out it is most unlikely that the carpet weaving came from Iran and the Near East. In looking at the migration of the Turks, we find that they came out of North China travelling westward into Central Asia. It should be noted that the Iranian nomads usually herded cattle, whose hair was unsuitable for carpet making. Although various other materials have been used to make carpets, undoubtedly sheep's wool, which has been used primarily throughout the history of carpet making, is the most suitable material.

Another important point is that Iranian geographers of the tenth century, Ibn Hudazbih, Istakhri, Al-Mukaddasi include among the products of the various regions and cities of Iran, a list of types of woven fabrics, identifying them by their local names. It is perhaps significant that while they record many textiles, they do not mention carpets. On the other hand, there are no Persian carpets surviving from the period before the sixteenth century.

The earliest knotted pile carpets from the Near East are the Seljuk carpets dating from approximately the twelfth or thirteenth century. In the eleventh century A. D., the Turkish Seljuks broke westward out of Eastern or Chinese Turkestan.

In 1037, they occupied eastern Persia and marched westward conquering the rest of Persia, Mesopotamia, Syria and Asia Minor. The Seljuks and their followers, the Atabegs (officers), established many local dynasties and became great patrons of the arts and crafts. The arabesque, one of the most characteristic ornaments of Islamic art, was fully developed in the Seljuk era. In Asia Minor, the Seljuks established, in the thirteenth century, the Kingdom of Rum. In their capitol, Konya, they erected splendid palaces and mosques, many of which are still standing. The Seljuk rulers established many looms for weaving of fine silks and for the manufacture of woolen carpets. Marco Polo who visited Asia Minor in 1270 reported that the finest and most beautiful carpets in the world were made in the Seljuk empire. Seljuk carpets were found in the mosque of Ala ad-Din in Konya, the major mosque of a Seljuk residence, built in 1219-1220, and another group of carpets was discovered later in the mosque at Beyshehir.

The decoration of these carpets is almost entirely geometrical consisting of all-over patterns of small octagons, lozenge-diapers, star-motifs, small oval medallions and interlacing combined with hooked motifs. The dominant motifs are almost always in lighter tones of dark blue, red or dark red ground of the central field.

The Pazyryk carpet employed curvilinear design techniques. However, all other known Near Eastern carpets made before 1500 A. D. are rectilinear. Only in the early sixteenth century do we see a sudden explosion of floral designs emanating from the Persian court manufactories. This could be seen as the phase of artistic and technological maturing from geometric and rectilinear designs to a more artistic flow into curvilinear design.

It can easily be seen that Seljuk carpets should stem as direct descendants of the Turfan fragments discovered by Sir Aurel Stein and Albert von Le Coq.[16] Since the Seljuks broke westward from East Turkestan and presumably brought carpet knotting with them, spreading this technique widely in Asia Minor, it becomes important to examine Eastern or Chinese Turkestan and her inhabitants.

Everything we know supports the idea that the knotted pile carpet was introduced into Islamic art and culture with and by the Turkish Seljuks. The history of the knotted pile carpet is closely connected with that of the Turks. It is conceivable that they invented the technique -- it is certain that they developed it and brought it out of Eastern or Chinese Turkestan westward to the Near East.

In Western Asia the Oriental carpet retained its original Turkish character until the beginning of the sixteenth century. The formation of the Safavid national state brought about the beginning of the separate development of the Persian carpet, although earlier traces can still be seen.

This view of the knotted pile carpet, as a specifically Turkish form of art, is based upon the excavations and studies of the last thirty or more years. Today the hypothesis is widely accepted that the history of the Oriental carpet began with the Turkish carpet and that its development evolved from the Turkish carpet tradition.

When we begin to study carpets from this point of view, many new problems come into focus which concern the development and transmigration of the Turkish peoples and the Turkish carpet. In part we can blame the present gap in our knowledge on early misconceptions, but these are only additional causes which apply to Turkish art in general.

In order to study the early Turkish carpets, we must turn to the areas of Eastern or Chinese Turkestan. Here in this isolated setting, early elements could still be found and studied.

East Turkestan and the Silk Route

Eastern or Chinese Turkestan, known as Hsi-yü in early Chinese documents, lies in the heart of Central Asia. Almost the whole region, stretching 1,000 km north to south and over 1,800 km east to west, is included in the Tarim Basin, named for its chief and vital river. This high desert plain, crossed by shifting sands, is bounded on the north by the T'ien-shan range, on the west by the Pamirs and on the south by the K'un-lun and Astingagh mountains. These are all steep mountain chains with peaks of 7,000 to 8,500 metres. All the streams rising in these mountains dry up in the sand of the great desert of Takla Makan; the Tarim after a course of 2,000 km is lost in the marshes of the land lock-ed Lop Nor. The extremely dry climate with violent changes of temperature only permits settlement in oases at the sides of streams on the edge of the uninhabitable desert. There irrigation brings good yields of grains, fruits, vegetables and cotton. A narrow belt of grass land along the foot of the mountains provides an environment for nomad economy. The populations of this enormous area consists of Eastern Turks, Kirghiz and Kazak tribes, as well as some Mongols and Chinese. The excellent wool from their flocks is the basis of the carpet production carried on in the workshops of the oases.

The old caravan trails of the "Silk Route" divided in west Turfan into two, one skirting the desert basin to the north and the other to the south. These trails link the distant oases with each other and join again in Kashgar on the western edge of the basin. This division into two routes arose because of the obstruction of the Takla Makan desert which made it necessary for the travellers to keep to the routes on the northern side of the Koulkum mountains or that on the south side of the T'ien-shan mountain chain. The "Silk Route" starts in Hsi-an, proceeds to Wu-wei and then to Tun-huang, were it is divided into two routes. The southern route follows the path from Tun-huang, in present-day Kansu, to Lou-lan, the Shan-shan kingdom to the northeast of Lop Nor, through Koten, So-sh'ê, past the Belaturgh mountains (Pamirs) to Ta-yüeh-shih, in the central part of Amu-Darya river basin in modern Afghanistan to An-hsi in modern Iran, continuing west to reach T'iao-chih in modern Iraq and proceeding to Ta-ch'in, Syria and the Roman Empire. The Northern route went from Tun-huang to Ch'ê-shih and Wang-ting, in modern Turfan to Kuei-t'zu, modern Kucha, Su-lê, modern Kashgar, to Ferghana.

In the period of over a thousand years from the Han (206 B. C. - 220 A. D.) to the T'ang (618 - 906 A. D.) dynasty, these were the major routes used to transport silk products to the west. Subsequently, Western historians called it the "Silk Road".

The name "Silk Road" is not Chinese and has never been used in China. Professor Baron von Richthofen was probably the inventor of this descriptive name. In his famous work on China, he speaks of "die

Plate II
Two sections of a handscroll representing the Four-grey heads of the
early Han period seated on rugs. Attributed to the artist Sun Wei.

Seidenstrasse", and, on a map, of "die Seidenstrasse des Marinus". In 1910 Professor Albert Herrmann published an extremely valuable work entitled *Die Alten Seidenstrassen Zwischen China und Syrien*. Henceforth the term became popular in the West.

The oases were often landmarks in the movements of people and civilizations, even of armies and traders, and their importance was emphasized by the "Silk Road" which in the age of the Caesars and the Han Emperors linked the Chinese Empire with the Roman Empire.

Government policy encouraged foreign trade by the Imperial Secretary during Han times. This is reflected in an interesting passage from the *Yên-t'ieh lun* or Discourses on Salt and Iron:

"Ju Han gold and other significant articles of tribute are means of inveigling foreign countries and snaring the treasures of the Ch'iang and Hu (i.e. Hsiung-nu). Thus a piece of Chinese plain silk can be exchanged with the Hsiung-nu for articles worth several pieces of gold and thereby reduce the resources of our enemy. Mules, donkeys and camels enter the frontier in unbroken lines; horses, dapples, bays and prancing mounts, come into our possession. The furs of sables, marmots, foxes and badgers, coloured rugs and decorated carpets fill the Imperial treasury, while jade and auspicious stones, corals and crystals, become national treasures. That is to say, foreign products keep flowing in, while our wealth is not dissipated. Novelties flowing in, the government has plenty. National wealth not being dispersed abroad, the people enjoy abundance."[17]

The importance of this passage is that it reveals a contemporary Chinese conception of Sino-barbarian economic intercourse in purely economic terms and it gives a preliminary account of the various kinds of foreign commodities imported to Han China.

It was sometimes a practice of the Han Emperors to send envoys abroad with gold and silk to acquire precious articles. This practice was also followed by the aristocrats. "During the reign of Emperor Chang, for example, when Li Hsün served as the Deputy Chiao-wei of the Western Regions, the barbarian hostage princes, as well as merchants, had several times presented him as gifts, slaves, Ferghana horses, gold, silver, incenses and carpets."[18] Although Li refused to accept any of these gifts because of his moral principle and integrity, the example nevertheless, seems to indicate that it must have been a well-established custom for the barbarians to present such treasures to the Chinese officials who had direct control over them.[19]

Another instance can be cited to illustrate the point. Ch'ên Shan was appointed Governor of Liao-tung in Emperor An's time (107 -125 A. D.) when the Northern Hsiung-nu were active in that region. Since Ch'en treated these barbarians reasonably, they were grateful to him and presented their precious articles to him before they migrated to other places.[20] It can be seen that Sino-barbarian trade in early imperial China was largely confined to the exchange of luxuries. This was especially the case with trade over the "Silk Road" and the Western Regions. Of these luxuries, coloured rugs and decorated carpets from the Western Regions, or Eastern or Chinese Turkestan are most distinguished.

The extremely high prices and regard for these rugs and carpets have already been touched upon previously with the citation of the imperial in-law, Mr. Tou, paying 800,000 cash for more than ten rugs.

The strong Imperial interest in foreign rarities had its repercussions in the Han high society. Following the Emperor's and the Royal family's example, officials and aristocrats also began to search for similar exotic luxuries.

In another lettre of Pan Ku to his brother Pan Ch'ao in the Western Regions, Pan Ku notifies him of the same Mr. Tou forwarding 700 pieces of coloured silk fabrics and 300 pieces of plain white silk to buy other luxuries from the Western Regions.

Inasmuch as many of these exotic goods were in reality luxuries that added nothing to the wealth of the empire economically, nevertheless, they were enjoyed by the Emperor. Quite a number of the literati petitioned the ruler claiming that these luxuries were useless things. In the *Yen-t'ieh lun*, we find such criticism:

" . . . Sable and marmot furs, wool and felt goods, do not add substance to silk. Beautiful jades and corals come from Mount K'un, pearls and ivory are produced in Kuei-Lin. These places are more than ten thousand *li* distant from Han. Calculating the labour for the farming and silk raising and the costs in material and capital, it will be found that one article of foreign import costs a price one hundred times its value, and for one handful, ten thousand weight of grain are paid. As the rulers take delight in novelties, extravagant clothing is adopted among the masses. As the rulers treasure the goods from distant lands, wealth flows outward. Therefore a true king does not value useless things, so to set an example of thrift to his subjects; does not love exotic articles so to enrich his country."[21]

The viewpoint of the Imperial Government and the Emperor is illustrated in an incident during the Three Kingdoms period. In 221 A. D., Emperor Wên of Wei sent an envoy to the Wu, the southern kingdom that had an active trade with and tribute from the peoples of the southwestern frontiers, asking for such precious articles as pearls, ivory, rhinoceros horns, tortise shells, and peacocks. The officials of Wu felt the request unreasonable and advised Sun Ch'üan their King to turn it down, but the King complied with the request, saying that "to me these are no more than tiles and stones".[22] Again, in 235 A. D., the Wei sent envoys to Wu with horses to trade for similar luxuries. Sun Ch'üan again granted the trade noting that "I have no use for all these things and yet I get horses out of them. Why shouldn't I allow such an exchange?"[23] This attitude of the King seems to have fully justified the criticism of the literati.

It is most interesting to note that coins and silk were used by the Chinese as media of exchange in this Sino-barbarian trade. It also indicates that this means was another important channel through which Han silk and Chinese textile designs were brought beyond the Chinese frontiers.

Another aspect of the Sino-barbarian economic trade and expansion relations, was the tributary system. This was an important aspect of the entire Han imperial system concerning not only the barbarians but the Chinese as well. "Local products" of various Chinese provinces were required to be presented to the court annually as tribute from the people of that area. On the other hand, it was equally common practice for Imperial gifts, from time to time, to be made to both meritorious Chinese officials as well as model citizens. Likewise, the chieftans of various friendly barbarian tribes were also accorded imperial gifts including embroidered silk garments with Chinese designs. The ultimate goal of the tributary system was to achieve political stability.

Rare products as tributary articles from the barbarians also had prestige value for the Emperor. Tribute symbolized submission. There-

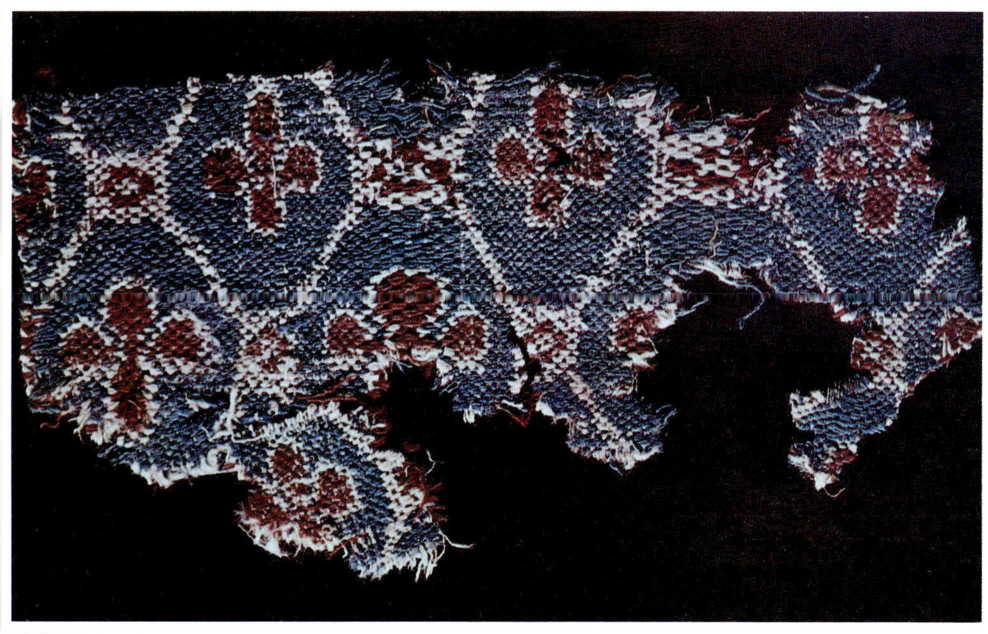

Plate III

A wool woven textile in a tortoise and four-petaled flower design called *kuei-chia-wên* discovered in the desert near Min-fêng in Sinkiang in 1959. Dated as Eastern Han, 25 - 220 A. D.

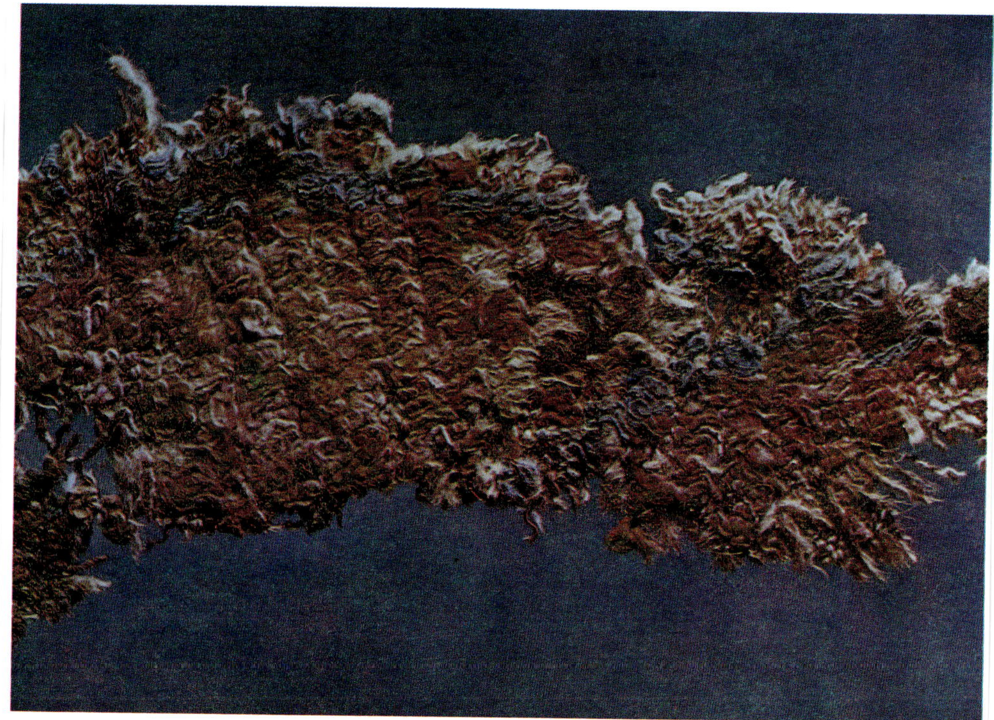

Plate IV

A fragment of a wool pile carpet excavated in 1959 from the desert near Min-fêng in Sinkiang and dated as Eastern Han, 25 - 220 A. D.

fore, the extant to which the Chinese Imperial rule was accepted by the barbarians was often judged by the variety of exotic curiousities in the Emperor's possession. Another high mark was to indicate or demonstrate the degree of Sinicization in either art of culture. Designs executed in Chinese flavour scored very highly.

In this system the Confucian principle of extension from the closest to the remotest can be seen. The closer a particular group of people stood in relation to the Chinese civilization, the greater was the attention given to it. It is easy to see why the Hsiung-nu and the Chiang of the Western Region or Chinese Turkestan received more immediate concern of the Han court and were treated more favourably than other groups. Through this same principle, it is easy to understand why overland trade through the Silk Road was much better developed than overseas trade. Sinicization was the key to the receiving of kindness, generosity and all favourable treatment. In the Oasal regions of Turfan, East Turkestan in the present-day Sinkang Province, and Kansu, where such contacts were most frequent, these developments and interchanges had left behind clear traces.

Sir Aurel Stein and other discoveries

Before the discovery of the Pazyryk and Bash-Adar finds, the oldest examples of knotted pile carpets were fragments from Eastern or Chinese Turkestan and Noin-Ula in North Mongolia. They came from the Turfan expedition of the Berlin Museum of 1906 - 1908, from Sir Aurel Stein, from the excavations of Albert von Le Coq in 1913 and the discoveries of Colonel P. Kozlov in 1924 - 1925 and published and studied by Sueji Umehara in 1959.

It is diasppointing that no fragment gives any indication of overall designs on the carpets, except for the use of small diamond shaped lozenges in half-drop arrangement and a stem scroll S-border which is more or less geometricized scrolls or single motifs popularly called 'running dog' motif. All these fragments date from the second-third to the fifth-sixth century and have a density of 500 knots to the square decimetre. The knotting have about half the density of the Pazyryk carpet. However, they were similarly woven with the Turkish knot, with only a few exceptions as one piece appears to have used the Sennah knot and contain features that are suggestive of later Turkish rugs and that of early Seljuk rugs discovered in the Near East.

Moreover, the same designs could be seen on early Chinese textiles. These designs could have entered these areas by either trade goods or through the tribute system whereby the Imperial government awarded friendly tribes, Chinese silks and other luxuries. However, these designs could be a development of an indigenous culture of the peoples of the "Western Regions" or they could be the result of acculturation and Sinicization.

Historic Ethnic Groups

According to Chinese tradition and chronicles, the peoples of these regions were the San Miao, who were the descendants of Ch'in Yün, a high-ranking official during the time of Huang-ti (2697 B. C.). They originally lived in Ch'ang-sha in Hunan Province.

There were also a number of Chinese settlements in Kansu in pre-Christian times. Emperor Wu-ti of the Han dynasty founded the province of Chiu-ch'üan in 121 B. C. so as to keep in touch with the lands to the north-west. This new province was populated with deported criminals and exiles. Then again, to the west, three more provinces were set up and the fortresses of Yü-men kuan and Yang-kuan were built in the north-westerly corner of Kansu. These were to be the solid basis of guarding the western frontiers which were gradually advanced to the West. Military posts were established and state commissions appointed to be responsible for the safety of the colonies and the provisioning of official embassies journeying to other lands.

The problem of feeding the occupation troops, which were the key to surviving colonization, was solved by combining agricultural cultivation with the military duties of the settlers. All other skills which were necessary to make the colonies self-sufficient were employed to further assure successful colonization.

From Yü-men kuan and Yang-kuan two main roads ran to Hei-yu which have been dubbed the northern and southern routes of the "Silk Road."

Within this area of North China live the descendants of a group of people called the San-miao who had migrated from China Proper. In the *Shu-ching* or the Book of History, we are told that this group of people had originally lived in the area encompassing Wu-ch'ang to Hupeh Province, Yüeh-chou in Hunan Porvince and Chiu-chiang in Kiangsi Province.[24] During the reign of Emperor Yao (2356 - 2256 B. C.), there had been hostilities with the Miao. These people "continued rebellions against the Emperor's command and so Emperor Shun (2255 - 2206 B. C.) drove the chief of the San-miao and his people into San-wei, and kept them there."[25]

Emperor Shun's punitive measure seems to have been to remove their chief and probably a portion of his people to another part of the country. San-wei was a district in the West, deriving its name from a prominent hill in the area. It was located near Tun-huang in Kansu. The San-miao were the first group of early inhabitants of China Proper to have been banished into the Western Regions. They were one of the "Ssŭ-tsui" or Four Criminals who were banished to the frontiers of China so that universal peace would prevail during the reign of Emperor Shun. Since they were disgraced by banishment later generations called them "Ssŭ-hsiung" the Four Bad Peoples. Subsequently they were also called "Hsiung-nu" whom Western historians collectively called the Huns.

From recent excavations at Ma-wang-tui in Ch'ang-sha in the province of Hunan, the ancestral home of the San-miao, a most important and significant discovery of a pile-loop brocade fabric was made.[26] It is woven with cultivated silk. The geometric designs on the surface are of pile-loop weave, which gives a three-dimensional effect to the textile surface. Within each motif, high piles alternate with low piles to produce sharply defined contours. These fragments which have been discovered were of fringes of a floss-wadded robe worn by the dead.

The structure of this loop-pile brocade is exceedingly complicated. It is a warp-backed weave consisting of four groups of differently coloured warp threads interlaced with one group of monochrome weft threads, which produce a varying surface on both sides of the fabric. These specimens testify to the advanced weaving technique mastered by the Chinese more than two thousand years ago.

It is most conceivable that the San-miao were familiar with weaving and brought the techniques of weaving, including pile fabrics, with them to San-wei. On their journey to San-wei, the San-miao may have taught the peoples along the route, such as the Wu-wei and Chang-yeh, their skills. These have all become important weaving centres. The only change was the substitution of wool for silk. From the accounts of the travels of Chang Ch'ien who visited the "Western Regions" during the Chien-yüan period (140 - 134 B. C.), it is clear that, "there was no silk or lacquer ware".[27] in these northern regions.

While he was in the land of Ta-hsia, Bactriana, prior to his return to China, Chang Ch'ien reported seeing "cloths and bamboo" which had come from Szechwan and other parts of Southern China. These articles were reported to have been purchased by their merchants from India. Thus, it appears the Western Regions were familiar with Chinese goods, even items from the far South and Southwest, before Chang Ch'ien's visit.

Chang Ch'ien's thirteen years travels brought to light the possibility of a trade route and intercourse with areas to the far west and he reported on new kingdoms in which the Han government was interested. He also called attention to the peoples living in the Western Regions who were in the path of Han expansion.

One of the largest groups of people living in the Western Regions were the Hsiung-nu, a Turkish-Mongol people who were called the Huns by Western historians. According to the *Shih-chi*, they were descendants of Chün-wei, a member of the Miao tribe during Emperor Yü's reign, (2205 - 2198 B. C.)[28]

The Hsiung-nu also lived originally in China Proper in the area encompassing the present-day provinces of Kansu, Shensi and Shansi. Having hostilities with the Chinese they were gradually pushed to the north into the Western Regions and beyond.

In 48 A. D., the twenty-fourth year of Emperor Chien-wu of the Han dynasty, the Hsiung-nu were divided into two separate groups due to famine and plague. The southern branch submitted their allegiance to the Han and were allowed to settle in the northern part of Shansi.

The northern branch migrated northward to Mongolia and Russia. They were troublesome to the Chinese government and Emperor Ho (89 - 105 A. D.) sent General Tou Hsien to campaign against them. General Tou was successful in driving the northern Hsiung-nu westward outside of traditional Chinese territory. This branch of the Hsiung-nu were the Huns who invaded Central Asia and Europe. In the fourth century, under the leadership of Atilla, they attacked Rome and other parts of Europe, and were greatly feared. After Atilla's death, these Hsiung-nu returned to the Western Regions and were defeated by the Ju-juan people.

The Hsiung-nu people divided themselves into clans, tribes and other units, with each group staking out their own territorial claims. These groups were often called different names at various periods of Chinese history, such as the Hu, Jung, Ti and other names. Although their ancestral beginnings were primarily the same, they differed in various practices and customs and had many conflicts among themselves.

In the beginning of the fifth century A. D. one of these Hsiung-nu chieftans, Ho-lien-pa-pa became so powerful that he established a kingdom for himself and called it "Ta-hsia". He claimed that he was a descendant of Emperor Yü of the Hsia dynasty. Taking on all the trappings of Chinese royalty, he built himself a Chinese palace with masonry walls instead of the nomadic felt tent. The naming of his kingdom Ta-hsia verifies, along with the Chinese chronicles and tradition, that these people were originally from China Proper.

Another group of Turko-Mongol people living in the Western Regions, who became sinocized were the Hsien-pei people who founded the Northern Wei dynasty (386 - 535 A. D.). These Turko-Mongol people, descended from the steppe nomads of the north and northeast, adopted more and more of the methods of government and cultural characteristics of the Chinese tradition. As they gained more power and prospered from the taxes of their peasant subjects, their upper class was even more drawn to the material culture, the arts and the style of life of the Chinese. By the early fifth century, a culture had emerged in North China that was a complex amalgam of Chinese and alien elements. In 439 A. D., when the Tartar Toba, who were related to the San-miao, had brought political unification to the north, they pushed further forward the full consolidation of regional power. The Northern Wei dynasty acted exactly like a Chinese dynasty by defending the northern frontiers and sending military expeditions that gained control of the Central Asian oasis kingdoms and the western routes of access to China Proper.

In 494 A. D. they even moved their capitol from the northern steppe frontier to Lo-yang. There they built a new city according to traditional Chinese plans. Moreover, the ruler, now calling himself Emperor issued sweeping order for Sinicization. The Hsien-pei imperial family adopted the Chinese surname, Yüan.

Plate V

Buddhist sacred symbols and the flowers of the four seasons surround
two central figures. The uniqueness of this rug is not only the representation of human beings which is uncommon but also the fact that the
figures are of a Han-Chinese lady with bound feet and a standing Manchu lady.

During the Northern Wei dynasty, a most significant passage in the *Pei-shih*, or Annals of the Northern dynasty, describes the coronation of the Emperor Hsiao-wu of the Northern Wei dynasty.

"In 532 A. D. Yüan Hsiu, Prince of P'ing-yang, was placed upon the throne as tenth Emperor of the Northern Wei dynasty by Kao Huan, who sent four hundred horsemen to meet him. The new emperor betook himself into a felt tent to don imperial regalia. He was then escorted to the east gate of the palace, and according to ancient custom, he was lifted by seven of the highest dignitaries of his court onto a black felt rug. Facing towards the West, the new Emperor implored and made obeisance to Heaven."[29]

This obscure passage from the *Pei-shih* brings to light that felt rugs were used in ancient China in ceremonies and rituals and that having contacts with the various Turkish and Mongolian peoples near her borders made this practice commonly accepted.

A closer scrutiny of the expression used by the Chinese annalist throws a flash of light into the darkness of those long-forgotten customs. The literary translation of the passage from the *Pei-shih* reads that the seven officials of the court "were covered by" (Chinese, *meng*) a black felt rug on which the new emperor made obeisance to Heaven". The precise wording of the *Pei-shih* shows that in the Chinese interpretation of the act, the Emperor was not lifted on the felt, but seven men were covered by it. The Chou dynasty has been elaborated into a symmetrical model of ideal government and this idealization was expressed in a Han compilation by Confucianists into the *Chou-li* or Rituals of Chou. The ritual of the new emperor using a felt rug imploring to Heaven was a practice recorded in the *Chou-li*: "The King sacrificed to Shang-ti wherefore he proclaimed his case with a felt."[30]

This ancient dynastic name is freighted with meaning: it was the name of the dynasty that had first swept out of the northwest and conquered the civilization of the North China plain; a period revered by Confucian ideologues.

Felt and Early Symbolism

The idea associated with the lifting of the Emperor on the rug is defined in the seventh century by Wên Yên-po, that "the Emperor is like the sky and the earth, which nourish all beings, cover them, support them, and grant them a complete security."[31] It seems certain that the traditional ceremonial described was intended to give visible expression to the idea of sovereignty and power.

As to the black felt rug, it evidently expressed the same concept of investiture, and represents the image of the heavenly curtain and celestial tent. This is similar to the Biblical passage when King David saw the heavens stretched out like a curtain,[32] and Isaiah praised God who "spreadeth them as a tent to dwell in."[33]

The lifting up of the new sovereign was not an act of submission but a warrant of protection and cooperation. This ritual established the hierarchical relationship between vassals and their suzerain in the sense that just as he was covered by the Eternal Heaven, so a sort of cosmic curtain was spread over the heads of the main feudatories. Just as the Emperor made obeisance to Heaven while lifted toward it, the highest dignitaries of the Empire made obeisance to him under a rug intended as a symbol of heaven.

The number of men who held up the felt rug with the Emperor is also significant. The fact that they were always either four or seven shows the fundamental affinity of those Oriental rituals and gives final evidence of the function of the black felt rug in the consecration of their sovereign. The constant recurrence of those numbers, four or seven, separated by many centuries and in circumstances totally independent of one another, attests the persistence of a tradition despite many changes in the constitutional structure of the widely varying kingdoms, dynasties and peoples.

The number of the chieftains who lifted the felt rug is explained by the cosmic symbolism of four and seven in old Chinese tradition and beliefs. The four corners of the felt rug, held up by four men, represent *ssŭ-fang*, the four cardinal points as conceived and expressed in Chinese cosmology and political symbolism with the Emperor as the centre. Again in the *Shu-ching*, Book of History, we find that there were four attendants or supporters, *Ssŭ-lin*, to the Emperor. The one standing before him was called, *i*; standing behind him was *ch'êng*, to his left was called *fu*, and to his right *pi*.

The seven men who supported the rug embodied the structure of the world and government of which the Emperor is the centre and the ruler. The highest dignataries of the empire particpated in that celestial power by virtue of that ritual of consecration. This number seven stemmed from the time of Huang-ti (2697 B. C.) who was aided in governing his empire by seven mythical personages. They were referred to as *Ch'i-fu*, or the seven assistants of the sovereign Huang-ti. Of these personages, Fêng Hou, was the fifth. His several functions are variously described by the legends, but he is usually represented as having knowledge of the system of Heaven, which signifies that he was well versed in astronomy. Fêng Hou is said to have assisted his sovereign in subduing the rebellion of Ch'ih-yu. As to the names and functions of the other six men, several different versions exist.

In 1206, when Têmujin assumed the title of Genghis Khan and was crowned emperor, he was placed upon a white felt and reminded of his duties in the following fashion:

"Direct thy eyes on the felt on which thou sitteth. If thou will well govern thy kingdom, thou will rule gloriously, and the whole world will submit to thy sway, but if thou will do the reverse, thou will be unhappy and be outcast and become so indignant that thou wilt not even have a piece of felt on which to sit."[34]

This custom of electing or investing the ruler upon a felt rug was also adopted by both the Turkish and Mongolian peoples who placed great importance on felt carpets.

Among the Mongols, white felt is a material endowed with a sacred character. Placing a person on a white felt rug means expressing to him good wishes for his welfare. For this reason a bride is seated on a white felt during the marriage ceremony, or people at the point of starting on a long journey receive this honour. An animal selected for a sacrifice to the gods is slaughtered on a white felt. Without a doubt the felt rug was regarded with high honour. This same honour was transferred to the knotted pile carpet with the evolution of the felt rug.

In the *T'ang Liu-tien*, a book on Chinese ritual and ceremonies, it is recorded that "on auspicious occasions, the Great carriage (in which the Emperor rides), three sets of curtains are required. These curtains are of black felt with red silk damask covering over." This same source, states that Yüan-hsia-chou and nearby places produced white felt and An-hsi produced a strawberry red felt.

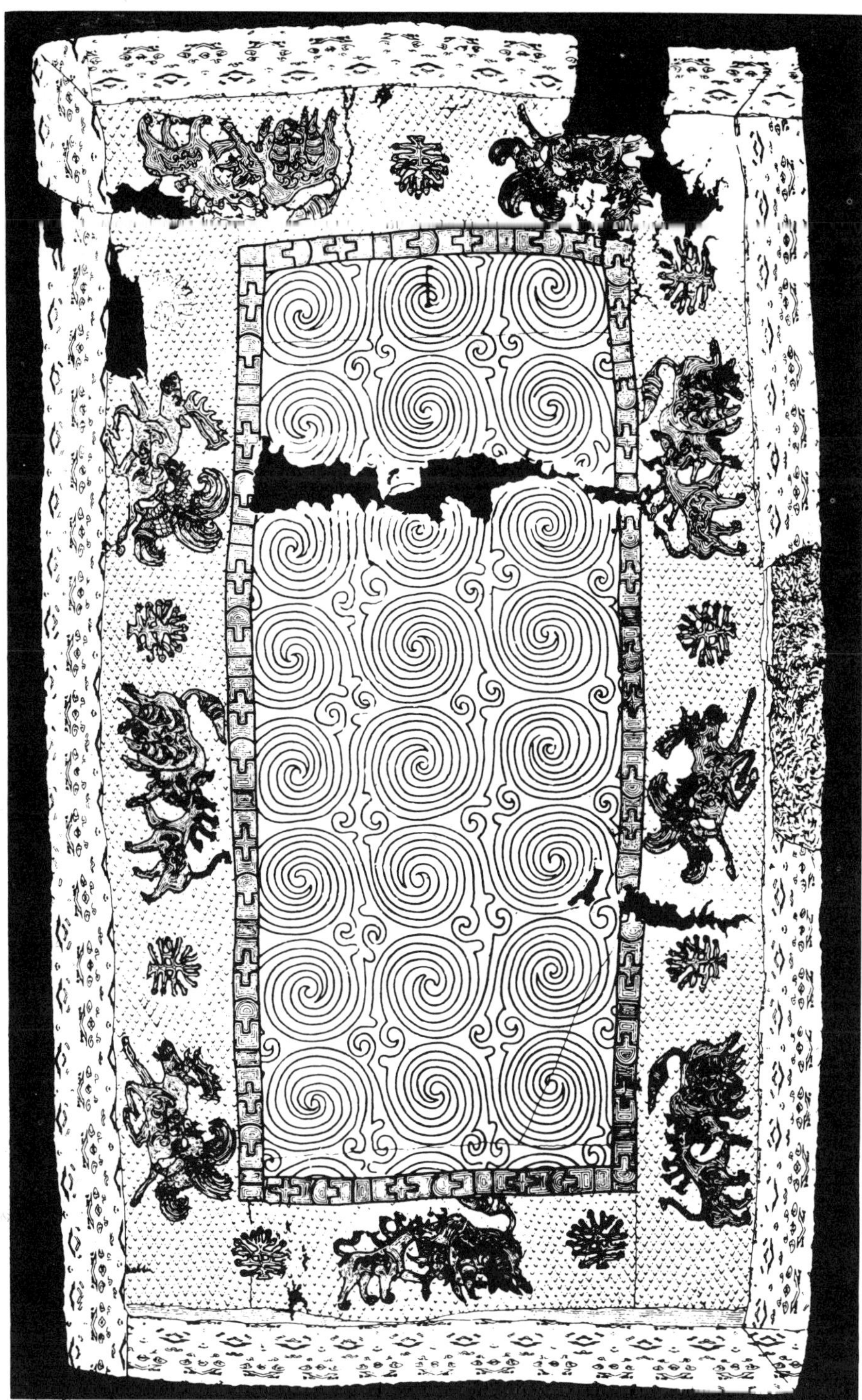

Figure 2
Large red woolen carpet bordered with quilted woolen stripe and mosaic applique work.   Found under the coffin in Tumulus No. 6, Noin-ula, Mongolia.

Felt rugs were also utilized in funerary practised as well as other important functions. Ma Tuan-lin, who lived at the end of the Sung and the beginning of the Yüan dynasty, included a detailed description of an imperial funeral of the Yüan period where there was an extensive use of felt in the ceremony. We learn that the "funeral car was of white felt and had curtains of blue and green and the coffin was also draped in that material."[35] On another instance, Marco Polo recounts how Nayan a chief and kinsman of Kublai Khan revolted and how he was put to death "by being enclosed between two carpets which were violently shaken until the spirit had departed from the body. The motive for this particular sentence was that the sun and air should not witness the shedding of the blood of one who belonged to the Imperial family." In the *Hsia-chi* or History of the Hsia dynasty (2205 - 1766 B. C.) which is included in the *Shih-chi*, we learn that a woolen woven material called *chih-p'i* was brought to China as tribute by the Jung and Chiang people living near the K'un-lun mountains.

It should be noted that as early as Chou times (1122 - 255 B. C.), felt was used in ceremonies and rituals. Felt, therefore, was not a material used only by nomadic peoples but was also used by the Chinese in ancient times. The Emperor Wên (179 - 152 B. C.) of the Han dynasty even wore a felt cap on his hunting expeditions. The use of felt however was mainly in evidence in the North of China, as alluded to by the philosopher, Huai-nan tzu who lived in the second century B. C. He noted that in his time felt was still unknown South of the Yangtze region.

Under the Han dynasty (201 B. C. - 220 A. D.), felt was well established in China and used in the form of mats and covers.

Previous Interpretations

The beginnings of rug and carpet making are hidden in the shadows of pre-history. The earliest evidence of the use of felt as well as knotted pile and flat woven carpets is contained in the Pazyryk burials. Later discoveries, though providing a series of examples, only emphasize that these types have been produced side by side for millenia over a large geographical area.

Under the circumstances only tentative assumptions can be made about the origins of rugs and few sound hypotheses have yet been put forward. Among these, the arguments of Kurt Erdmann, are the most convincing. Concentrating exclusively on the evolution of knotted pile rugs, he believes pile to have been an imitation of animal pelts and associated its production with early herdsmen of the steppe area. This development, he argued, rendered it unnecessary to kill an animal in order to obtain raw material for fabric. Erdmann distinguished these herdsmen from the hunting nomads who always had an abundance of furs at hand to clothe themselves and cover their living quarters.

Erdmann was unaware of or gave little importance to felt in the evolution of carpets. While knotted pile carpets may have evolved as an imitation of pelts, the production of felt would have been an even earlier innovation. Felt could be manufactured quickly and without any particular equipment or technology.

Felt, which requires large quantities of animal hair, especially wool, must have appeared in the Steppes with the domestication of fur-bearing animals in Neolithic times. The art of making felt by rolling, beating and pressing the animal hair or flocks of wool into a compact mass of even consistancy is assuredly older than the art of spinning and weaving. The making of felt naturally presupposes the existence of wool-bearing animals like sheep, goats and camels. While it is true that felt can be made and has been made from the hair of wild animals, the supply of such hair is not plentiful enough to establish the industry on a large scale. It is therefore clear that only those peoples who possess large herds of wool-bearing sheep and camels could develop a flourishing felt industry. This reason alone, however, would hardly be sufficient to ascribe the invention of felt to the nomadic population of the Steppes and to disclaim it for the Chinese, who had domesticated sheep. The ancient Chinese, although they had sheep, never utilized the wool as a popular form of clothing as there were many other materials, such as silk, velvets, hemp and cotton. The Chinese most assuredly understood the process of making felt, and produced some themselves, but the manufacture of felt had less importance than other materials. Eliminate felt from the Chinese and they would still remain what they are without any significant change. However, if this material was eliminated from the life of the nomadic populations of the Steppes, they would suffer greatly. With these peoples, felt was a fundamental part of culture, an absolutely essential feature and necessity of life. While with the highly civilized nations like the Chinese, it is a side issue, an element of occasional and minor importance.

Another interesting point of difference is that to the urbanized nations felt was simply a utilitarian product which they adopted because it was useful and practical, whereas among the nomads it was associated with religious and ceremonial practices. It was part and parcel of their life, inseparable from their inward thoughts. It is in this light that the invention of felt can be attributed to the nomads of the Steppes.

Although these people may have invented felt, they could have been influenced by an urban nation like China in design and the evolution of felt-making into carpet making, from flat-weaves to knotted pile rugs. It must be remembered that in order to make flat weaves or knotted pile carpets, spinning and weaving and the technology of looms must be introduced. Many of the peoples of the Western Regions had earlier lived in the area of China Proper, some were driven North by the Chinese, some like the San-miao were exiled and some like the Hsiung-nu escaped to the North after the fall of the Hsia dynasty (2205 - 1766 B. C.).

Yüeh Ch'an wrote in the *Kua-ti p'u*: "Chieh, the last ruler of the Hsia dynasty improperly conducted himself, so that T'ang banished him to Ming-t'iao where after three years he died. His son, Hsün Chu, took all his father's concubines and fled with them to the Northern wilderness. They became nomads and were called the 'Hsiung-nu'." Ying Shao confirmed this statement in *Fêng-shu t'ung* in that "those who were called Hsün-chu during the Shang dynasty (1766 - 1066 B. C.) were later called Hsiung-nu."

According to Chinese tradition, silk spinning and weaving had been discovered by Lei Tsu, the wife of Huang-ti who lived from 2698-2598 B. C. By the time of the migration of tribes mentioned to the Western Regions from China Proper, it is very possible that they could have brought with them the technology of spinning and weaving. However, since the material most abundant to them was wool, not silk, they utilized it as the basic material. At the same time, the turning to wool was not only a necessity but a practical need as they migrated from a more temperate climate to a cooler and harsher area.

The early cut-out felt patterns and appliques that have survived clearly show Chinese influences. A felt rug with an applique was found

Plate VI

Eighth century floral design as a central medallion with subtlc gradations of green, brownish red on a pale blue ground.

in the Pazyryk burials. Also a felt applique rug with similar designs of the Pazyryk knotted pile rug was discovered in Tomb No. 6 at Noin-Ula in Northern Mongolia. It is of great interest to discover how far back in time the Chinese had known about or used rugs and carpets, including felt, flat-weaves, cut-loop napped fabrics, and knotted pile textiles.

The rug or carpet evolved from modest beginnings into a work of art of a high order.   In the course of its development the multiplicity of its technical forms, the laws governing its design, and the wealth of its ornamentation were perfected. This is simply the initial, but decisive, chapter in the history of rugs. Rugs reflect both symbolistic, and ritualistic practices as well as the history and culture of the peoples who created them. It is apparent that the Chinese have contributed much and have greatly influenced the usage of rugs and carpets from a period pre-dating the Christian era.

Expanding Kurt Erdmann's thesis, the nomadic shepherds, who descended from the nomadic hunter tribes, must have come upon the idea of producing artificial pelts by first inserting, then knotting, long threads of wool into woven textiles. Although we have no knowledge when the technique was developed, we may be certain that it was more than two thousand years ago. It is very probable that spinning and weaving along with woven textiles were introduced by the Chinese to the peoples of the Steppes. In any case, it was on traditional Chinese soil and territory that this textile medium, which was destined to play such an important role throughout the world, was first developed. Textile floor coverings were of course, known and used by the Chinese in ancient times.

Etymology of Terms

In searching the Chinese literature and early traveller's accounts for evidence on the provenance or history of Chinese rugs, it becomes apparent that the terminology is fluid and inexact. Neither the early dictionaries or encyclopediae nor early literature are clear as to the precise or special meaning of the various words in current use for "rug", or some kind of special rug. This is not remarkable, for words in all languages suffer continual change, if only through shift of emphasis. In today's American speech, a "biscuit" is no longer something "twice-baked:: but rather something "half-baked"; a "steinkrug" is not an "earthen jar" but in the abbreviated form, "stein" is applied to what the Germans call a "seidel". We must expect therefore, from time to time, and from place to place, some shift of meaning or emphasis in the Chinese words for "rug" or "carpet".

Moreover, words that have to do with commodities in international trade, and with fashions that come and go, must necessarily be numerous and variable in their meaning. The name of a material may easily become the name of a kind of rug made from that material. The boundary line between coverings for the floor, the bed, the wall, the altar, the seat, the saddle and the body is a shifting one. A thin carpet may be used to cover a bed or a wall. A blanket may be worn by day and slept under by night. A thick rug may be used as a saddle cushion. This situation is further complicated by the circumstances that the dictionaries use the English word "rug" in the double sense of "carpet" and "blanket". In modern American slang, the word "rug" could even mean a "wig" or "hair piece"

In Chinese literature, various terms for different objects denoting rug, carpet, and blanket can be found dating from very early times. We have already seen that felt rugs were known and used during Huang-ti's time (2698 - 2598 B. C.), and in rituals in Chou times (1066 - 221 B. C.). The most often quoted terms are *Ch'ü-yü*, *Ch'ü-sou* and *T'a-têng*.

In an early second century A. D. work, *T'ung-su wên* by Fu Ch'ien (d. 189 A. D.), both the terms *Ch'ü-sou* and *T'a-têng* are mentioned.

"Delicate wool is woven and the material is called *Ch'ü-sou*. The finer form of *Ch'ü-sou* is called *T'a-têng*. They are spread out before the large bed."

With this brief description, we know that both terms represent woven woolen textiles which were used as coverings or rugs, and that one is of a better quality than the other.

In a third century A. D. work *Nan-chou I-wu chih* by Wan Chên, an even more specific description is given:

"For *Ch'ü-sou* sheep's wool is used, mixed with wool of other animals. Designs are woven into it depicting birds, animals, grasses (plants), trees, people and other objects, clouds and mist. Parrots are also worked in so that from a distance it seems that they are in flight."[36]

Adding even more to this description, the *Wei-lüeh* written by Yü

Huan (ca. 239 - 265 A. D.) notes that:

"In the kingdom of Ta-ch'in[37] from the silk of wild cocoons[38] are woven into *Ch'ü-sou*. There are ten different colours employed which are: fire-red, white, black, green, red, mauve (deep red), gold, blue-green, blue and yellow".

In addition to the colours of *Ch'ü-sou*, a foreign place name is given. However the term "Ta-ch'in" is a problematic one for Chinese historians as it is used for a number of places. Nevertheless, another source, *Kuang-chih* by Kuo I-kung[39] gives us an even more precise location.

"*Ch'ü-sou* is a fine woolen material which comes in recent times from Nan-hai . In ancient documents there are references to *Ch'ü-sou* from the northern Han -- but it is not these areas which produce it."

Hans Bidder misread the term "Nan-hai" which he literally translated as "southern shores (probably from India, Kashmir)"[40]. It is located in present-day Ch'ing-hai and Kansu near the K'un-lun mountains.[41]

This quotation from an early Chinese literature suggests that *Ch'ü-sou* originated in northwest China or areas just beyond her borders. As for the term *Ch'ü-yü* the eleventh century dictionary *Kuang-yün* compiled by Ssŭ-ma Kuang (1009 - 1086) gives the definition as "a thick woven woolen covering or mattress". This is also the definition found in the work *Fêng-su t'ung*, a late second century A. D. work by Ying Shao as a chronicle of popular customs of that period.

In the *Ku Yüeh-fu*, it states that "In honouring guests, felt and *Ch'ü-yü* cushions were used as seats."

In later encyclopaedic works such as *T'ien-kung k'ai-wu* it is recorded that:

"As for such terms as *Ch'ü-yü* carpets, *P'ang-lu* rugs, and the like, they are simply the names derived from many dialects both Chinese and foreign. The coarsest kind of blankets or rugs are made with horsehair and shoddy mixed with sheep's wool."[42]

During the fourth century B. C., the father of Mêng Ch'ang-chün, who was a powerful vassal of the Prince of Ch'i, used as floor covering of his palace, *Ch'i-hu* which is a woven silk, crepe-like textile."[43]

This extragavance may have been the cause which led the first emperor of the Han dynasty, Kao-tsu (206 - 195 B. C.) to issue in 199 B. C. decrees to forbid merchants from the usage of six different textiles: *Chin-hsiu* silk brocade, embroidered or embellished, *Ch'i-hu*, silk crepe-like material for floor covering, *Ch'ih-chü*, fine and coarse hemp, and *Chi*, carpets made from the hair of animals.

Chi was one of the articles of tribute known during the time of Emperor Yü of the Hsia dynasty (2205 - 2198 B. C.). This is the same *Chi* carpets that had been mentioned by the historian Pan Ku in a lettre to his younger brother, General Pan Ch'ao of a certain Mr. Tou, paying a sum of 800,000 cash for more than ten *Chi* carpets. During the epoch of the Three Kingdoms, Emperor Wen (220 - 226 A. D.) of the Wei dynasty presented the King of Wu two *Chi* carpets as gifts.[44] Without a doubt, *Chi* carpets were both expensive and prestigious to own. In this same period, to emass gold, such comodities as *Chin-hsiu*, silk brocades, embroidered or embellished, *Chan-ch'i*, appliqued felt rugs and *Chi* carpets was considered a measure of wealth.

This concept of wealth continued into the T'ang dynasty (618 - 906 A. D.) as related by Li Chao (fl. 806 - 820 A. D.), in his compilation *T'ang-kuo shih-pu*:

"Wei Chih fell ill and Marshall Fang sent his son to make inquiries. On being invited to enter the bedroom, he had to walk across a flowery carpet (*Yin-t'an*) on the floor. Fang's son quickly removed his footwear before treading on the carpet. All of the slave girls in attendance broke into laughter. The entire court was full of derision -- as if from this one could take Mr. Wei for wealthy and prosperous, leaving Marshall Fang to appear simple and modest."

Inasmuch as *Chi* was usually made of wool or animal hair, it could also be made of silk as in the case of Mêng Ch'ang-chün's father who covered his palace floors with these carpets. In the *Li-chi* or Book of Rites, *Chi* is defined as dyed silk threads that have been woven. Therefore, *Chi* is a woven textile which could be made from either silk or wool. During Han times a compound term was used *Chi-hu* to allow for the two different materials used, as reflected in Emperor Kao-tsu's royal decree which was noted earlier.

China under the Han was perhaps the greatest civilization in the world at that time. People beyond China's borders with any pretense to civilization or culture derived much from contacts with the Chinese. The farther away from China they lived, the more barbarious they became. The Han Empire spread throughout the Asian continent and their influence extended into Central Asia. States from Korea to Ferghana sent presents and tributes, pledging their allegiance in return for military protection. The court welcomed their tribute and wallowed luxuriously in its reputation.

By the late second century A. D., T'ang Chung-ch'ang described China thus: "with the mansions of the great landowners stretched in rows by the hundred. Dealers and merchants move about in their boats and carts in all directions. The grandest houses are not big enough to contain all their jewelry and gems; the hills and valleys are not wide enough to contain all the horses, oxen, sheep and pigs." There was great wealth during Han times and with the flow of money and wealth, the theory of class broke down so that laws restricting the wealthy merchants had to be promulgated. Besides silk brocades, they were forbidden to have *Ch'i-hu* to cover their floors and also *Chi* carpets.

Han Artifacts

The Han Emperor Wu pacified the Western Regions and opened the "Silk Road", establishing military garrisons in strategic places, these settlements have yielded many Han dynasty artifacts. Recent excavations in China have brought forth many examples of textiles and rugs which enable us to study the designs and technology of weaves, dyes and materials employed.

A most notable feature, however, is the diverse structure of the many fragments now known. Considering that fragments of knotted pile carpet have been found in many separate sites in North China including Sinkiang and Mongolia, it is reasonable to assume that during the Han dynasty, and the next several centuries, knotted pile rugs and carpets were well known and used extensively throughout these areas. These fragments are evidence also of different weaves and knotting techniques with both the Ghiordes and Sennah knots represented along with examples of at least three different kinds of single-wrap knots, and some examples of cut-loop weaves.

Plate VII
A mural painting from Tun-huang showing a high court official, perhaps a royal family member offering incense. Note the rug on which he
is standing.

The question arises as to whether these fragments were actually woven in the places where they were found or whether they were actually trade goods. Some of the fragments show signs of Chinese design and colour preference. Furthermore, these discoveries were made in known Chinese settlements which were under Chinese administration. In addition to carpet fragments, a number of other Chinese artifacts were found all indicating the influence of Chinese culture.

As the powerful Han waned, the guarding and maintaining of garrisons on the frontiers diminished and the "Silk Road" held less importance as it was no longer a safe route. Although land routes were still used, a newly charted sea-route, which was safer and more profitable to operate, slowly took over. The Western Regions began to be by-passed. Patterns and designs of textiles seem to have frozen in development and each area preserved their own patterns in making carpets and rugs with a most distinct flavour.

The successors to the Han were unable to recapture its power and glory and the several shorter, less capable dynasties brought foreign invasion and division of the country. The period between 220 A. D. and 580 A. D. when China was reunited, cannot be dismissed as insignificant. It witnessed important developments in literature and in the other arts and was the time when Buddhism spread most rapidly and took on distinctive Chinese forms. However the achievements of those years are most easily seen as part of the inheritance of China's greatest dynasty, the T'ang.

T'ang Dynasty

From the seventh century onward, merchants and diplomats alike were attracted from all over Asia by the stories of the glorious T'ang Empire. Its capitol, Ch'ang-an (meaning 'lasting peace'), and its large ports became cosmopolitan centres where many people from various areas jostled in the streets and markets. Both land and sea routes were open and the glory of the T'ang Empire flourished. Scholars and pilgrims came too, as China superseded India as the centre of the Buddhist world. Their destinations were often the rich libraries of Ch'ang-an or the monasteries of the two holy regions, Mount T'ien-t'ai in the southeast and Mount Wu-t'ai in the north. In July, 838 A. D. two Japanese monks, Ennin and his disciple Ensai, set out to make the journey to

Mount T'ien-t'ai.

They had been given titles as part of an official mission to the Chinese Court and intended to visit the sacred mountain while the Japanese ambassador was in Ch'ang-an. After a year's time, Ensai was allowed to go to T'ien-t'ai and to stay there as a student, however, Ennin was supposed to have returned to Japan with the ambassador. He was given shelter by some Korean monks in a small monastery and so remained in China. Chinese authorities gave him permission to visit Mount Wu-t'ai. Moving among the monasteries on the holy peaks, Ennin played a full part in the busy life of the holy communities. His diary shows that in addition to working in libraries, he attended ceremonies, feats, and lectures; went on excursions to shrines and places of interest and had interviews with leading monks. He was not by any means the only visitor. For in the early ninth century Buddhism was an important element in the life of the people, and laity as well as visiting clergy attended functions on Wu-t'ai.

Among his observations, he noted the use and importance of carpets and rugs. In the city of Têng-chou, Ennin described the elaborate ceremonies when "an Imperial Rescript by the new Emperor has arrived from the capital. Two carpets were spread in the court in front of the gate of the mansion inside the city wall . . . The Magistrate called out, 'the common people', and they chanted a response all together. The Magistrate stood on one of the carpets and an administrative officer stood on the other, both of them facing west. Then the Commissioner who had brought the Imperial Rescript walked up in front of the Magistrate and bowed again, whereupon the Magistrate stepped off his carpet and stopped him with his sleeve."[45] The importance and use of carpets is indicated and the act of facing to the west reminds us of the court investiture ceremonies for an Emperor.

In recording his experiences in the various monasteries, Ennin reports that:

"In response to the invitation we went to the ritual place and saw the religious arrangements for worship . . . Valuable banners and jewels in all the beautiful colours of the world were spread out and displayed, and carpets of varied colours covered the whole floor."[46]

On another occasion, Ennin describes a more specific use of the carpet as he relates that:

"Next they opened up the Wan-shêng (myriad saints) Ordination Platform, and we looked around. It is made entirely of white jade and is three feet high and octagonal. The base of the platform is filled in with plaster (made from powdered) incense, and on the platform is spread a silk carpet of five colours, also octagonal and made to fit the platform exactly."[47]

The monasteries, as described by Ennin contained great amounts of treasures. Among them were carpets.

" . . . each year the Imperial Commissioner, on separate Imperial command sends incense, flowers, precious baldachins, pearls- (decorated) banners and baldachins, jades, jewels, precious crowns of the "seven treasure",[48] engraved golden incense burners, large and small mirrors, flowered carpets . . ."[49]

These references clearly show not only that the Chinese had known and used pile carpets and rugs but that they were considered items of wealth and necessary in high ceremony.

Besides written evidence of Ennin's diary there are also many examples of Chinese carpets and rugs found on the mural paintings on the walls of the Tun-huang caves. Here we see not only dignitaries standing on carpets but dancers dancing on them and muscians sitting on them. We also see depicted, Buddhist altars covered with carpets as well as gifts of jewels and precious commodities and offerings very much as Ennin had described them.

Shosoin Repository Rugs

Among the inventory of treasures of the Shosoin in Nara, Japan which were donated by the Empress Komyo, the widow of Emperor Shomu, in the mid-eighth century, sixty kasen, patterned or decorated rugs are listed. The rugs existing in the Shosoin are thirty-one kasen (decorated rugs) and fourteen shikisen (coloured rugs which are monochrome or plain) which are all housed in the North section of the repository. Besides these there are a few damaged ones which are kept separately. The rugs are mostly rectangular in shape but there are a few square ones. These rugs must have been made for the use at the Todaiji, for many of them bear the inscription, "Todaiji" or seal marks of that

Plate VIII
Detail of a Chinese felt rug from the Treasury of the Shosoin, Nara,
Japan. Birds form the central medallion and are surrounded by floral
designs and clouds.

temple.

Some problem has arisen about these rugs as there is a notation that they were taken out of the repository at the time of a religious service at the Todaiji in the third year of the Tempyo-Hoji (759 A. D.) and there is no documentary evidence of their return. Therefore it is unknown how the present rugs came into the repository.

However, this notation confirms the use and importance of carpets in religious ceremonies described earlier by the priest Ennin.

The designs of these rugs are clearly Chinese in both colour choice and flavour and reflect T'ang dynasty tastes and style. They were also described on inventories as being Chinese rugs, an attribution totally consistant with their designs.

The most famous of these rugs is one depicting a central medallion of two birds each with a floral spray in their bills; and clouds, mountains and floral sprays and flowering plants arranged in vertical symmetry in the surrounding space of this rectangular-shaped rug. The main motif of parrot design is similar to the quote from *Nan-chou I-wu chih*: "Designs . . . depicting birds, . . . grasses (plants), trees . . . clouds and mist. Parrots are also worked in so that from a distance it seems that they are in flight."

Roundels of this sort must have served as proto-types of "roundels of birds and animals" and other such motifs which were later to be established as "mirrored" of "facing" patterns.

At each end, and scattered about the field, is a three-hill form with a flowering plant at the top. It is strongly suggestive that this is the proto-type of the sacred mountain motif used in later carpets.

The intriguing matter is that the entire design is executed by the embedding of coloured wool felt pieces which create a very colourful, luxurious effect. Little is known about this technique of felting. Perhaps coloured wool fibres were inserted between something like knit-bamboo folders and rolled tightly, the masses of wool being pressed into previously prepared hollows of the ground which formed the design. Whatever the technique may have been, the design is worked out with remarkable precision. The backs are usually plain white and have no pattern.

Several rugs in the collection are covered with floral patterns and scrolling vinework while others have large medallions called *kara-hana* by the Japanese meaning "artifical flower" and lozenge-shaped designs all similar to later nineteenth century examples. The stylization is well thought out which gives a more fluid, billowing sort of design that re lates to space by occupying it rather than by delineating form through line and formal arrangement. These designs could be seen in contemporary paintings and also on the murals of the Tun-huang caves.

The question arises of the terms *kasen* and *sekisen*. The term *sen* or *chan* in Chinese modern usage would denote the meaning of felt. Most of the rugs in the Shosoin that have been published appear to be felt rugs. However, the term *sen* or *mōsen* meaning carpet is not a native Japanese word and was imported from China during the T'ang times or earlier. In modern Chinese, the term *t'an* or *t'an-tzu* is used for carpet or rug and the term *chan* is used for felt.

Of the two Chinese terms *chan* and *t'an*, the former is an older term, and is found in the *Shuo-wên* dictionary while the latter is not. Hans Bidder, in his *Carpets from Eastern Turkestan*, states that " in the Sung period the ideogram *t'an* had not yet acquired the meaning of "carpet".[50] He continues by saying that "on the other hand it can be shown that the word *t'an* had been used to indicate 'felt rug' from much earlier times"[51] and he quotes a passage from the *T'ang-kuo shih-pu* by Li Chao (fl. 806 -820 A. D.), which we have referred to previously. Here Bidder refers to the term *yin-t'an* which he translates as "signifying a coarse material"[52] This is a mistranslation as the term *yin* refers to the delicate pattern of the carpet. Therefore *yin-t'an* should be translated as "a flowery carpet". On the other hand, Bidder has also referred to the term *yin-t'an* as a modern composite word for carpet.[53]

Bidder is correct when he quotes the Sung dynasty work *Hsi-shang fu-t'an* by Yü Yen in his definition of the term *t'an*. *T'an* is another expression for an underlay, mattress of wool, that is, carpet.[54]

And he gives the reason for this new term, by saying that the earlier terms *Ch'u-yü*, *Ch'ü-sou* and *T'a-têng* were archaic words and difficult to understand.

One point that Bidder does not touch upon is that during the

T'ang dynasty, both the older term *chan* and the new term *t'an* were used interchangeably to mean carpet. Even today in Southern China, particularly in Kwangtung, the Cantonese use the term *chan* which they pronounce as *chin* to mean a rug, carpet or even a blanket. This pronounciation is consistent with the pronounciation in earlier times in the *Shuo-wên* dictionary. Moreover, we should realize that the Cantonese dialect was that used during the T'ang dynasty. It is also interesting to note that in the Hokkien dialect, spoken in the province of Fukien, this term is pronounced similarly as *chin* with the same meaning. Also many Japanese terms for things Chinese were imported during the T'ang period. Therefore, the Japanese term *mōsen* to mean a carpet is in accordance with T'ang dynasty usage.

Besides the terms *chan* and *t'an* and the other terms that we have examined, there are a number of additional terms that have been used in Chinese literature to denote rug, carpet, blanket, bedding and cushion. Some of them are: *Ju, Lo-ho, K'o-mao, T'o, Pu-lo, T'o-lo* and *Ti-i.* The numerous terms used throughout Chinese history, merely indicate carpets and rugs were used by the Chinese people.

Literary References

By the time of the T'ang dynasty, rugs and carpets became so widely used that a number of poems have been written about them. A notable one is by the Poet Po Chü-i (772 - 846 A. D.), one of the most famous among the poets of this period. He had also held various high offices, among them that of governor of modern Hankow, where he constructed one of the great embankments of the beautiful West Lake. His verses resemble in character those of Li Po, and like Li Po, he was enthusiastic in his praise of the wine cup. At the same time he involved himself in the human equation. When he looked at a luxurious rug, he thought of the hardships of the weaver and concluded that it was best to use the thousand silken strands to clothe the poor in the locale in which the rug was made.[55] In protest he wrote the famous poem, *Hung-hsien-t'an* or the "Red-thread rug."[56]

Plate IX
Brocade with an evolved jewels and flower design discovered in Turfan in 1968 and dated from a burial mound as T'ang dynasty. The date of the burial mound is the thirteenth year of Ta-li (778 A. D.). Both colour scheme and design, especially the mirrored-images, are similar to Near Eastern rugs.

The Red-thread Rug

Silk cocoons are selected, in clear water boil them and reel them,
Picking and twisting the silk into threads, dye them with saf-
*   flower,*
Dyed threads in red are better than in indigo-blue.
Woven into a carpet, it is to be spread out on the palace floors
Unrolled on the palace floor, the space is more than ten mea-
*   sure.* [57]
This red-thread carpet covers the entire palace floor.
The coloured silk is soft and fluffy, there is a lingering fragrance.
Soft, fluffy threads allow the flowers and designs to float to the
*   surface, truly a superior product.*
Beautiful ladies step on it, singing and dancing
Silk stockings and embroidered slippers, they are lost in its pile
The rugs from T'ai-yüan are harsh; the material is rough and stiff
Szechwan mats are thin, their embroidered designs are cold
They are not like this rug which is warm and pliantly soft.
Yearly in October, orders for rugs are dispatched to Hsuan-chou,
The prefect of Hsüan-chou had them woven with increasing style
Claiming that he had done his utmost.
A hundred men are needed to carry the rug into the palace.
The threads are substantial and tight, making it difficult to roll
*   up (fold)*
Is the prefect of Hsüan-chou aware that a thousand ounces of silk
*   is needed to weave one measure of rug?* [58]
The ground does not know coldness but people need warmth
Do not take away the people's clothes in order to make rugs to
*   clothe the ground.*

From Po Chü-i's poem of protest, we learn a number of significant facts. Foremost is that there were both silk and wool rugs in common usage, and that they were made in several areas: Hsüan-chou in
modern Anhwei, Szêchwan, and T'ai-yüan in modern Shansi. In the
T'ang-shu or History of the T'ang dynasty (618 - 906 A. D.), under the
geographic section, it states that "among the native products of Hsüan-
chou that were presented as tribute to the Emperor are silver and bronze
wares, *Ch'i* silk, white sack cloth, red brocades and red rugs." There
is also this line of poetry by Mei Yao-ch'ên (1002 1060 A. D.) who is a

native of Hsüan-chou: "Weaving the red floss silk, it becomes a carpet to cover the palace floors." This further confirms that Hsüan-chou was noted for the production of red-coloured rugs. T'ai-yüan in modern Shansi, is no longer a major rug producing place. Nevertheless in the early period of the Ch'ing dynasty, under Emperor K'ang hei, in a reference to the city T'ai-yüan, capital of Shansi, Father du Halde noted that: "Besides the silks which are wrought here, as elsewhere, they make fine carpets, such as the Turkey ones, of all sizes".[59]

Szêchwan, as the ancient kingdom of Shu, had been famous for their woven textiles since Han times. It is also significant to learn that red was preferred over indigo and that red dye was made from safflower.

The organization plus the equipment and technology to weave a carpet to cover an area of ten measures.[60] suggests that the area of carpet weaving was very well developed. In fact weaving looms were exported to Persia.

In recording the process of the transmission of the art of silk weaving to the west, Tu Huan, living in the mid-eighth century wrote a journal where he noted that:

"From the tenth year of the Emperor T'ien-pao (731 A. D.) to the first year of the Pao-ying Emperor (762 A. D.), Tu Huan visited the capital of Ta-shih, Arabia, called Yü-chü-lo which is the modern Meshrd-Ali in Iraq. He described this city as 'the hub of the universe, with markets filled with all manner of goods in abundance, embroidered silk brocades and precious pearls'. He also saw Chinese looms for silk weaving, *ling chüan chi chu*, and met the Chinese weavers, Lo Huan and Lu Li from Ho-tung."[61]

The area of Ho-tung is in the Shansi province and is also an area that had produced rugs. Fan Sun (fl. 566 A. D.), a noted literati, hails from Ho-tung and in the *Wên-yüan chüan* it is recorded that "his brothers were engaged in rug-making". Also T'ai-yuan, the capital of Shansi province was one of the major areas of rug production in T'ang times.

Po Chü-i, in another poem continues to reflect the same sentiment of his earlier work. The poem entitled, "The Big Rug" contains these lines:

That so many of the poor should suffer from cold
What can we do to prevent it?
To bring warmth to a single body is not much use.
I wish I had a big rug ten thousand feet long,
Which at one time could cover up every inch of the city. [62]

In North China, the Chinese used rugs as blankets and mattresses as well as floor coverings from ancient times. In a poem entitled: "Being visited by a friend during illness", Po Chü-i mentions the use of a rug in a manner customary with us:

I have been ill so long that I do not count the days.
As the southern window, evening and again evening
They took my couch and placed it in the setting sun.
They spread my rug and I leaned on the balcony pillar. [63]

Throughout the poems of Po Chü-i, there are many references and allusions to the various types of rugs and carpets. The poetry mentions a variety of usages, all indicating that rugs were much in vogue during T'ang times.

The T'ang dynasty was heir to the Ch'in unification and the imperial system founded by Ch'in and Han. Of all the native dynasties, with the possible but doubtful exception of the Han, it was the one in which martial or military arts were most prominent and played the greatest role. The Imperial family had originated in the western or frontier regions and Li Shih-min, the second emperor called T'ai-tsung, was brought up with constant contact with the peoples of the Steppes. Moreover the powerful families that supported and helped found the T'ang dynasty were Northern families which had strong military traditions. The skills of horsemanship, archery and the hunt held more importance than book-learning among the Northern aristocrats. One of Li Shih-min's brothers remarked, "I would rather go three days without eating than one day without hunting." [64] The sons of these great houses were given the rudiments of literacy and perhaps a brief exposure to a Confucian classic or two. But their training was utterly different from the bookish up-bringing which in later dynasties was *de rigueur* for young men with ambitions. Perhaps it was this martial tradition of the élite of this Northern society and the close contacts with the peoples of the Steppes that helped foster an overwhelming fondness for rugs and carpets.

Plate X

Design of equestrian hunters. This motif resembles what is commonly known as *Shitenno monki* of the Horiyuji. A hunter is shown being attacked by a beast while pursuing a deer. The motif is surrounded by a pearl border and an outer floral tendril or scroll. This eighth century design is also found on a number of Near Eastern rugs.

All classes of T'ang society were suffused with Buddhism. Its monasteries and shrines dotted the landscape, and from the great and powerful monasteries, it penetrated economic life and affected the customs of every village. Buddhist festivals, with their sumptuous ceremonies, punctuated the ritual year. This is quite evident as recorded in Ennin's diary. To Confucianists of this period these excesses were appalling and the rug may be seen as a symbol of their protest.

Perhaps it was a rebellious thought of Po Chü-i and other Chinese poets who tried to guard against pure native Chinese traditions as the T'ang dynasty was a Northern dynasty and had little respect for Chinese literary tradition. Southerners rightly sneered at Northern literature noting that it was "like the braying of donkeys and barking dogs". While choosing the rug as a symbol of protest, Po Chü-i evidently forgot that rugs and carpets were used in the grand palaces of the Chinese in ancient times.

During the T'ang period, as China itself was once more united, there were great military problems. Inasmuch as there were no more independent sovereign Chinese states to combat, there was still the frontier. Consequently, there was also the continuing tendency to resolve the frontier problems by extending territory to incorporate the source of conflict into the larger whole. T'ang imperialism attempted to subjugate the nomads, as well as other peoples of Central and East Asia, such as the oases city dwellers of the Tarim Basin and the Koreans. We should not forget that the T'ang had its roots both as a state and a dynasty in Western Wei-Northern Chou, the last of the non-Chinese dynasties of the period of division.

Western Wei-Northern Chou, as part of its propaganda to be regarded as the legitimate heir of ancient Chou, had adopted a deliberate policy of racial and cultural intermingling. As a result of this policy, the T'ang royal family, though Chinese in the male line, had a good deal of Hsien-pei blood in the female line. They were still not very far removed from nomadic traditions in T'ai-tsung's reign, as reflected by the atavistic predilections for the Turkish life style of T'ai-tsung's eldest son.

T'ai-tsung's conquests of the Turks and the city-states of Central Asia were achieved with great rapidity, and were much more extensive and thorough than those of the Han. The T'ang government made alliances with various nomadic groups hostile to the Turks, especially the

Toquzoghuz, of whom the leading tribe were the Uighurs. The victorious T'ai-tsung brought under his rule the entire Steppes and this was symbolized in the title, T'ien K'o-han "Heavenly Qaghan" which was proferred to him in 630 A. D. by the chieftans of the various nomadic tribes.[65] With this new title, came the asumption, quite contrary to Chinese traditional attitudes, of the equality of barbarian and Chinese as subjects. This was a point of view consciously maintained and expressed by T'ai-tsung.

The Northern peoples were the only neighbours of the Chinese who possessed the mobility to penetrate into the great mass of China and conquer it. Their way of life, pastoral nomadism, was in almost every way antithetical to the sedentary, village-based world of the Chinese.

The incompatibility of the two ways of life had to be reconciled. The economic and cultural preponderance of China was so great that even the ruling aristocracy was inexorably pulled away from the lingering remnants of its nomadic traditions. Woolen rug and carpets changed into silk ones and designs which had been stagnant during the Han period were revived and developed. With rugs and carpets made in silk, and better looms and weaving technology, along with aristocratic patronage, the rug weavers were able to execute more flowing and complicated designs, thus freeing themselves from geometric and angular designs.

Under the T'ang emperors T'ai-tsung (626 - 649 A. D.) and Kao-tsung (649 - 683 A. D.), Chinese policy toward the Turks of Inner Asia was aggressively offensive. The two emperors carried the warfare out into the Turkish heartland with overwhelming success. With the Chinese conquest of the Eastern Turks, the Western Turks also vowed their allegiance to the T'ang Emperor. Communications with the Western Regions were re-opened. Once the Inner Asian peoples had arrived at the stage of "pastoral-urbanization", an overwhelming need for Chinese goods and services developed. The fragile ecology of nomadism could not support urban centres. The sinocization of these areas became more rapid, although there remained pockets in Inner Asia of nomadic populations that remained loyal to their folk cultures and customs. Buddhism came into this area and spread rapidly, influencing the daily lives of these peoples, even in art and rug design. Later in 762 A. D., there was a conversion to Manicheism as a result of an Uighur's visit to Lo-yang and the conversion made by Soghdians.

The T'ang policy of cultural intermingling along with elaborate rites and ceremonies gave greater importance to the use of carpets and rugs, and this importance even penetrated into the daily lives of the people. Documents discovered in the Tun-huang caves in Kansu, during the 1890's and in the vicinity of the Turfan oases in the more Western region of Central Asia give us considerable more detail which contribute to our understanding of various aspects of T'ang social, political and economic life. Among the discoveries were included many specimens of popular literature -- ballads and stories -- of a genre that was not previously known to exists. From this popular literature we learn of the various uses of the rug and carpet.

In the story of Hou Hao,[66] who performed a good deed in giving burial to a set of exposed bones, the hero was repaid by a ghost who obtained a wife for him. On the wedding night, "he made his way home and on entering his bedroom found a girl of eighteen or nineteen installed there along with bed-curtains, rugs, coverlets and everything she would need for her toilet, all in the handsome style." Here the rugs and coverlets are part of the bedroom furniture and a bride's trousseau.

Also in marriage ceremonies, the decorated rug played an important part as reflected in the "Marriage Songs" which in 781 A. D. were banned by the government. However, these customs are said to be universal,[67] extending from the Imperial family down to ordinary officials and the common people. The songs, though here modified to fit with a Tun-huang wedding, probably originated in Central China. The prescribed upper class form of marriage was for the bride to be brought to the bridegroom's house for the consummation of the marriage; but it is evident that in these songs the marriage is consummated at the bride's house. In these songs, rugs and carpets are referred to as embroidered cushions, coverlets, mattresses and brocades. When the groom on horseback rides up to the bride's house, the women sing:

Golden saddle and prancing steeds,
Embroidered cushions in plenty!
From what quarter is this gentleman
Who has come to our gates. [68]

Plate XI

A marriage rug with symbols forming the rebus *T'uan chieh i chih -- Ju-i hao chieh*. "To cohere and be united -- A blessed union". The varied and multi-floral borders herald the begetting of many offspring. 96x52 cm.

They later sing:

> *A waiting guest is hard to send away;*
> *We have spread cushions and stretched brocades across the bed.*
> *We ask his lordship to dismount and come,*
> *Then we can talk matters over quietly.*[69]

The men reply in singing:

> *The Governor rides on golden stirrups.*
> *In his hand he holds a white jade whip.*
> *On the ground you must first spread brocade*
> *Otherwise he won't be willing to dismount.*[70]

The women reply:

> *A length of brocade already has been spread;*
> *The embroidered mattresses have not been taken away.*
> *The governor must now make up his mind to dismount*
> *And lodge paired in the purple upper room.*[71]

Sung on reaching the hall gate:

> *The hall gated is fenced (?) on it four sides;*
> *Within there is a four-box couch,*
> *Surrounded by a twelve-fold screen;*
> *The brocade coverlet is decorated with patterns.*[72]

In the collection of Sung colloquial literature called *Ch'ing-p'ing shan-t'ang hua-pên*, there is an extemely lively account of the wedding of the shrew, Li Ts'ui-lien. The piece is in fact a sort of burlesque cantata rather than a story. Verses very similar to those in the Tun-huang manuscript are recited. Here it is found that "the bride treads on a long green carpet or mat without letting her feet touch the ground" as she descends from the sedan (outside the groom's house). She is led by someone holding a mirror and walking backwards; she is helped on to a saddle, which she must bestride and climb down from the other side, stepping over a pair of scales. This is a reversal of the previously cited ceremony, as here the bride dismounts at the groom's house instead of a vice-versa situation. The same marriage customs were observed centuries later as recorded in the thirteenth-century account, *Mêng Liang lu*, which refers to the lifting of the bridal veil, and also describes a chorus of verses being intoned outside the houses of a bride and groom -- a custom surviving from T'ang times.

In another story from the Tun-huang discoveries, "The Story of Catch-Tiger", we find that the rug or brocade bed-spread had magical powers

"Having taken leave of the Emperor and all the ministers of the court, Catch-tiger came to his own house and gave final instructions to his wife and son, and his whole household, freemen and slaves, and said farewell to them. He then ran to his bed, lay down (and died). Then, taking only the brocade bed-spread to cover him, he rubbed down his horse, saddled it and rode on it up into the clouds, waving farewell to his Majesty the Emperor Wên of Sui as he passed by the palace."[73]

Reference to the magical power of rugs is found also in the story of "The Wizard Yeh Ching-neng" who used magic to cure a young girl's illness which was caused by a fox spirit.

"A neighbour said to K'ang T'ai-ch'ing, 'At the Hsüan-tu monastery there is a monk from far away who knows how to cure illness caused by fox-spirits'. When K'ang T'ai-ch'ing hear this, he and his wife went to the monastery, bowed down before Yeh Ch'ing-nêng and described the case to him. 'If by any chance your Reverence can cure her', they said, 'we shall be grateful till our dying day'. 'It is certainly an illness caused by a fox-spirit', said Yeh Ch'ing-nêng, 'If you want her to be cured all you have to do is to get a piece of serge-matting (rug) and four big nails, and she can be cured at once'."[74]

Besides these Tun-huang stories, we find numerous incidents in popular Chinese literature of the magical use of rugs and carpets, even incidences of magical flying carpets.

Magic or alchemy was also practiced by Buddhist monks who quarreled and competed with the Taoists. However, in the beginning of the T'ang dynasty, they enjoyed Imperial patronage as a result of the continuation of the earlier Northern Wei-Western Chou tradition. As Buddhism was also adoped by the Turks in the Western Regions, especially by the Uighurs (who were the closest Chinese allies), the power and wealth of the Buddhist temples grew immensely. This situation later created an imbalance both socially and economically. Artistically, in the early T'ang, Buddhism made its greatest impact. By the late T'ang, Buddhism was replaced by Taoism. The Turks likewise turned away from Buddhism in the eighth century, converting to Manicheism and later to Islam.

As early as 841 A. D., the Emperor's disfavour with Buddhism was evident. Ennin reported the first signs of this when on the occasion of Emperor Wu's birthday, the Taoist priests present were rewarded by being granted the priviledge of wearing the purple robes while the Buddhists were not so rewarded. This was repeated during the birthday celebration of 842 A. D. In the same year a Buddhist monk, Hsüan-hsüan, claimed that he could defeat the Uighurs who were invading the northern frontiers by a magic sword, but when he was put to the test, he was found to be an imposter.

Therefore, the Emperor issued a decree in the tenth month to the effect that all monks and nuns who practiced alchemy or magic had to return to the laity and that all monetary wealth and property, such as estates and gardens were to be turned over to the government. The Anti-Buddhist movement became more repressive and many Confucian scholars such as Han Yü and Li Ao presented memorials to the Emperor advocating the suppression of Buddhism. All small temples and shrines were closed and all monks under forty years old were ordered to return to the laity and later those under fifty were laicized. The order was given for the destruction of all Buddhist establishments in the land with certain exceptions. In each of the major prefectures one temple was to be preserved, usually the one which was most beautiful and artistic. In each of the two capitals, Ch'ang-an and Lo-yang, four Buddhist temples were to be permitted, each one to have thirty monks. The disposition of the temple wealth followed. Bronze images and bells were to be converted to coins, iron statues were to be melted into agricultural implements, and images made of gold, silver and jade were to be turned over to the bureau of public revenue.

Extreme repressive measures were taken to quell this foreign religion under Emperor Wu-tsung's reign. When the Imperial Scepter was taken up by Emperor Hsüan-tsung (847 - 859 A. D.), action was initiated to call off the anti-Buddhist movement. An official edict which was promulgated noted that inasmuch as Buddhism was regarded as a foreign religion, it had not damaged the fundamental principles of the empire, and therefore should not be abolished, especially since the Chinese had practiced it for such a long time. Buddhism was allowed a revival how-

Plate XII
This religious painting from the early T'ang dynasty depicts a scene remindful of Ennin's diary. The Pure Land Sect of Buddhism scene features flowery designs on altar drape, and dancers and musicians on rugs.

ever there was a loss of Imperial patronage. In rug and carpet designs, the anti-Buddhist period allowed many Taoist designs to be adopted and developed. Nevertheless, the period of the early T'ang and the extravagence of Buddhism have left in the Tun-huang caves and elsewhere, many murals depicting luxurious and elegant ceremonies with the ever-present rugs and carpets, a conspicuous element. In addition, some of the T'ang paintings of important personages also feature the use of rugs and carpets.

During the period when the religion was so widespread and influential in China, Buddhism made such deep inroads into the national life of China and coverted so many pious devotees, that when there was a governmental ban, Buddhist designs and customs changed somewhat, but were not completely replaced. Thus, the mystic Buddhist emblem, the Swastika, was given another meaning and read as *wan* because all good fortune and virtue were embodied in it. Since the power of the T'ang Emperors was also felt in Central Asia, many of the small states, in an attempt to be on good terms with the Chinese, adopted Chinese designs in a wholesale manner.

The Central Asian peoples had also been influenced since the third century A. D. by the flourishing colony of monks at Tun-huang in Kansu province. Dharmaraksha, one of the most important monks and translators during the formative period of Chinese Buddhism, resided at Tun-huang. Dharmaraksha was of Yüeh-chih (Turkish) ancestry but was born in China. Since he was proficient in Chinese, as well as, Asiatic and Indian languages, he was able to translate a prodigious number of sutras. Through his translations and his religious activities, he played an instrumental role in the spread of Buddhism in Northern China and Central Asia. During the fourth century A. D. numerous monks fled to Tun-huang to escape from the political and military disturbances in the rest of North China. Their literary scholarship and religious activities further enhanced the reputation of Tun-huang as a Buddhist centre.

The most famous treasures of Tun-huang are the murals painted on the walls of the caves. The dry climate of the region has preserved these murals in remarkable good condition. Covering as they do over a thousand years of Chinese history, spanning the fourth century A. D. on to the end of the Sung dynasty, these murals provide an invaluable record of the history of Chinese art and record aspects of daily life and ceremonies. Added to the manuscripts found there, the murals provide a rather complete portrayal of the life of the common people as well as high society. In these depictions the development of rug and carpet designs from the fourth century A. D. down to the end of the Sung dynasty can be seen. The textile fragments discovered by Sir Aurel Stein could be compared to these examples.

In addition to the mural paints on the Tun-huang caves which clearly depict rugs and carpets, there are preserved today some of the paintings of the T'ang artist, Chou Fang. These paintings vividly illustrate the common use of rugs and carpets, showing both their delicate colour and design. Chou Fang was a figure painter who had a predilection for upper-class femine models. He specialized in depicting the manners and bearing of noble ladies who never seemed to lose their air of pensive serenity even during the decadent years of the T'ang. Along with being a court painter, Chou Fang had also served as a prefect of Hsuan-chou, which had produced rugs and carpets for the T'ang palaces. Thus, he must have been very well versed in rug designs and decoration. His brother, Chou Han, had served as a military man in campaigns in Turfan. Chou Fang accompanied him while he served as governor-general of Shih-pao. In one of Chou Fang's most famous paintings, entitled: *Chih-shan shih-nü t'u* or "Palace ladies and their servants in various occupations", there is a vivid depiction of a rectangular rug on which several ladies are seated. Likewise Chang Hsüan, a contemporary of Chou Fang, painted a scroll entitled "Ladies preparing silk" also showing court ladies seated on rugs. These paintings of the T'ang period clearly show that by this period rugs and carpets were not only known but were in general use both in domestic life as well as in ritual and ceremony.

Contacts between China and Central Asia appear to have been far more varied and more reciprocal during the T'ang dynasty than during earlier times. During this period many aspects of T'ang culture and art were adopted by people as far west as Persia and Asia Minor. The era of the T'ang dynasty was, indeed, a period of most intensive contacts between East and West Asia. It was natural that, as in the past, these exchanges should take place along the Silk Road and also in Central Asia.

In the Oases regions of Turfan, East Turkestan, and Kansu, where such contacts were most frequent, these developments have left behind clear traces. It is known how important the spread of Buddhism in the sixth and seventh century and later Islam in the eighth century, became for the culture of that region. Yet it was Buddhism and traditional Chinese culture that have influenced the art and design of rugs and carpets. The dragon and phoenix design, for example, was even taken over by the Iranians as seen in the Anatolian rugs of the fifteenth century.

The Sung period

After the downfall of the T'ang dynasty, there followed a half-century of turmoil, disunity, and struggle that was finally ended in 960 A. D. by the unification of the Chinese Empire under the Sung dynasty. The Buddhism which developed under the Sung differed greatly from that of the Sui-t'ang era, and only Ch'an (Zen) and Pure Land Schools remained active under the new dynasty. In Buddhist art and architecture, including rug designs and decorations, it appears that the great advances were already in the past, so that the main Sung contribution was one of continuation and minor changes. The emergence of Neo-Confucianism as a strong intellectual movement contributed to the decline of Buddhism. Taoism also moved to the foreground with the Sung Emperors who fostered the Taoist papacy in Lung-hu shan Kiangsi province.

Even after the downfall of the T'ang the tradition of rug making continued to be strong. In literature we find this work by the famous poet Li Yü (937 - 978 A. D.):

The red sun has risen in the sky
And the golden incense burners give off incense
Walking on the red brocade floor clothes (rugs),
My foot steps leave wrinkles.

Just as our knowledge of Persian rugs has been expanded and documented by the study of Persian miniatures in which rugs are depicted, so also we can learn much about Sung dynasty rugs from contemporary paintings of that period. Certain scrolls and paints of the Sung dynasty are of greatest importance to us because they depict a number of rugs in minute detail.

The importance of these paintings extends beyond the information they yield regarding contemporary rugs and usage, for they also provide clues to the origin of certain geometrical designs found in Turk-

Plate XIII
A detail of a Sung dynasty painting of Wên Chi's return from Mongolia
to China showing a pile rug with fringes on the ends, geometric designs
and a pearl or fish roe border. Attributed to Ch'ên Chu-chêng.

ish rugs of the fourteenth and fifteenth centuries.

One of these paintings that depict rugs is located in the Palace Museum in Taiwan and is attributed to the painter Ch'ên Chu-chung, dated c. 1205. This painting depicts Ts'ai Wên-chi's return from Mongolia to China.

Wên-chi was the daughter of Ts'ai Yung, a statesman from the Han dynasty. She was abducted by the Hsiung-nu, from her father's home in Ch'ên-liu, in present day Honan province in 195 A. D. She was made to be the wife of the *Tso-hsien wang*, the chief of the tribes-left. Years later a Chinese embassy was sent to Mongolia to ransom Wên-chi, who then had two children. The painting in Taiwan is a scene of the reluctant parting of Wên-chi from her Hsiung-nu husband and her children.

Although the original colours of this painting have faded, we are still able to distinguish the patterns and colours of the rugs. The central figures, Wên-chi and her husband are seated on a large carpet with fringes shown on either side depicting a knotted rug. The predominant colours are red or reddish-brown, white and turquoise. Within an outer border of small rounds or pears, is an inner border with a repeat pattern of double brackets. A square compartment in the centre of the red field is bordered by a band of blue linear motifs and frames a lozenge which is decorated with a geometrical pattern of Chinese symbols made up of triangles and crosses in white on the red ground. The lozenge has a separate border with a zigzag pattern, and outside it, in the four corners of the square compartment, are triangles framing heart-shaped or trefoil motifs. At each end of the rug are six bands of scrolls and palmettes in blue, three within the field and three separating the field from the border. The texture, as depicted by the painter, is that of a pile rug.

The other rug on which the Chinese envoy is seated has a pattern of narrow bands with different designs: a lozenge pattern in white on red, a geometrical scroll with half palmettes in white on tan with angular renderings. This is most probably a flat weave or kilim rug.

Two other paintings of the same Wên-chi story exist, which show more scenes and details of life during this period. In the Museum of Fine Arts, Boston, are four badly damaged album leaves of the twelfth century illustrating Wên-chi's life in Mongolia and her eventual return to China. Also in the Metropolitan Museum's collection is a more complete handscroll which illustrates the entire story and is a copy of the earlier Boston album leaves. The Metropolitan scroll is shown in its entirely in the book *Eighteen Songs of a Nomad Flute*. All these works, the Taiwan, Boston, and Metropolitan Museum's paintings attempt to illustrate Liu Shang's poem of the lament of Lady Wên-chi called *Hu-chia shih-pa p'o* or commonly known as the 'Eighteen Songs' written during the T'ang dynasty about 773 A. D. The Taiwan scroll is attributed to the T'ang painter Ch'ên Chu-chung while the artists of the other two works are unknown. These paintings accurately reflect early twelfth century Chinese and Mongolian life. The illustrations shown in these paintings were made by men of the Sung. Their visions and understandings of life in the Northern Steppes, rich though they are in exotic details, clearly show a Chinese viewpoint of that period.

Recounting a historical drama in contemporary details, these pictures give us a vivid image of rug and carpet designs and usage of the Sung period. Both pile and kilim rugs are illustrated along with rugs used as saddlebags and saddle covers and blankets on horses and camels. One of the saddle blankets shows an octagon design, contained in a square, and decorated with a geometrical design of crosses and angular motifs, and "t" pattern, similar to the designs on Chinese bronze mirrors. Also included in this saddle blanket are trefoils or a sort of *ju-i* motifs. Some of the other saddle covers are decorated with Chinese scrolls, trefoils or *ju-i* designs, flying clouds, a flaming fire wheel, cloud motifs, a flying goose, a zigzag band, crosses, a running "Y" and pearls.

The different rugs and saddlebags and saddle covers shown are in the predominant colour of reddish-brown, with red, white, light tan, light blue, and dark blue accents. The patterns of these rugs are particularly significant, as we find a geometrical pattern which also appeared in Anatolian rugs of the fourteenth and fifteenth centuries, and to some extent in Persia, as seen in some miniature paintings.

The pictorial revelations of Sung dynasty rugs are supported by historical documents and literature which add to the details.

Mei Yao-ch'ên (1002 -1060 A. D.) in his collection of poems, writes: "Red silk threads are woven into rugs to cover the floors of the palace." Mei is a native of Hsüan-chou which we have already learned was an important rug weaving area in the T'ang dynasty and also that red coloured carpets were their most famous products. Thus we know from Mei's writings that the rug production in Hsuan-chou continued to flourish in the Sung period.

In the *Sung-shih*, the Official History of the Sung dynasty (960 - 1206 A. D.), under the section of ceremonies and rites, there is a note that: "whenever the ruler should give a feast to his minister below the rank of councillor (and magistrate) [the place setting] should include two layers of rush mats over which is heaped over with *Chi* carpets and rugs". As in earlier times, both flat weaves and pile rugs were utilized. It can be seen clearly that in Sung times, rugs and carpets were essential pieces of furniture. In his *Short History of Chinese Civilization*, Dr. Richard Wilhelm states that: "Chairs did not exist at that date (Sung dynasty) in China. People sat on mats as they do still in Japan." Chu Hsi (1130 - 1200 A. D.), the great Sung scholar, even wrote an essay entitled *Kuei-tso-pai shuo*, on the proper and ceremonious way of sitting on mats for the instruction of his students of the Pai-hu t'ung School.

Moreover, the terms *t'an* or *t'an-tzu* were in greater common usage replacing the more archaic terms for rugs and carpets. However, the use of the term *chan* continued as an alternate but less frequent choice. The rug with explicit placement as a piece of furniture evolved from the T'ang dynasty term *Ti-i*, clothing for the floor (which was still used in the Sung period) to the modern term *ti-t'an* meaning floor carpet or rug. This new term, *ti-t'an* first appeared in the *Yüan-shih* or the Official History of the Yüan dynasty (1206 - 1368) and henceforth grew into popular usage replacing all earlier terms. The term *chan* took on the sole meaning of felt throughout China except in the provinces of Kwangtung and Fukien, where it is popularly still used and pronounced as *chin* meaning a rug, carpet, or blanket.

The Yüan period

Under the rule of the Mongols, a policy of racial discrimination and institutionalized double standards was made effective that caused the Chinese gentry great pains. In the arts and crafts a universal humiliation and frustration was felt by the Confucian scholar-gentry, and they vented their feelings in various forms in both art and literature. Therefore it is not surprising that native Chinese scholars would treat the Yüan period only as a passing, or even as a *declassé* subject not worthy of much attention.

Although the conquering Mongols continued many of the Chinese court practices and customs, they also integrated many customs of their own. According to the *Liao-shih* or History of the Liao period (916 - 1168), the Liao Emperors ruling Northern China, dressed in Chinese style while their Empresses wore Khitan costumes.[75] The Liao dynasty was ruled by the Khitans and later was absorbed by the Nuchen and in turn by the Mongols.

During the Mongol period great favour and preference was placed on the felt carpet, and it grew to be a luxury article. The beauty of its colours and applique patterns and the perfections of the silver-brocaded felt gauze were prized and the large quantity of carpets delivered from the Ordus region and Kansu to the court are noted in the official record.

Friar John of Pian del Carpine, generally known as Carpini or de Plano Carpini, who visited the Mongol imperial camp near Karakorum in 1246, recorded many of their customs in his *Historia Mongalorum*. His writings show the importance of felt in Mongolian life. Felt is the universally employed material of all nomadic tribes of Asia and above all else the characteristic mark of their rudimentary pastoral civilization. It was used in different qualities, shapes, and colours for the making of tents, weapons, clothes, rugs, mats, mattresses, blankets, door curtains, boots, headgear, and many other utensils of everyday life during time of both peace and war. Felt was so important that when a Mongolian emperor died, a felt flag or standard was flown from in front of his tent. Friar John reported that "when any one of the Mongols sickens unto death, a spear is put at his tent, and around it they wrap a black felt; and thenceforth no one who is a stranger dare enter the bounds of his dwelling."[76] Friar William of Rubruck, who traveled and lived in Tartary from June, 1253 to the end of 1254 explains that warning by their "fear lest an evil spirit or some wind should come with those who enter."[77] This use of felt which was replaced later by woven rugs to ward off evil was later taken up by the Mongols and also adopted by the Tibetans in pillar rugs used mainly in temples.

The part played by felt in the rites and ceremonies of the Yüan dynasty and the Mongolian nobility had both a practical and a symbolic function to remind them of a nomadic past and their life in the Steppes.

Yet that humble material ceased to be exclusively employed in Mongolian life when the contact with China made the conquerors familiar with, and fond of silk, artistic embroideries, and textiles of all kinds including cotton, linen, woven carpets, and pile rugs. As a matter of fact, the authentic contemporary descriptions of the residence of a Mongolian chieftan clearly show that felt had almost disappeared in favour of more elaborate and costly materials. Marco Polo mentioned felt only incidently.[78]

With the disappearance of felt from the refined environment of wealthy Mongolians, its symbolic function and significance increased in proportion to the decline of its use at court. A generation after Genghis Khan there was hardly an object in an imperial palace or tent that was of Mongolian make. Felt appeared there only as a door curtain at the entrance to the dwelling and thus protecting, as does every door in Asiatic tents and homes, the sanctity of the inviolable threshold. This curtain remained one of the few national symbols that connected the Mongolians with the old traditions of the nomadic tribes. Yet, after contact with China, even these curtains were replaced by rugs and embroidered textiles.

Chinese designs and motifs were taken over without any change or alteration so that they became static and lost their meaning. However, since carpets and rugs in many cases replaced felt, their value became paramount and they were in great demand. So much so that a manufactory of rugs for the Imperial Court was established in a northern suburb of Peking.

The essence of the orthodox Mongolian tradition is, however, represented in a miniature painting appearing in the famous manuscript of Rashis al-Din's *Jamiel-Tevarikh*, illustrated under direct Chinese influence, and perhaps collaboration. The miniature depicts an episode in the funeral rites of Chagatai, a ruler of Central Asia who was the second son of Genghis Khan, and who died in 1242. Felt and rugs appear in the characteristic forms and functions; a tent, a door curtain, and a cover over the coffin. Whether those rites implied that felt has some symbol of humility in the face of death or of the transitoriness of human power and glory, is not certain. The coarseness and rapid deterioration of that material would certainly justify its symbolic function in contrast with the finer textiles used by the nobility. As a matter of fact, the Mongol princes of the Yüan period, who were guilty of crime or misdemeanor, had to wear a simple felt garment instead of their richly or-

Plate XIV
A cloud design rug with simple patterns enhanced by subtle shading and
outlining. The plain lines of the framing borders are given depth with
the same shading technique employed in the cloud forms. 78x169 cm.

nate courtly attire. Therefore, in contrast with the drab and dull funeral vestments, carpets and rugs for the living were rich and vivid in colour as a symbol of power and glory. Red and reddish-brown was preferred. Light blue with floral designs were also favoured. Trefoils or *ju-i* motifs as well as soaring clouds and flames took on magical significance and are seen on saddle blankets and covers. In an anonymous poem, *Mu-lan tz'ŭ* or the "Ballad of Mu-lan", who was a young girl disguised as a male in order to substitute for her father who was called to join the Khan's army, there is a line, "At the Eastern market, she purchased a fine steed, at the Western market, she bought a saddle and saddle trappings."

The various wars and military campaigns of the Yüan emperors created such a demand for saddle trappings that a whole market and thus a whole industry of weaving and creating saddle covers and saddle blankets arose. At the same time, the Mongolian chieftains who vied with the emperors in the display of luxurious textiles, taxed the supply of rugs and carpets, always demanding the exotic and the unique. Inasmuch as design and motif remained static, nevertheless, there was great variety in the execution of these patterns.

The Ming period

The Mongols founded the Yüan dynasty and inaugurated a governmental regime based superficially upon the T'ang and Sung. By rearranging architectural elements inherited from the T'ang and Sung dynasties, the Mongol rulers created a highly centralized and intricately articulated government. The surveillance and restrictions over the people combined with the harsh treatment, racial discrimination, and double standards made them a hated group. Finally in 1368 they were overthrown and a native Chinese dynasty was restored.

The Ming dynasty (1368 - 1643), governed China and dominated the whole of East Asia during the time when Europeans were suffering from instability and turbulence of wars and the Black Death.

With the Mongols out of the way, the Ming self-consciously set out to restore and reassert the glorious traditon of the past -- notably of the T'ang and Sung eras. They had no wish to participate in adventures or to make progress toward anything new. The important thing was to shake off the bad memories of the Mongol rule. In doing this, they committed themselves to a conservative mode of thinking and living, being satisfied that their stability was undoubtedly comfortable.

The unusual self-satisfaction and conservative outlook of the Ming does not suggest that they had lost all their flexibility and creativity. The general stability that marked life in Ming China was achieved by many changes in traditions, which showed realistic adaptability. In rug and carpet designs, the geometric style favoured by the Mongols gave way to the floral patterns and other more recognizable Chinese art motifs. Hans Lorentz in his book *A View of Chinese Rugs from the Seventeenth to the Twentieth Century*, illustrates in *Plate 22* a seventeenth century rug displaying a vase full of *ju-i* fungus sprigs, the symbol of Taoist immortality and the five-claw dragon with five floating clouds, a symbol of ruling the five directions. Yet the borders are reminiscent of earlier Sung and Yüan designs. Over the years the designs and motifs took on more symbolism readily understood by the native Chinese gentry. These symbols were taken more from porcelain decoration rather than from earlier bronze mirror motifs. Since the government moved to standardize certain symbols and motifs to signify rank and status, a uniformity of design developed with a new visual vocabulary.

Under the ultra-conservative Ming government, the square "Mandarin" badges of *p'ŭ-tzŭ* were invented, with different species of birds for different civil officials and various animals for nobles and the military.

Ch'iu Hsün, a famous Ming statesman in his *Ta-hsüeh yên-i-pu* wrote that the birds were intended to symbolize the literary elegance and the animals the fierce courage, of their respective wearers."[79]   The right to wear robes with these insignia had to be bestowed by the Emperor, according to Ch'iu Hsün. An official could not automatically adopt the robe appropriate to his rank. After he was granted the right to wear a particular insignia, the official had to have it made for himself. No doubt, the many variations of insignia can be traced to their having been made by different artisans in various parts of China.

With this restriction of birds and animals, rug designs were mainly floral, stylized Chinese characters, and some geometric designs which were used in lattice work. Only birds and animals not covered by governmental ordinances were utilized. Vases and various objects formed "rebus" as well wishes to continue the magic of the rug, sometimes even with Taoist talismanic language.

From various depictions in Ming paintings and woodcut prints, we discover that many of the early Ming dynasty rugs had a field that contained all-over patterns. Oftentimes the repeated designs are of octagonal shape and arranged in both horizontal and perpendicular lines so as to leave small diamond-shaped spaces between diagonally placed octagons. Within these designs are often emblems of happiness or longevity, floral motifs or archaic hydra or dragons.

Another popular rug pattern has a field that is completely covered with a swastika-fret and marked at regular intervals with diagonal rows of bats, a symbol of happiness.

Sometimes there is a field of plain colour containing an irregular arrangement of objects used for sacrificial or sacred purposes. Again, it may be covered with an all-over pattern of small archaic animals similar to those found on ancient bronzes. It is also commonly marked with an all-over diaper pattern.

An essential feature that is most common is a central medallion surrounded by a field that is either plain or patterned. The medallions may be either octagonal, or as is more frequently the case, rounded. But the defining lines are angular and generally represent frets. Sometimes they contain archaic dragons executed in geometric shapes similar to lattice work, called *K'uei-lung* motif, in a rigid angular pattern forming a medallion.

On the other hand there is also the lively depiction of the dragon and even the phoenix as in the rug in the Metropolitan Museum of Art. This badly faded rug is described in Museum records as having a red pattern on a yellowish-brown ground. The design consists of a huge five claw dragon and an equally large phoenix, with a flaming pearl between them. Bats are represented in the upper corners. Of particular interest is the repetition of the double character *Hsi* which forms the border. This is an example of a rebus of marital bliss and best wishes, *Lung-fêng ch'êng-hsiang*.

With the exception of this border, Ming rugs have borders that are invariably narrow, and generally consist of a single stripe which is figured and surrounded with a coloured edging. The most common border design is that of a stripe with a pattern of swastika-frets, Occasionally some form of the "key pattern" appears in the inner stripe, but almost all Chinese rugs that have two border stripes with figures belong to a later period. Many of the oldest borders are without figured stripes and consist merely of one or more stripes of plain colour.

Although the palette of colours used in the rugs of this period is limited, nevertheless the colours used have deep and rich tones. Natural dark brown or fawn or blackish wool was often used in the outer edging that surrounded the field or in the narrow border stripes. Natural fawn wool was also used as a solid plain field especially in rugs used in K'un opera performances. However, frequently corrosive brown dyes were used that over the years have eaten the wool almost to the foundation of the warp and weft. Other colours used were soft dull yellow and various shades of blue in the borders, while the same colours are often dyed richer if used in the central field.

In the early twentieth century art connoisseur's book *Ku-wan chih nan* it states that:

"In Ming rugs where the field is white, its borders are usually black and the decoration is mostly executed in the colour blue, however, sometimes other colours are also utilized, but they are no more than ten or twenty percent. The decoration follows that found on Ming porcelains and the blue is dark as indigo."[80]

Both dark and light blues, sky blue, clair-de-lune and robin's egg blue were used. These colours were quite similar to the various shades of blue and white porcelains of that period. Various greens, such as jade green and apple green were also found in Ming pieces, however, green was considered a rare colour. Soft yellow and various shades of yellow including apricot and varying hues of brown and reddish browns were also popularly utilized. Since red was the colour of auspicious occasions this was also very popular. However since red was the Imperial colour of the Imperial household, reds were defined in many shades such as, *Fei,* a strawberry red, *Chih,* a fire red, etc. with certain red hues restricted to royal usage as was yellow in the Ch'ing period. In silk rugs metallic threads were also used, adding lustre to colours and thus giving a richer appearance.

Ming carpet designs like that of Ming porcelains in general, were lively and in flowing rythmn such as depicted in a painting by the fourteenth century painter Wang Chên-p'ing in the Boston Museum of Fine Arts. An excellent example of this rythmic design and sensitive colouration is to be seen in the early Ming carpet fragment with lotus blossoms and foliage in the Museum fur Kunsthandwerk in Frankfort, Germany.

Even before the Manchus penetrated the Great Wall to become the masters of China Proper, it is correct to state that they had already become acquainted with both Chinese culture and institutions. Like the Mongols before them, they favoured the brand of Lamaistic Buddhism, which they felt was closer to the Shamanism they believed in. The Manchus, who were called Ju-chên at that time looked upon Nurhachi, founder of the Ch'ing dynasty as an incarnation of Mañju'ṣri.

After the conquest of China, the Manchu emperors continued to patronized Lamaism, with the added incentive that such a policy would aid them in winning the allegiance of the Mongols and Tibetans. To manifest their support of Lamaism, the early Manchu emperors, especially K'ang-hsi, made numerous visits personally to Wu-t'ai-shan, the holy mountain of Lamaism, to pay their respects to Mañju'ṣri and the temples dedicated to him. Many Lama temples were also constructed, with the largest and finest concentration in such areas as Fêng-t'ien, Peking, and Wu-t'ai-shan. Those in Peking included such famous ones as Yung-ho kung, Ch'ung-chu-ssŭ, and Huang-ssŭ. Prosperous Lama temples such as the Pai-ling-miao in Inner Mongolia and the Kumbum in Ch'ing-hai, housed over five hundred and a thousand lamas respectively. The building of a vast number of Lama temples brought about an overwhelming need to supply and furnish them with pillar rugs, prayers rugs, and rugs and carpets for the performance of various rites and ceremonies. Following the Ming custom, most pillar rugs were dedicated with a coiling dragon with five claws as a sign of Imperial patronage and favour. The colours of these pillar rugs, either red or yellow, were basically in accordance with the religious sect, with the main division between Tibet and Mongolia. The division was basically the *Nying-ma-pa* or the Sect of Red Caps and the *Gê-lug-pa* or the Sect of Yellow Caps.

In addition to their interest in Lamaism, the early Manchu emperors Shun-chih and Yung-chêng, were also favourably diposed to the *Ch'an* (Zen) School of Buddhism. Emperor Yung-chêng, 1723-1735, who called himself the Perfectly-enlightened Layman was most deeply committed to *Ch'an* Buddhism and published the *Yü-hsüan yü-lu* or selected Imperial Sayings, whereby he looked with favour on the harmonizing of Taoism and Buddhism. His purpose was to popularize them among the people.

Plate XV
A pictorial rug in shades of tan, brown, beige and blue. The T'ung and
pine trees with the deer, peony and crane express *Shou-lu t'ung-ch'un*.
"May you enjoy happiness, longevity and robust health". The swastika
border has flowers set into the corners. 158x258 cm.

This fusion of *Ch'an* Buddhism, Lamaism, and Taoism created a wealth of designs for rug and carpet weavers who were busy furnishing the many temples that were erected. However, a number of rugs continued to be woven with the traditional designs of the Ming and earlier periods.

A Japanese woodcut print by Nishimura Shigenaga, ca. 1697-1756, entitled *Haru Hanami no Sakura Ayashiki Fu* or "Spring Flow Viewing: The Style of Cherry Damask", reveals vividly the design of a late Ming-early Ch'ing rug. It depicts a young woman standing beneath a flowering cherry tree, lifting one side of the cloth screen to reveal a patterned carpet on the other side. The carpet seems to be substantial in size and has a border of fret work and pearls with curling vine-like scrolls. The main colour of this rug is red, with a yellowish border and black lines outlining the designs.

Ming designs of a field of octagonal shapes are frequently seen on ancient portrait paintings including portraits of the Ch'ing emperors and empresses.

The Ch'ing Period

The Ch'ing emperors, even before their conquest of China, had adopted many Ming dynasty customs and institutions. The famed eight-banner system of military organization was a direct copy of the Ming system as was the use of birds and animals in Mandarin squares as insignia denoting rank and status.

From the reports of Jesuits in China, Peré J. B. Du Halde, in his description of T'ai-yüan, the capitol of Shansi province, states that "besides the silks which are wrought here, as elsewhere, they make fine carpets, such as the Turkey ones, of all sizes."[81] T'ai-yüan, flourishing as a carpet centre, is not surprising as we know from Po Chü-i's poem that this area was a carpet weaving centre during the T'ang dynasty (618 - 906 A. D.).

An eye-witness account by Father Gerbillon, who accompanied Emperor K'ang-hsi into Kansu in 1697, is most interesting. He noted that when the imperial entourage visited Ninghsia, "they also presented to his Majesty several floor rugs, somewhat resembling our rugs of Turkey, only more coarse. They are made here, and the Emperor was curious to see them worked in his presence, as he had been with the paper made at Ninghsia from hemp . . ."[82]

It is interesting to note that both these accounts referred to similarity to Turkish rugs. Fathers Gerbillon and duHalde were from aristocratic backgrounds and their familiarity with rugs may be assumed. Both of these accounts were written in the Emperor K'ang-hsi's reign when transitional designs of the Ming and earlier periods were in vogue. These designs were also exported into Central Asia and the similarity of designs should not be surprising. Authors, including Murray Eiland, have tried to correct " . . . those who insist that the Chinese rug is a modern innovation extending back only into the nineteenth century". As he states: "These seventeenth century references should conclusively refute such a notion."[83]

The rule of Emperor K'ang-hsi was, for the most part, tolerant and conciliatory. In comparison with the Emperors of the late Ming dynasty, K'ang-hsi was frugal, practical and conscientious in the discharge of his responsibilities. During his reign the empire increased in wealth and, most of the time, enjoyed peace and prosperity.

The K'ang-hsi period is noted for advancement in learning to which the emperor himself made significant contributions such as the compiling of the *K'ang-hsi tzŭ-tien* or K'ang-hsi dictionary. Desirous of lessening the opposition of recalcitrant Chinese scholars to the next regime, he solicited their help in the compilation of the *Ming-shih* or the History of the Ming dynasty (1368 - 1643). He selected learned men and good calligraphers to be his personal secretaries and many famous works on literature and art were compiled by his order. The emperor patronized the arts. In the palaces of Peking, the hall known as *Ju-i kuan* in the Court called *Ch'i-hsing Kung,* (later called *T'ai-chi kung*), was set aside as a studio and repair shop where the Emperor gathered the painters, mechanics and architects who were in his service. The Emperor encouraged not only fine printing and the manufacture of porcelain but all the fine and applied arts in general which would have included weaving and rug and carpet making. The *Tsao-pan ch'u* was created including the *Kung-i chü*, which was a headquarters or department in charge of various artistic workshops or the "Office of Arts and Crafts". These workshops were attached to the *Yang-hsin tien*, the Hall to which the Emperor retires for relaxation. The Imperial Office of Weaving and Dyeing, *Chih-jan chü*, was separate and supervised by a prince or Minister of the Household called *Kuan chih-jan chü ta-ch'ên*, Director of the Weaving and Dyeing Office. Subordinate to him, in addition to the usual officials, was a group of officials called *Chien-shê chih-jên chü-wu ssŭ-kuan*, which included inspectors, overseers and clerks.

In weaving, as in porcelain making, many of the products of the late Ming were copied but with a freer use of colour and a more decorative ornamentation. Inasmuch as curls and vine-like scrolls were utilized, many of the designs were angular and geometric. Most conspicuous were the use of frets in the central field of the rugs. The use of the dragon design was favoured although it differed from the distinct Ming design which was more in line with ancient rendering of this mythological animal.

Often two or more dragons were utilized to form a medallion in the centre of the field, surrounded by other dragons which were either around the central design or occupying the corners. Sometimes the fields are covered with various objects, such as scrolls, books, vases and flowers.

The borders of these rugs, frequently have an outer edging of brown and a single border stripe with swastika-fret. Sometimes the border is a repeat of the design in the central medallion. The colour scheme of the late Ming, including the golden browns and deep blues was largely followed.

Conscious of being a foreign dynasty, the early Ch'ing emperors first turned to T'ang and Sung examples and later even to the Han dynasty institutes. Large literary works were ordered to be compiled and every effort was made to become stereotype Chinese. Porcelains and the other applied arts followed Sung dynasty examples as did the fine arts, however, with technological advancements and differences in tastes, there were distinguishing characteristics to show these developments.

In rug and carpet design and decoration some changes were made from the adopted Ming examples. Frequently, the fields were covered with sub-patterns of fret-work on which medallions appeared more prominently and strikingly.

Angular and geometric figures were softened and supplanted by tendrils and foliated forms and often the fields were covered with delicate scroll or foliate sub-patterns that support floral forms resembling

Plate XVI

Japanese print entitled: "Spring flower viewing: The style of Cherry Damask". A young woman drawing aside a fabric screen beneath a cherry tree in blossom. A patterned carpet appears behind her on the fround. The carpet has a border of key-fret and pearls with an all-over trellis design in the centre. Woodcut print by Nishimura Shigenaga.

the lotus or peony. Sometimes, the foliate or floral designs no longer appear as sub-patterns, but become the prominant feature in the decoration of the field. The rug depicted in the Japanese woodcut by Nishimura Shigenaga is a good example. Flowers, bats and roundel shapes oftentimes are conventionally arranged with precision in diagonal or perpendicular lines.

There is in Ch'ing dynasty rugs a blending of pictorial and symbolic ideas, as well as being a rebus, such as a flight of storks, flittering butterflies, bunches of peaches or a deer with the *ju-i* fungus all emblematic and symbolic of longevity and happiness.

In a portrait painting of Emperor K'ang-hsi in the Metropolitan Museum of Art, an ornate rug with flying cranes, peaches and flowering foliage can be clearly seen. All of Emperor K'ang-hsi's deeds were performed with great flair and an understanding of Chinese culture and traditions. As he was a scholar, everything had to have a deep inner meaning including the naming of his pleasure palace or country villa. Just outside of Peking near the little town of Hai-tien, K'ang-hsi restored a country villa named *Ch'ang-ch'un yüan*, the Garden of Joyful Springtime, and he often spent several months there each year. The whole villa was 10,600 Chinese feet in circumference, or about one half of an English mile on each side. [84] This figure, however, does not include the walls of another Imperial garden which he granted to his heir apparent, called *Hsi Hua-yüan* or West Flower Garden, which adjoined the *Ch'ang ch'un yüan*. We can only surmise the quantity of rugs and carpets necessary to furnish the huge country estate where the Emperor was in residence for so much time each year and where he conducted and received official audiences. As official functions were performed here, a throne room and furnishings appropriate to his station were required.

On the celebration of his sixtieth birthday, 1713, the royal procession started from this garden and paraded to Peking, a distance of some six miles. Court painters including Wang Yüan-chi, and Wang I-ch'ing painted a long commemorative scroll known as the *Wan-shou Ch'ang-t'u* or *Wan-shou-t'u* to illustrate this historic event. [85] Depicted in this scroll is the great use of saddle rugs, saddle coverings, rugs and carpets used in an Imperial procession.

In the last part of K'ang-hsi's reign and thereafter, although traditional old patterns and designs were followed, there was a tendency to adopt more ornate forms and more brilliant colours. This vogue continued so that by the time of Emperor Ch'ien-lung (1736 - 1796), the style and practice ripened.

Ch'ien-lung's reign may be divided into several periods, marked by various events and individuals. The first thirty years of his reign was a period of peace and prosperity in which gains made by his father and grandfather were consumated and the princes of the Imperial clan remained docile and submissive. As prosperity continued, the court began the luxurious trend which soon spread throughout the empire. Emperor Ch'ien-lung was very successful in his military ventures and the territorial expansion of the empire. In an essay entitled *Shih ch'üan chi*, he enumerated ten great victories of his reign. He boasted of conquering the Sungarians in two campaigns, 1755, 1756-57; of pacifying the Mohammedans of Turkestan, 1758-59; of annihilating the Chin-ch'üan rebels in two wars, 1747-49, 1771-1776; of surpressing a rebellion in Taiwan, 1787-88; of subjugating the Burmese, 1766-70; of bringing under his suzerainty the Annamese, 1788-89; and twice conquering the Gurkhas, 1790-92. These wars made heavy drains on the treasury, however despite these drains the national treasury was far from being exhausted. This apparent prosperity is in part attributed to the efficient readjustment of national finances by his father, Emperor Yung-chêng and in part to an enormous increase in population and arable land.

In connection with the completed conquest of the whole region of Chinese Turkestan which came to be known as Sinkiang of "New Dominion". there is a story associated with the conquest of Yarkand about a concubine of Khozi Khan who was captured and taken with other spoils to Peking. This Mohammedan beauty came to be known as Hsiang-fei,[86] the "Perfumed Consort", because she is said to have had a natural gift of emanating perfume. According to contemporary legends, she never yielded to the emperor's advances, although he was so anxious to win her favour that he built a Mohammedan quarter southwest of Nan-hai or the Winter Palace. He also built a tower inside the palace grounds from which the disconsolate Hsiang-fei could view her fellow believers passing in the nearby mosque and bazaars. It is also said that the emperor built for her a Turkish bath which came to be known as *Yü-tê t'ang*. Legend has it that she always carried with her a sharp weapon with which to resist the emperor's approaches. Finally, the emperor's mother, fearing for her son's safety, summoned Hsiang-fei and ordered that she commit suicide by self-strangulation during the emperor's absence. From this story have grown many tales of Emperor Ch'ien-lung's furnishing the palaces built for Hsiang-fei with Sinkiang rugs of Muslim designs to please her. This may have been so, however no records could be found to prove this to be a true story. In the *Ch'ing-shih* or History of the Ch'ing dynasty (1644 - 1911), there is no biography of Hsiang-fei.

The Palace Museum in Peking has two portraits of a lady in European military armour, which are pruported to be likenesses of Hsiang-fei, painted by P. Joseph Castiglione. While there is little doubt that such a person actually lived, many of the fanciful stories about her are probably imaginative creations, grown into romantic myths and legends. Nevertheless, they are the favourite tales recounted over and over by Western writers on Chinese rugs and carpets, who mistakenly call her Ko-fei.

Emperor Ch'ien-lung, like his grandfather K'ang-hsi, patronized not only the scholar but also the artists, craftsmen and literary men of his day. Though he himself painted with indifferent success, he was a confident critic and accumulated an enormous collection of art. He was also interested in music and drama. Owing to his encouragement and the demands for luxuries made by the Court and the aristocracy, procelain, cloisonne wares and the applied arts as a whole, made great advancements particularly in decorative design and technology. Workmanship in jade and ivory also improved as did carpet and rug weaving. At the age of sixty-five Ch'ien-lung began to look with favour on a Manchu named Ho-shên, who was appointed his last chief minister. Ho-shên, though intelligent, was unfortunately unscrupulous. As Emperor Ch'ien-lung grew older, Ho-shên used his vast power for personal gain. Corruption, which usually accompanies a luxurious court, went to extremes. The huge accumulation of gold, silver, precious gems, art objects and other forms of wealth that was emassed by Ho-shên, rivaled the Emperor's own collection.

After the death of Ch'ien-lung, the power of Ho-shên came to an end, leaving the foundations of government permanently undermined. The later Ch'ing emperors were unable to repair them.

From the beginning of his reign in 1736, Ch'ien-lung wished to emulate, and perhaps surpass the achievements of his grandfather K'ang-

Plate XVII
Portrait of Ch'ien-lung's mother, the Empress Dowager. The floor is
covered with a rug having an all-over repeating pattern with a single
band border visible behind the throne.

hsi. He ordered many literary compilations and revisions on a variety of subjects. The greatest achievement being the compilation of the *Ssŭ-k'u ch'üan-shu* the famed four-treasure library comprising more than 36,000 volumes.

Also during his lifetime, Ch'ien-lung was particularly pleased with the art, mechanical, skill and knowledge of the European missionaries who came to China. Several Jesuit missionaries served as architects in designing the buildings and landscape garden in Italian style, which formed part of the Old Summer Palace, *Yüan-ming yüan*. [87] The Emperor had first used this as a palace retreat and later it became one of his three main residences -- the other two being in Peking and Jehol.

Describing *Yüan-ming yüan*, the artist Attiret writes:

"It is in the apartments which form this palace that there are to be seen all that can be imagined which is most beautiful; furniture, ornaments, paintings -- I mean in the Chinese taste -- precious woods, lacquer of Japan and of China, antique vases, porcelains, silks, and cloth of gold and silver. Here has been brought together everything which art and good taste can add to the riches of nature." [88]

The Rococo architecture of these palace buildings recalls the extravagances of Italian art at the end of the seventeenth and the beginning of the eighteenth centuries as seen in the work of Borromini, Guarini, and Bibiena. [89]

Inasmuch as the *Yüan-ming yüan* was looted and burnt down, we may assume that the furnishing of rugs and carpets must have followed the main scheme of the Italian style architecture. In one of the palaces, we are told, which was built in the style of Louis XV, there were seen a series of chambers hung with Gobelin tapestries." [90] In several paintings in the Palace Museum, we see more evidences of this. In the portrait of Empress Hsiao-shêng, the mother of Ch'ien-lung, the pattern of the rug is unique. It consists of stylized floral shapes with trefoil centres, arranged in diagonal rows with a geometric floral border. A similar carpet with diamond shapes is seen in the portrait of Emperor Ch'ien-lung's Empress, his principle wife. Both the carpets and the ornate furniture in these portraits should fit well with the Rococo architecture of the *Yüan-ming yüan*.

As for Emperor Ch'ien-lung's personal taste, it was surely catholic, however he was somewhat superstitious and unfaultingly followed Chinese literati traditions. He was motivated not only by a desire to promote sound historical scholarship, but also to set example for later generations. In a move to preserve tradition, and to set the stage for later emperors, he had a strong desire to expunge from literary works all slanderous references to the Manchus. Even early Manchu chronicles, and their Chinese versions, were rigorously checked and the Chinese words chosen for transliteration of Manchu names, were often changed to avoid any covert disrespectful meaning. Like the founders of the dynasty Ch'ien-lung did not want to set himself apart as being of non-Chinese origin. The first Ch'ing emperor to rule China, reigned under the title "Shun-chih" meaning "a continued rule" avoiding the fact that they were actually invaders.

While Ch'ien-lung was proud of his Manchu heritage, he considered himself to be a Chinese sage-king and conducted himself accordingly. He enjoyed hunting and riding horseback and the practicing of the martial arts and skills. In behaviour he acted Chinese. Van Braam, an eyewitness to the life of the Emperor wrote, " . . . toward a great open space in the wood, where a large tent of the Tartar kind, in the form of a dome, had been pitched for the Emperor. A square yellow tent was erected in front of the other, while six little tents, which stood on the two sides, were destined for the Ministers and Grandees of the Court.

The Emperor's tent was exactly similar in the inside to the halls which I have several times had occasion to mention, and in the middle was an estrade and a throne. I remarked that the instruments and other appendages of the music had been conveyed hither from Peking.

His Majesty came a little after sun-rise in a palanquin borne by four Mandarins of the gold button. He alighted under the yellow tent and went on foot to his arm-chair. As soon as he was seated, all the guests performed the salute of honor. The Envoys sat upon cushions placed upon the carpet under the yellow tent in front of the Emperor's, with little breakfast-tables before them as at the preceding fetes." [91]

It is clear from this description that Ch'ien-lung preferred to sit in a Chinese arm-chair rather than on cushions placed upon a carpet on the ground. This is certainly an indication of his departure from nomadic practices. Ch'ien-lung was pre-occupied with ceremony, superstition and tradition which was stereotyped Chinese but which he well understood and mastered.

After his mother's death, being a devoted son and exercising filial piety, he built a temple in her honour on the east side of a temple built by his father, Yung-chêng to honour his grandfather, K'ang-hsi. He was extremely careful to have the same architecture so that nature and tranquility should not be disturbed. Nearby is a small stream with a rather inconspicuous bridge, the *Lu-tou ch'iao*, or Stove Peck Bridge. Ch'ien-lung chose this strange name and it illustrates his great belief in *fêng-shui* or the supernatural influences of the wind, water, and natural configuration of a place. This name choice was his method of devising a charm to counteract the good *fêng-shui* of his neighbour when he thought it dangerous to his own good luck.

No wonder he adhered strictly to the correct use of symbols and followed prescribed guidelines for auspicious signs so that he could benefit from properly complimenting the *fêng-shui*.

After a sixty year reign, Emperor Ch'ien-lung abdicated. The abdication ceremony took place on Chinese New Year's day, which fell on February 9, 1796. He had ruled a complete cycle of sixty years. The reasons which were given for this nominal abdication were that he had made a vow at his accession to abdicate if he should be granted a reign of sixty years, and that he did not want to be so unfilial as to outdo his revered grandfather, K'ang-hsi who had reigned sixty-one years. However, even after his abdication he continued under the title, *T'ai-shang huang*, or "Exalted Emperor who has vacated the throne." He held the reigns of power in his own hands, making decisions and occupying the central seat at audiences while the young Emperor Chia-ch'ing sat on his left.

Emperor Ch'ien-lung, at the age of sixty-five, looked favourably upon a Manchu, Ho-shên, who he appointed his last chief minister. Although Ho-shen was intelligent, he was also, unfortunately unscrupulous. Ho-shen was known to the Western residents of China by the names Ho Chung-t'ang or Voo-tchong-Tang. As the Emperor grew older, Ho-shên used his vast power for personal gain. Corruption ran rampant in the luxurious court. Ho-shên's ill-gotten wealth was so overwhelming that it rivaled the royal collection.

Since Ch'ien-lung still held power, it was not possible for Chia-ch'ing to rid himself of the powerful and corrupt minister Ho-shên, un-

Plate XVIII

The superb design of this rug gives it a richness and dignity which makes it the most represenive sample of the art of the Ch'ien-lung era. The four decorative borders include a floral outer border, a dimensional swastika border, flowers and antiques along with the four literary joys and a running T pattern inncr border.

til Ch'ien-lung died in 1799. Ho-shên's fall is closely associated with the Summer Palace, for one of the charges brought against him was his presumption in riding his horse through the central gate of the *Yüan-ming yüan*. He was forced under torture to admit that he had buried most of his treasure in his country villa and later investigators reported on 26 out of 109 schedules of Ho-shên's possessions which amounted to the enormous value of 223,000,000 taels. [92] On the same basis his total wealth must have amounted to about 900,000,000 taels. After the death of Ch'ien-lung, the power of Ho-shên came to an end. This episode left the foundations of government so permanently undermined that the later Ch'ing emperors were unable to repair them.

The extravagances and luxuries enjoyed during the period of Ch'ien-lung's reign, as a whole, brought about the most ornate Chinese rugs. The blend of Chinese, Manchu and Western tastes resulted in decorative designs in carpet weaving and related applied arts which reflect a luxurious style. They represent in the drawing of leaf, flower, birds, butterflies and emblems of early philosophy and faith and the colours that blend with rare harmony, the most elaborate and voluptuous expression of native craftsmanship. Although many of the old patterns and designs were followed, the tendency to adopt more ornate forms appears to be the rule. The use of colours and ornamentation followed broader lines and designs became less conventionalized and more artistic. Many of the designs showed delicate shading that is not observable in earlier rugs.

In the best examples, the geometric and many of the stiff conventional forms which continued through the seventeenth and the early part of the eighteenth centuries, disappeared. In their place was a greater refinement of design, a greater accuracy for drawing which found expression in floral forms that reached their highest development at this time and became characteristic of it. Some of them, such as the chrysanthemums, lotuses, peonies, sunflowers and orchids are most dainty and naturalistic. The fields are often covered with such flowers which are carefully arranged in harmonious groupings of leaf, bud and flower but never with the formal, symmetrical and exact balance of Persian carpets.

An excellent example of this type of Ch'ien-lung rug is a rug belonging to Mr. M. Shiobara of Tokyo and illustrated in the publication *Shina Kogei zuran*. This rug has a central phoenix standing with four others flying around it clockwise. Four additional phoenixes are repeated in the corners. Floral sprays in groupings cover the field with two butterflies flittering about. The borders are unique. There is a band of running "T" design, a band of swastika fret (meander), and an outer band of small blossoms which is very unusual. A wider band is decorated with flowers in vases, brush-pot with brushes, books and an upper and lower band with symbols of the four literary joys. [93] The execution of the phoenix is certainly a Ch'ien-lung innovation and style. The design is rendered in a much more realistic and ornate fashion.

Quite frequently, both Ch'ien-lung innovations and the more conventional designs mingle in the same piece. Sometimes there is a single central medallion and occasionally there are multiple medallions. Generally, the medallions are entirely floral, with their ornamentation becoming more elaborate as time passes. Infrequently animals, birds and mythological creatures appear as the central design.

Another quite common Ch'ien-lung rug design is to have the central medallion surrounded by various objects or symbols such as Taoist and Buddhist symbols, longevity and happiness symbols, emblems of honours and the literati as well as fruits, bats and flower vases. The most typical Ch'ien-lung rug design is a central medallion with the four corner pieces all having the same design. Sometimes the entire field is completely covered with a pattern of intertwining and continuous foliate stems and flowers. Other examples have the field completely covered with an all-over pattern of small hexagonal and other geometric figures containing a conventionalized flower similar to T'ang and Ming textile patterns.

During this period, the borders were executed in the same distinctive manner as the central field. The most predominate design is the running "T" pattern, the Greek key pattern and pearls or dots. Sometimes the swastika meander is found but it is not as frequent. Almost all the rugs produced during this period have two ornamented stripes, one is floral while the other is geometric. The wider strip is most often geometric and serves as the outer border while the inner, narrower strip is most often floral. It is unusual that the borders should be two floral stripes. Whenever pearls or dots are used, they are almost always the inner border.

Ch'ien-lung rugs are also unique in that they have particular colour schemes one of which is blue and white with an ivory or ashy white ground and designs executed in varying shades of light and dark blues. Another distinctive colour scheme is a yellow or buff ground with overlaying designs in blues, whites, reds and yellows. Still another colour combination is a reddish ground with overlaying designs in blue, white, yellow and even green. The colours of both field and border are occasionally similar but more frequently they are complementary. These colour schemes are but a group that is most typical and by no means the only ones. As a whole, Ch'ien-lung period rugs have elaborate designs, delicate shading, and rich colours which rank among the most beautiful of Chinese rugs. So much so that the Indian weavers imitated them in a group of rugs that they call "Keen-lung". While we have not found any concrete evidence or documents to substantiate our suspicions or beliefs, it is, nevertheless, most probable that during the period of Ch'ien-lung, rugs with eighteenth century French 'Aubusson' designs were created most likely as furnishing for the *Yüan-ming yüan*. Contemporary designs of cloisonne support this supposition.

After Ch'ien-lung's time the following reigns merely copied and repeated the designs with only slight modification of the earlier patterns. However, there was the tendency to use larger and coarser designs as opposed to the finer lines and workmanship of the Ch'ien-lung era. The colours, although similar, lacked the deep richness of earlier dyes. This collapse of a refinement of technique is perhaps understandable as there was a larger population and new territories added to the empire during Ch'ien-lung's reign. Toward the end of his reign, corruption ran rampant and at least three provinces were devastated by rebellion. The Manchu bannermen were weakened by luxury and no longer a fierce fighting force. The national treasury was heavily drained, as the population had nearly doubled and China was plagued by floods, famine and war as various ethnic, religious and oppressed peoples rose in rebellion.

The emperors following Ch'ien-lung were not as energetic, strong and capable and thus were not able to cope with or remedy the mounting dilemmas and catastrophes. The war alone was costly as from 1796 to 1801 it drained the treasury of one hundred million taels. Pirates were active in ravaging the South China coast and it required ten years (1800 - 1810) in order to suppress them.

Plate XIX
A portrait of Hsien-fêng, the sixth Emperor of the Ch'ing dynasty. The
rug is decorated with an all-over diaper pattern in the centre and four
distant borders.

China, in such a lamentable state, saw no great expenditures for court life which was in fact quite austere and Emperor Chia-ch'ing was accused of being a miser. Therefore, with the court and the aristocracy no longer demanding costly carpets and rugs, with hostilities evident everywhere and a curtailment of an active export and import by sea, it was inevitable that the quality of the product should suffer. Although there was some trade with the West, it was mainly with the English and rugs were not a commodity of high value, since rugs could be obtained from the Middle East which was closer, less expensive and more accustomed to the Westerners. The appreciation for rugs and carpets was mainly a European tradition and the war with Napoleon was emptying many European treasuries.

In the mid-nineteenth century, China found herself engaged in war with England after suffering many foreign incursions that had threatened her traditional life and society. Weakened by a protracted war, the T'ai-p'ing rebellion, China was unable to defend herself and therefore fell to the demands of the West which drained not only the national treasury but also the national life of the Chinese. When aniline dyes were introduced into China, they were considered another foreign incursion and were resisted by many Chinese dyers. This was most fortunate as unlike the Middle East, the use of aniline dyes was not so widespread and not common for such a long period.

With the wars and the turbulence in the second half of the nineteenth century, a number of carpet weavers moved to Peking as it was considered both safer and also closer to the ready market for their products. This location avoided the cost and liability of distant transportation. Not only were there Chinese who would buy their rugs and carpets, there were also many Westerners and their legations and staffs. Since Tientsin was the port city for Peking, some carpet weavers ventured there to be near export facilities.

During this time, to give credence to Peking rugs, an oft-told story was circulated as to how carpet weaving was introduced to Peking and the standards of quality. This fabricated story relates that in 1860, a Lama priest by the name of Ho Chi-chang started a carpet weaving school out of pity for the poor in the city of Peking, while he was on vacation. The first looms were set up in the Pao-kuo Monastery. The West court, *Hsi-yüan*, or in some versions of the story called the West gate, *Hsi-mên*, was used as a showroom. The poor people were so eager to learn the craft that applicants clamoured for admittance. The East court, *Tung-yüan*, or East gate, *Tung-mên*, was then fitted with looms, and workers were taught the art of rug making.

The priest's vacation was limited, and, doubtless, due to the earlier start and longer period of training, the West gate, *Tung-mên*, carpets were considered better than the East gate, *Tung-mên*. From this there developed two "schools" called respectively, the *Hsi-mên* and the *Tung-mên*, the former refers to Peking rug weavers and the latter to Tientsin. The notion remained that *Hsi-mên* rugs were better than *Tung-mên* rugs as their makers' training had been longer.

This fabricated story allows rug dealers to concoct all sorts of claims and to raise their prices on *Hsi-mên* rugs. This particular story circulated in China when rugs from elsewhere in China were not readily available due to hostilities and poor conditions. This form of propaganda which was readily acceptable to many people in Peking helped greatly to sell the local products.

During the closing years of the nineteenth century, the Western world began to appreciate Chinese carpets. German exporters sent some of these Chinese rugs to Germany, where they received immediate admiration. It was like a breath of fresh air to the Europeans, who were only familiar with Persian rugs, to see an exciting product so artistic and well-coloured. During this period, aniline dyes swept over the Near East and became such a menace that Persia banned their importation. These early aniline dyes were extremely fugitive and not fast to either light or washing, and rugs dyed with them soon became two-toned beige and grey. The Persian government's ban on importing these dyes was never fully effective and was eventually lifted. Not only were cheap fugitive dyes used in Persia in the late nineteenth century but they are still used today especially for the mauve and orange combinations and the strident turquoise green that most Persian villagers seem to love. The particular disadvantage of these Persian dyes is that they fade very unevenly, the tips of the pile turning grey while the rest retains its original colour and blotches appear where one part of the rug is exposed to more light than another.

The Chinese rugs of this period, compared to the Persian ones, were certainly superior and became more sought-after and desired. The

West was in the Victorian Era and the sombre and subtle tones and colours of the Chinese rugs with their natural plant dyes were more favourably accepted than the harsh and garish colours of the fugitive aniline dyes on Persian rugs. By the closing years of the nineteenth century near the Hopeh-Shansi border, now on the Chên-tai railway, called Huai-lu, a very good quality rug was produced which was very popular with the foreign missionaries who purchased them as they travelled past that area. Some of these rug weavers went to Peking where they had set up their looms as to be closer to the foreigners and Chinese aristocracy.

Both Hopeh and Shantung provinces became centres for the rug industry. In Hopeh, Tientsin and Peking were the important centres while in Shantung, Chefoo was the centre. Shantung is one of the great wool-producing areas in China, and it is also an important area for silk-production.

Adolf Hackmack in his *Chinese Carpets and Rugs* writes that: "With such exceptionally great wealth of wool and silk materials to hand it was only natural that the provincial government of Shantung should show in a practical form its interest in the industry. About 1900 the Industrial school (*Kung I-chü*) for carpet weavers in Tsinanfu was established and a suitable place set apart for actual carpet weaving. A teacher from Kansu was engaged to instruct the youth of Shantung in the art". [94]

The *Kung I-chü*, to which Hackmack refers is really the *Kung-i chüan-shou-so* which was established by the government to teach carpet weaving. During the boom of the rug industry as a result of World War I, a rug factory was set up in Chefoo as a subsidary of the Shantung Silk and Lace Company. This firm exported all their products to the United States to Alfred Kohlberg and Company of San Francisco, California. After the boom subsided, this factory closed its doors in 1919.

With the Mediterranean blockade by the Allies; with fighting in the Near East and in the lower Balkan states, it became impossible to ship rugs and carpets from the Near East to the great markets in London or New York. Into the Peking and Tientsin area poured many merchants, bent on making easy profits. These were mainly Armenians from the United States, well schooled in the rug business, but thinking only of immediate profits. The Western world was wealthy and would

Plate XX

A nineteenth century picture showing a Chinese official purchasing rugs from the Turkish peoples living in Sinkiang. The designs on the rugs are basically from Khotan.

purchase anything that had the stamp of luxury on it.

It is a comparatively simple matter to start a Chinese rug factory. Anyone who had learned the art could easily set up his own loom, there being no complicated mechanism or machinery connected with it whatsoever. The chief requirements are a knowledge of dyes, and some good designs to follow in the manufacture of the articles, which are entirely handwoven. Naturally the quality of the product and the design it bears varies considerably. The foreigners had a knowledge and control of the export market and they merely followed a system of combining Chinese motifs with a Western treatment. Chinese labour was plentiful and also cheap so that factories could almost be set up overnight.

The Republican Period

After the collapse of the Ch'ing dynasty in 1911 and under the New Republic, foreign influence increased in the political sphere and is also reflected in the carpet designs which led up to the establishment of the New Chinese Style, mainly by American importers, in the 1920's. This new style of the era reflects the direct influence of the Art Deco Movement.

During and after World War I the rug factories in both Peking and Tientsin profited greatly form the mushrooming demand caused by the closing of Mediterranean ports. Westerners quickly seized the opportunity to exploit not only the trading in Chinese rugs but also to dominate and own the carpet-weaving industry of China. Immediately, a number of foreign owned and supervised firms were established first in Peking, then in Tientsin, and later in Shanghai such as the Fetté Rug Company, The Shoemaker Art Looms, and the Nichols Super Yarn and Carpets, Incorporated. All these companies had showrooms in Shanghai as well as in Peking. Nichols rugs also had operations in Tientsin. All these companies primarily produced rugs in Peking to be sold abroad.

Nichols Super Yarn and Carpets, Incorporated was the largest and the most unique firm. They had adapted a Manchu palace to serve as a showroom for their Chinese rugs. The palace once belonged to Prince I and the reception hall was used by Nichols as the showroom and for serving tea to visitors. The audience hall where Prince I once received official calls was decorated with Nichols' principle stock of rugs amidst a replica of the throne chair placed on the dias to lend an impression of an Imperial setting.

The once magnificent prince's residence was now reduced to a rug factory by the Nichol's Company. To add insult to injury, this foreign concern had all their workers wear suits of Manchu blue with red sashes. Suits of Manchu blue or *lan-san* were worn by graduates of the former first degree or *hsiu-ts'ai* and the red sash, or *hung-tai-tzŭ* was a distinctive badge worn by members of the collateral branches of the Imperial clan. Nichols took these steps in order to give their products an aura of luxury and Imperial quality for which the wealthy West clamoured. However, these actions were considered insults and humiliations by the Chinese.

The Chinese had just completed a revolution which overthrew the Manchus. After a period of chaos and adjustment to a Republican form of government, a strong feeling of nationalism swept over the country with young students leading and forming the backbone of this movement. Foreign companies and firms in China were looked upon as a strangle-hold on China and a vehicle to reduce the Chinese to a population of slaves, impeding any development of the Chinese nation. Students returning from abroad compared working conditions in the West and the degrading and harsh conditions of the Chinese workers employed by Western firms or firms doing business with the West.

We must understand that China had not been a highly industrialized nation and her factories and manufacturers were no more than cottage industries. There was a somewhat paternalistic attitude of business and a strong tie to a guild system which oversaw and mediated all disagreements and ill-treatment. There was also a set practice in working conditions and vacations. Workers had their meals at the shops and some even lived there. On the first and fifteenth of each month of the lunar calendar they had chicken on the menu. On important festivals and holidays there was time off, such as ten days vacation for the Chinese New Year season, three days for the Full-moon festival and several days for the Dragon boat festival. Otherwise they worked seven days a week throughout the year.

Although Western owned and operated firms had a six-day work week, they did not respect the Chinese practice of holidays. Since small Chinese shops producing rugs had to depend on the Western export firms to sell their products, these shops were supervised and dominated by the foreigners who had a strong hold on them. These small Chinese shops had to find ways of producing carpets and rugs far cheaper than those of the large Western-owned and operated firms or else they would not be able to compete. This led to a deplorable situation for all the carpet weavers in the large cities and also affected the quality of their products.

From the 1924 publication *Peking Rugs and Peking Boys* we learn that child labour was one of the main blots on the escutcheon of the Chinese rug industry. The Peking apprentices, for the most part, came from the country-side where "guarantors" would find the boys. It was felt that these children having no city connections, made "less trouble" for their employers. The majority of the young boys came from Hopeh, although some came from Shantung province.

These young boy apprentices, during the time of their contracts, which usually ran a little more than three years, were bound to the will of their employers. After this initial contracted period, they may be given a small amount of money as salary and became employees of the shop. During their period as apprentices, the boys lived and worked in these shops sleeping on wadded bedding on the floors and working twelve or more hours a day. The young apprentices began by sorting and winding wool and learned weaving at small looms where they work-ed at what were called "hit or miss" rugs.

The mortality rate amongst these young boys was high due to the carpet lint which they breathed into their lungs. Also many of them be-came malformed and developed spinal disorders due to their having to sit for hours each day on a plank suspended in the air without any back support. Dust and lint caused irritation to their lungs and eyes. It is not surprising that many suffered from tuberculosis and trachoma un-der these working and living conditions. A day's work for a weaver was to complete between five to six inches of carpet on the loom which took between twelve and fourteen hours.

The long hours of work affected these adolescent boys, whose constitutions were so undermined that they were poorly suited to carry on an active life. Additionally the poor food tended to make them sus-ceptable to colds and weakened them against other infectious diseases. Inspite of these hardships and deplorable conditions which arose in the rush to satisfy the market, many small shops were unable to continue operations and were absorbed by the larger foreign-owned rug factories.

The rugs of China not made to the requirements of Western purchasers soon disappeared. Traditional patterns and designs were obsolete as the foreign-owned rug companies designed their own exotic "Peking" and "Tientsin" rugs drawing from some elements of Chinese design but with a totally Western feel so that any Western home could find patterns which blended in with its scheme of decoration. Firms such as Fetté Rug Company boasted of having their rugs personally supervised and designed by Mrs. Franklin C. Fetté, who was a Vassar graduate. To give the appearance of an old rug, these firms introduced a chemical washing to the finished product. Nichols Super Yarn and Carpet, Incorporated became a completely self-sufficient company with its own facilities for all processes from spinning the yarn to the chemical washing of the completed rug done under one roof. A colour chart and pattern of every rug made was filed and any order could be duplicated.

Although these foreign firms brought new capital and new life to the rug industry, they did little for art. They produced a rug that had no more reason to be called Chinese than they did; they merely supplied a demand and were bent on making easy profits. These early reorganizers did one thing well. They standardized the wool and the dyes to be used in the rugs. Sadly they also brought about a change in the organization of the Chinese workshop and the centralization of goods for export was brought totally under foreign domination. As part of their "marketing" they disregarded and defiled Chinese customs and traditions and like the Nichols firm even used a palace for a rug factory. Their monopolization caused take-overs and closing of smaller Chinese shops. The disregard for the young Chinese boys and their harsh treatment, spurred the young nationalistic Chinese to take action against these foreign-owned and foreign supervised firms. In the late 1920's the politically active students urged the weavers to go on strike when a deaf ear was turned to the workers' request for better working and living conditions and just compensation. These nationalistic students were condemned as labour agitators by the foreigners, and their presses. Nevertheless some concessions, like not allowing children under fourteen to work, were made to end the strike so that this most profitable industry would not be hampered.

To combat future labour problems, the foreign owned and supervised firms began a program of decentralizing their operations and having their workers separated into smaller units and firing some of the more politically active employees. The various foreign export firms then took on the position of "sales department" except that the foreign salesmen were responsible for and had the final word to say as to the quality of the manufactured product. They acted as clearing houses and central inspection and grading headquarters. Thus, most of the foreign companies continued to operate in a most profitable setting.

After the conclusion of World War I, as Persian rugs returned to the markets, many predicted the doom of the Chinese rug industry. But by then the Chinese rugs were better able to meet the Persian competition. Not only had quality standards fallen in Persian rugs, Chinese rugs had improved in quality.

The firms which had been hastily set up in wartime for quick profits now dropped out of the business and new faces appeared. Several distinctly Chinese firms started producing rugs and while their products were not at first as good in quality as some of the firms headed by foreigners they added something that had been lacking. These Chinese firms produced rugs for a Chinese market and used old Chinese motifs. By 1930 some of the best rugs of North China were being produced by firms in which the capital was wholly Chinese. These rugs now began to appear in the export markets. The American market responded quickly to this new rug that carried with it some of the feeling of the ancient East. Soon all manufacturers sensed the trend and a revival took place. Just before the outbreak of World War II, the Chinese were producing rugs in quality equal to anything produced in Persia in designs and colours. In fact in dyes they were far superior to the Persians who were still using aniline dyes.

Of the two major types of rugs, "Peking" and "Tientsin" which the Chinese call *Hsi-mên* and *Tung-mên* respectively, there was very little difference in the early products. However, soon the "Tientsin" rug became more adventuresome in both colour and design. "Peking" rugs often adhered to the traditional blues, buff, tan and white colours with very little red colour used. However, "Tientsin" rugs in contrast engaged bright hues of reds, oranges and greens. In earlier times, blues were only used as designs, however in the "Peking" and "Tientsin" rugs, they were used in the field also. Dark blue, grey and tan colours were also used for the central fields. There was less importance given to the borders and later the designers sometimes eliminated them. Both these two major types of rugs had designs which were more or less oriented around a central medallion. However, by the 1920's pictorial scenes arranged asymmetrically across the carpet became an innovation that proved very popular.

"Peking" rug weavers tended to create more complex designs while the "Tientsin" rugs were more varied in shapes and sizes and had a thicker and stiffer pile. Both of these rugs wore extremely well and in some of the "Tientsin" rugs machine-spun wool was also utilized which was supplied by three foreign firms in that area, Nichols, Elbrook, and Karaghlusian. These machine-spun wools were called "super" yarn by the trade. The foreign-owned rug companies all used this "super" yarn which was both durable and wore well. Had not the Japanese invasion of China taken place, which completely disrupted the Chinese rug and carpet industry, it is more likely that Chinese rugs would have become the most popular rug in the Western market.

The war with Japan caused a great need for blankets which led the Chinese government to make mass-purchases of wool in Kansu and in the surrounding territory. This greatly curtailed any development in rugs in the Peking-Tientsin area. The Japanese first subjugated Manchuria and the Northeastern provinces and gradually extended into other parts of the country. The Japanese also blockaded Shanghai, shutting off foreign trade to the extent that industry was disrupted and rug production came to a halt. Many firms were forced to quit business, while others transferred their headquarters to more hospitable regions in the South, such as Hong Kong and Indo-China. A rug factory was even tried in Western China in Chêng-tu in Szechwan province. Due to wartime conditions and the difficulty of acquiring chrome dyes, the dyers reverted to the use of natural plant dyes. However one innovation that was most popular in Cheng-tu was using plain natural wool with perhaps a darker pattern of natural wool -- no dye being required.

The Modern Period

After the defeat of Japan with the closing of World War II, Civil War broke out in China between the Nationalists and the Communists. On October 1, 1949 the Communists became victorious and established the People's Republic of China. Shortly thereafter the rug-industry was established in six centres: Peking, Tientsin, Shên-yang, Ta-lien, Shanghai and Tsingtao. Of these locations, Tientsin and Shên-yang in Liao-tung province are the leading manufacturing centres. The range of size, colour and designs has remained much the same since the Revolution.

Tastes and fashion changed somewhat in the world so that in the late 1950's when these rugs appeared on the market, they were met with no more than lukewarm response. Perhaps in part it was the world situation as the Korean Conflict caused a certain amount of anti-Chinese feelings. Also the United States government had imposed a trade embargo against Chinese goods and items resembling Chinese products had to have a "Certificate of Origin".

By the late 1960's and early 1970's, the climate changed again so that things Chinese had become more fashionable. President Nixon's visit to China in 1972 was the catalyst that created a tremendous boom in the interest in China and things Chinese. Although the trade embargo against Chinese goods was lifted, the tariff was so high that the rugs were quite expensive. Nevertheless, the superior quality and aesthetics of Chinese rugs carved out a niche in the international marketplace and in turn older Chinese rugs were sought after and collected.

There was a period during the Cultural Revolution in the mid-1960's when dragons, flying horses, mythical dogs and similar motifs strongly associated with China's ancient culture were not considered suitable for use in carpets and other hadicraft products, and for some years dragon designs disappeared from the market. However, subsequent political changes led to a reprieve for these old designs and they were again adopted for use.

In modern Chinese rugs there are four basic designs: Self-toned and embossed, "Peking", Floral and Aesthetic. The self-toned and embossed rug is characterized by deeply clipped designs in which the main flowers are cut in a higher pile to give an embossed effect. Sometimes these embossed designs are clipped from a field of a single colour. This treatment is unique to Chinese rugs. "Peking" designs take as their themes natural scenery and people, though some tradtional symbols such as the Four Joys of the Literati, "Happiness and Longevity", and so forth are also frequent motifs. Bat, butterflies and pine trees appear occasionally. Pandas have also been popular.

Floral pattern rugs are based on the "Peking" designs but include flowers not usually used in traditional designs, such as roses and morning glories. There is no border on this type of carpet and the pile is embossed to create a three-dimensional effect.

Plate XXI
An assortment of modern rug designs which show traditional Chinese design features blended with various influences of Western taste. Note the obvious French-Aubusson flavour.

The Aesthetic pattern was created in the 1920's and incorporates European design influences such as full-blown roses and peonies. This carry-over of the 1920's style is created with a heavy warp and weft, a firm ridged back and a thick pile. All designs are carved.

Although the standard sized rug manufactured today is 3.6 x 5.5 metres, manufactured out of machine-spun wool and chrome-dyed with 90 to 120 lines per square foot, modern carpets are generally made larger than traditional ones. The texture has been made finer by the use of more knots per foot. The colouring effect has been improved since the last century by chemical washing processes, which the manufacturers claim mellows the dye colours and gives them a sheen. However excellent this processing, it cannot compete with the effect produced by natural vegetable dyes. The Chinese government has centralized their exporting and distributing organization with the China National Animal By-product Import/Export Corporation which has sole charge over the industry. Since Japan is the largest importer of Chinese rugs, buying 40 percent of the output, this governmental unit has appointed Nissho-Iwai Trading Company Ltd. as its sole agent in Japan to better facilitate their export trade. Besides Japan's 40 percent, the United States buys 20 percent with the United Kingdom, West Germany, Canada and Hong Kong buying the rest of the output.

Taiwan's rug factories which were also established in the 1950's have not been able to develop a clear identity in the world market. As might be expected Taiwan rugs invariable are woven in classic Chinese patterns, particularly the "Peking" design. In addition to the traditional colours there are a number of rich deep background and soft shades. The main wool used comes from New Zealand and other foreign sources. There is a wide range of standard sizes and Taiwan rugs are generally of decent quality. However, Taiwan is finding it difficult to maintain weaving centres in their steadily industrializing nation, despite the fact that weavers earn equal or better pay than factory workers. This situation, coupled with the normalization of American relations with the People's Republic of China, would seem to create an insurmountable challenge for the rug industry of Taiwan. Considering the construction, quality of wool and the investment potential of Taiwan rugs, they can only be compared to Indian rugs at best.

Current events may seem to be a repeat of history. The Chinese rug industry was created and given world attention and acceptance with the closing of the ports of the Near East in World War I. Now with the United States embargo on Iranian goods due to the Iranian Revolution and the seizing of the United States Embassy in Tehran, the Chinese rugs become once again the beneficiary of the world political situation.

From a purely practical viewpoint, Chinese carpets are a good value in that they are soundly constructed of outstanding materials and refreshingly free of those "deliberate" mistakes which are endearing in some Persian rugs but which in others are no more than evidence of plain shoddy workmanship.

The progress that is being made in the rug industry in China, such as the close-back weaves, embossing and carving, is so great that it is unlikely that Iranian carpets will be able to re-enter the market in the volume and price that they once commanded. Even if Iran goes back to its pre-Revolution schedule of production, the demand for carpets world-wide is so great that China is assured of markets even if she doubles her present output. Inevitably the older and more classic Chinese rugs will become even more valuable and sought after.

COLOURS and DYES

Different colours evoke different sensations and emotions and the Chinese are very sensitive to them. Also each colour has its appropriate meaning and purpose in Chinese symbolism and may be emblematic of rank, authority, virtues and vices, joys and sorrows and so forth.

From ancient times the Chinese conceived of five primary colours termed *Wu-sê* to correspond to the points of the Chinese compass or *Wu-fang*. [95] In turn these five colours compliment, reflect and embody the five elements *Wu-hsing*.

Black	North	Water	Mercury
Ch'ing (Blue/Green)	East	Wood	Jupiter
Red	South	Fire	Mars
White	West	Metal	Venus
Yellow	Centre	Earth	Saturn

The derivation of these primary colours is reflected in a statement by Sung Ying-hsing in his seventeenth century compilation, *T'ien-kung k'ai-wu*, observing that "in the sky the clouds are of different hues, and on earth the flowers and the leaves are dissimilar in appearance. What Heaven has established as model, the Sages then followed. Dyes of variour colours therefore were invented, which are derived from the five [primary] colours. Who can say that Emperor Shun [96] has not deliberated carefully in this matter? Among the many birds of the air the phoenix sports a red colour, and among the multitude of animals, the unicorn is blue-green. The same principle underlies the decision that vermillion and yellow should be the objects of obeisance by the multitudes of dark-robed literati. Lao-tzu once said, 'The bland will absorb a mixture of tastes, and the white will absorb the rainbow colours', All the silk, hemp, fur, and woolen stuffs are naturally plain, yet when dyed in various colours, their value can be much enhanced. Is there one who contends that the Power of Creation had not exercised great care in its undertakings? I certainly would not believe him." [97]

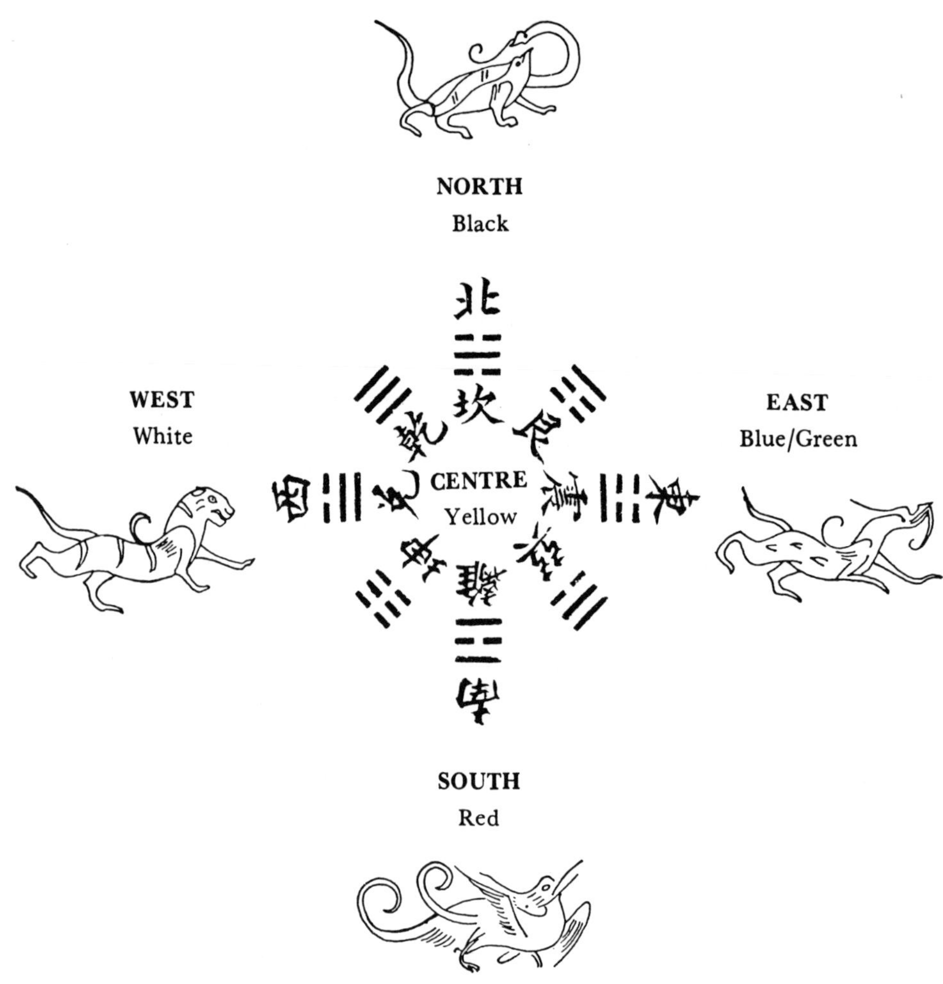

Figure 3
Points of a Chinese compass with corresponding animals and colours.

Colour is of such importance that various dynasties issued decrees to forbid the use of certain colours or shades by any but Imperial family members, i. e., green in the Ming and Yellow in the Ch'ing period. In annual ceremonies of making sacrifices to Heaven and Earth, the Emperor wore robes of an azure hue in allusion to the sky and yellow robes to indicate the yellow earth. Therefore magical charms and talismans as well as petitions to Heaven and Earth were either inscribed on

Plate XXII
The swastika-fret ground softens the brilliant red of this stunning rug.
Stylized floral motifs make up the central medallion. Three decorative
borders are surrounded by a final plain red stripe. 128x176 cm.

red or yellow paper as they were the embodiment of the *Yin* and *Yang* forces.

The five primary colours were traditionally used in paper charms and talismans since spirits moved in all five directions, suitable colours or combination of colours were needed to control them. Yellow represented the centre, blue the east, red the south, white the west and black the north.

Of these five colours, red was especially important as it symbolized blood, the life force, the embodiment of the *Yang* element, and was considered to have supreme magic power. Red talismans protected the entire family from pestilence and ills. The belief that red brought good fortune and longevity is reflected in the extensive sue of cinnabar in Taoist alchemy in the perpetual search for the elixir of life. With all these qualities and attributes red became the most auspicious colour in Chinese daily life.

Certain colours were also symbols of humiliation and indications of inferior status. In the *Ming hui-tien* or Statutes of the Ming dynasty, it is recorded that "a green scarf was worn by the actors belonging to the *Chiao-fang-ssŭ*, and black gowns were worn by government runners, the so-called *Tsao-li*. In the *Yüan-tien chang*, Statutes of the Yüan period, we find, "it was required that a male member of the family of a prostitute wear a blue scarf." Green was used on a painted board carried before a criminal going to the execution grounds. This board had inscribed on it the authority for his punishment.

The outward sign of a colour whose meaning was readily understood by all served the Chinese in maintianing what was viewed as the proper order of society. This is in keeping with the Chinese belief that what is not said is more important than what is obvious, *Yên yu chiang, I wu-k'ung*. This tradition and practice is also carried into theatrical make-up and costume. In the Peking Opera, colours reveal the inner characteristics and personalities of the roles portrayed. Like official government regulations there are also very strict rules as to what kind of costume should be worn depending on the status and personality of the roles being played. Oftentimes the colour scheme becomes more important than the design or pattern. The costume rules are so paramount that actors usually follow the axiom *Yüan ch'üan p'o-i, Pu ch'üan ts'o-i*. Better to wear a worn and torn costume, rather than make the mistake of wearing the wrong costume."

On the Chinese stage red indicates a character displaying loyalty, sincerity and bravery or a sacred person. Purple does the same but to a lesser degree. Black signifies a good, vigorous character who may also be rough or crude. Blue symbolizes savageness and fierceness but may also indicate arrogance. Yellow is a sign of the same negative traits as blue but not so pronounced. It also denotes a clever thinker who hides his thoughts. Green is the colour of an unstable character as the faces of devils are painted green.

With this sensitivity in mind, Hans A. Lorentz in his book, *A View of Chinese Rugs from the Seventeenth to the Twentieth Century*, has made a most profound observation the "the colours of a (Chinese) rug are more important than its pattern. A harmoniously blended rug will please even if it has not much of a pattern; whereas ill-chosen colours spoil the best design." [98]

Colour or *Se* is of such importance that it had become a part of words used to denote appearance and quality, such as *Ch'êng-sê*, meaning quality, and *Ch'u-sê*, meaning outstanding.

As we examine closely the colours of Chinese rugs, the most striking point is the paucity and simplicity of the materials with which they produce so many brilliant effects.

The beauty of their appearance depends largely on the colours which are produced naturally. Natural dyestuffs, properly used, are unquestionably the best. They are rarely garish in themselves and usually produce subtle and harmonious combinations. However, they are not fully fast, and are subject to change either by light or by washing. Nevertheless, they produce magnifent, rich, glowing colours when exposed to daylight over a long period of use. It is the use of natural dyes which was the secret of resplendent colours of antique carpets for until about 1850 all dyestuff used anywhere in the world were of vegetable, animal or mineral origin. In antique Chinese rugs the dyes used were almost exclusively vegetable dyes.

Although the Chinese speak of five primary or basic colours, in practice, many varieties and shades of colours exist and were used in varying degrees. Inasmuch as certain colours such as green and yellow were proscribed during the Ming and Ch'ing periods, these rules basically restricted a particular shade of these colours which have been popularly called, Ming green and Imperial yellow. Various colours which we look at as separate colours were considered by the Chinese as a shade or hue of one of the basic five colours. Therefore, brown, tan, apricot colours were grouped as yellow while purple, violet, mauve and maroon were considered to be shades of red. The unique practice of toning one colour into gradations, which the French call *broché ton-sûr-ton* is very characteristic of Chinese art. An early writer on Oriental rugs, Jean Henri d'Ardenne de Tizac observed that "the most original method used for the lovely Chinese rugs culminates in applying different shades [nuances] of one colour . . . The rug artist clings to the tone which is in his ear and does not let it go before he has exhausted its scale sufficiently."[99] The subtle tones of colour, soft harmonies with the different shades gives a lyrical treatment to the design and pattern, resulting in a marvellously soft effect yet giving a subdued appearance, in spite of the lustre of the material.

"From the T'ang dynasty textiles excavated from Turfan, there is a total of twenty-four colours [or shades]. Aside from black and white there are five shades of reds: vermillion, clear pale pink, scarlet, crimson, and purple; six shades of yellow: canary [gosling] yellow, tan, apricot, golden yellow, earth brown and tea brown; six shades of blue: eggshell [Robin's egg] blue, deep sky blue, peacock blue, sapphire, mauve, and Mohammedan blue; five shades of green: bright green, grass green, fruit greet, dark green and pale green."[100]

Thus there seems to be quite versatility in colours during the T'ang times. What is more significant is that this versatility of colours indicates the high and sophisticated level of the dyeing technology in the seventh century. In examining literary sources, we find that in the *Chou-li*, Rituals of the Chou Period (1122 - 221 B. C.), vegetable dyes were known and used. "Indigo is used for blues, *Ch'ien* (madder) for reds and *Hsiang-tou* for black". Inasmuch as the ancients preferred to use blue, yellow and red colours for dying, various other colours, deep or pale, may have been produced by mixing the main dyes or using them at various strengths. By the end of the first century A. D., we find in the *Shuo-wên* dictionary, over twenty different dye colours that are listed.

In the T'ang dynasty statues, *T'ang Liu-tien*, it is noted that: "There are six basic or principle colours of a dyer's art. *Ch'ing*, blue;

Chiang, crimson or red; *Huang*, yellow; *Pai*, white; *Tsao*, black; and *Tzu*, purple."[101]   Of these six colours, all are obtained from plant or vegetable dyes except white which is obtained by soaking and bleaching.

Indigo

Of the various dyes, Indigo is the most extensively used blue dyestuff. It is mentioned in the *Êrh-ya* and the *Kuang-chih* that it was used as a medicine and a dyestuff as early as the Chou dynasty (1122 - 221 B. C.). It is important to note that in one of the earlier books the *Shih-ching*, the Book of Poetry, there is mention of Indigo: "All the morning I gather the indigo plant. And do not collect enough to fill my apron."[102]   Chao Ch'i, in the late second century A. D. described in the poem, *Lan-fu* the people cultivating indigo. Indigo was a commercial crop that was both used by the Chinese and also exported by them as a commodity. Since the T'ang dynasty favoured the colour red, the growing and cultivation of safflower were encouraged by the government, both for domestic use and for export. The cultivation, preparation and use of indigo as a dye are fully described in the *Ch'i-min yao-shu*, an early agricultural encyclopedia written by Chia Ssŭ-hsieh in the first part of the sixth century A. D.

There are five kinds of plants which yield indigo *Mu-lan* or tea indigo *Isatis tinctoria* is a plant that is propagated by spring planting. The other varieties, *Ma-lan* horse indigo, *Polygonum tinctorium* and *Wu-lan* Kiangsu indigo *Indigofera kiangsu* are all seed grown. The commonly used indigo plant in China is the tea indigo which is chiefly found in the central and northern part of China as well as in Manchuria. It is harvested in the eleventh month of the year, by cutting off all the leaves and some of the stems, and placing them into a pit for processing into Indigo. The tops and bottoms of the stems are trimmed off so that only a few inches near the roots are left, which are dried in hot air and then covered with earth for storage and used for the planting in the spring.

The preparation of indigo blue was generally carried out in the seventh month of the lunar calendar. The leaves and stem of the plant were put into a pit, vat or jar according to the quantity to be prepared. They were covered with water and pressed down by means of some heavy wood or stone and allowed to stand for seven days. A fermentation took place causing a rise in temperature which released and hydrolyzed the indigo juice. In the *Ch'i-min yao-shu*, we find the water extraction of *Indican* was accomplished by the use of hot water. It was possible to recover 80 to 85 percent of the *Indican* by hot water extraction, as against only 40 to 50 percent by oridinary steeping.

The greenish-yellow liquid was separated from the plant residues, lime was added and the mixture was violently stirred and splashed by workmen for several hours in order to thoroughly aerate and oxidize the soluble, colourless indigo white. The insoluble blue colour indigo was precipitated and after settling to the bottom, the liquor was drained off. The precipitate was washed, filtered, and finally pressed into cakes. When used, it was mixed first with ashes of burnt rice stalk and water and again violently stirred repeatedly.

For many centuries Wu-hu on the Yangtze River in Anhwei province was famous for its deep blue colour. Another area well-known for a dark blue was Sung-chiang in Kiangsu province.

All blues in old Chinese rugs have been dyed with indigo which produces varying shades from pale sky-blue to almost a black colour. Indigo is fast to both light and washing, but it is not fast to rubbing. Even the best dyeing allows some transfer of colour. Nevertheless, with continued use, the colours become a clearer, lighter and a more shimmering blue. The richness and various shades of the blues on Chinese rugs are undisputed and unparalleled among handmade rugs.

Safflower

Hung-hua or safflower or bastard saffron has been cultivated and used as both a red dye and a drug in China since ancient times. According to Li Shih-chên's (1518 - 1593) *Pên-ts'ao kang-mu* and the *Chung-hua ku-chin chu*, safflower juice was first used for make-up rouge in the time of the ruler chou of the Shang dynasty (1154 - 1122 B. C.). On the other hand, the *Po-wu chih*, a third century A. D. work relates that the seeds of a "barbarian safflower" were brought into China from the "Western Regions" by Chang Ch'ien in 126 B. C.

Safflower is the dried petals of *Carthamus tinctorius* which contains a considerable amount of a very brilliant red colour, *Carthamine*. Its seeds are sown at the beginning of the second lunar month and the plant begins to blossom in the early summer. The blossoms must be picked early in the morning while they are still moist with dew, as the flower will close up into a solid ball as the sun rises high in the sky and the dew dries. In this state it is not fit for picking. The plant will con-

Plate XXIII
Simple four petal silver-blue persimmon flowerettes termed *Shih-t'i wen*
form a pleasing repeating pattern across the ground of this two-colour
rug. The borders are a running-T and swastika-fret surrounded by a
plain outer stripe. 116x222 cm.

tinue to bloom every day for an entire month. Those flowers destined for use in medicine, need not be made into cakes. However, for dyes, they must be made into cakes so that the yellow juice in the flower is eliminated and the red colour obtained.

The cultivation, preparation and utilization of safflower were fully described in the *Ch'i-min yao-shu* as follows:

" . . . after picking [the flower], immediately pound to a paste [with a foot pestle]. Wash. Wring out the yellow juice by means of a filter bag, and pound again. Wash with clear sour rice drink [a slightly fermented rice meal soup containing lactic acid] and again wring out the juice. (This juice is to be kept as a red dye, so don't throw it away). Place the [residue] in a porcelain container and cover loosely with a cloth. [In the early morning], take out and pound again. Spread on a mat to dry. This is better than rolling to a lump, which owing to a retained moisture, makes the flower swarthy. . . Burn caltrops (*Tributus*), tumbleweeds and pigweeds (*Chenopodium*) wormwood (*Artemisia*) sometime ahead and keep the ashes (ordinary kitchen ashes may be used in lieu) now steep with hot water to obtain a clear *Lixirium* (if the primary steeping is too strong, the flower will be destroyed; so it is better not used for this purpose but keeping it for laundry. The third steeping is mellow; when used with the flowers, it will give a brilliant colour). Mix with the flowers and knead (for a dozen rounds until flowers give up all their pigments). Wring out the rich extract into procelain bowls. Take two or three sour pomegranates. Remove the seeds, pound, add some extremely sour clear rice drink and mix with the flower extract. (If no pomegranates available, use good vinegar with sour rice drink or even rice drink alone if vinegar also failing). [The acid treated mass] is then put in a sack, soaked in water, and finally squeezed to remove its decomposed yellow matter. Then for one night this solid residue is covered with branches of *Ch'ing-hao* or *Artimisia apiacea*, after which it is shaped into cakes, dried in the shade, and stored. When dyers know the correct method [of preparing safflower cakes] brillant will be our red colour. This is the colour known as *Hsing-hung* or scarlet."[103]

Briefly stated, the principle was to start the extraction with an alkaline solution (lye), and then finish with an acid. Chia Ssŭ-hsieh wrote his treatise before mineral acids were made, so polybasic acids in unripened fruits were the best available agent and in lieu of this they even resorted to the use of acetic and lactic acids.

Safflower was used extensively as a red dye for rugs and a particular shade called *Fei*, a dark stawberry red was developed in Liang-chou in Kansu province. In the *Pei-shih* or History of the Northern Wei dynasty (386 - 532 A. D.), it states that: "The *Fei* or dark strawberry red colour of Liang-chou is the most superior [colour] ". It is during this period safflower was used as a cash crop for export. In Ming times (1368 - 1643) the particulars of safflower were fully described by Sung Ying-hsing in his work *T'ien-kung k'ai-wu*.

One of the peculiarities of the safflower dye is that it has a lovely scent but "it is most allergic to *Ch'ên-hsiang* garu-wood *Lignaloes* and musk, i. e. perfumes. If safflower-dyed materials are stored together with these scents, the colouring will be ruined within a few months. If the removal of the colour after dying is desired, it only needs to be moistened with a small amount of the aqueous solution of caustic soda or rice stalk ash, and the red colour will be completely withdrawn and return to its original form. This liquid is stored in green lentil flour and can be released again for dyeing with no loss. Information about this process is not obtainable from dyers; who regard it as a trade secret."[104]

Besides safflower, *Tzŭ-ts'ao* (*Lithospermum officinale*), a plant yielding a red dye was also used in ancient times. Both safflower and *Tzŭ-ts'ao* were very weak dyestuff and did not produce a fast dye. However the colours were also brilliant and with fading a magnificent rich glowing colour appears which enhanced the softness and beauty of the rug. With the knowledge that safflower dyes could be manipulated with various scents to cause an artificial fading, the richness of the aged red was sometimes induced by the skilled Chinese dyers who possessed the trade secrets.

Su-fang-mu or Sappanwood

During the Sung dynasty (960 - 1206) as sea-routes were opened, a new dyestuff was imported into China called *Su-fang-mu*,[105] Brasil-wood, *Caesalpinia sappan*. The dye from this wood is colourless but when dissolved in boiling water, with mordants added, it then oxidizes and gives off a variety of vivid reds. According to Li Shih-chén, *Su-fang mu* was used by the Chinese for dyeing fabrics in the Western Chin dynasty (265 - 316 A. D.) and possibly earlier. It is described in the third century work *T'ang Pên-ts'ao*. However it became widely used since

Sung times due to better means of commerce and transportation.

Logwood *Itaematoxylon campechianum* was also used as a red dye. It is also found colourless and oxidized in hot water with proper mordants added it gives a variety of red-blues that verge toward violet brown and even "Midnight blue" or blue-black.

Of these two dyestuffs, Brazilwood or *Su-fang-mu* was more commonly used especially after Sung times. It produced various interesting red shades. The colours, however, are extremely fugitive to light but somewhat fast to washing. As a common practice the Chinese usually dye the wool first with a yellow dye before dyeing with *Su-fang-mu* in order to obtain a variety of fruity red shades such as apricot, peach, red- orange or persimmon. Since *Su-fang-mu* is fugitive to light, after a long period of time, the red would fade and the yellow under-colour would surface giving a mellow and attractive shade. A case in point is the famous "Fo-dog" design rug in the Victoria and Albert Museum. In 1922, it was described as having a rose field by Kendrick and Tattesall in their book, *Hand-woven Carpets, Oriental and European*, although now the colour is clearly more a yellowish-red shade.

Ch'ien or Madder

Another dyestuff that the Chinese used is *Ch'ien* or Madder *Rubia cordifolia var. mungista*. This variety of madder differs from Near Eastern madder as it contained a higher percentage of *Purpurin*. This produces reds that are subdued and more bluish in tone. *Ch'ien* was used in ancient times in China and by the beginning of the Han dynasty, third century B. C., it was not only widely used but exported.

Madder dye is different from the other red dyestuffs used by the Chinese, in that it is fast to light but less so to washing. Cochineal dyes from the dried bodies of insects, which were widely used in the Near East were rarely if ever used by the Chinese.

Huai and Other Yellow Dyes

Yellow was an important colour to the Chinese however, it has always been a problem for the dyer inspite of the many available natural dyestuffs. Many writers on Chinese rugs make references to a "Mandarin yellow" and an "Imperial yellow" which are terms dealers favoured as they suggest a provenance of an Imperial household. It has been suggested that this particular colour has been obtained from the *Huai*

Plate XXIV

A dragon pillar rug with sacred Buddhist symbols surrounding the dragon and a devil's mask above. This dragon coils around the pillar when the rug is properly wrapped. The lower border features the mountain and waves motif. 107x158 cm.

flower buds or *Sophora japonica*. Although *Huai* was used as an ordinary yellow dyestuff, it was not used to develop the "Imperial yellow" hue.

Huai or *Sophora japonica* is a large and beautiful tree belonging to the *Leguminosae* family which grows abundantly throughout China. In the *Êrh-ya*, it is recorded that in the Chou dynasty (1122 - 211 B. C.) *Huai* was considered the most appropriate tree for the Imperial palace as well as the meeting places of the very high officials. The cultivation of *Huai* trees and the use of their flower-buds as an ordinary dyestuff are respectively mentioned in the sixth century work *Ch'i-min yao-shu* and the eighth century work *Pên-ts'ao shih-i*.

"A *Huai* tree will not blossom and bear fruit unless it is over ten years old. The immature, unopened blossoms are called *Huai* flower-buds, which are a necessary ingredient in dyeing green colour, just as safflower is in dyeing a red colour. To gather the buds, bamboo mats are spread closely under [the tree] to receive them [as they are picked]. The buds are then boiled once in water, strained and fashioned into cakes; they are now ready for use by dyers."[106] *Huai* contains *Flavonol quercetin* and a wide range of yellow shades could be obtained. The yellows are relatively fast to the light and usually have a greenish tinge.

When applied to wool, the *Huai* dyes give a dull orange colour with chromium as mordant, a yellow of moderate brilliancy with aluminum, a bright yellow with tin and a dark olive with iron. To obtain the "Imperial yellow" colour in ancient times, dyers followed an elaborate process. A full description is found in the *Ch'i-min yao-shu*:

"The Ho-tung Method to obtain 'Imperial Yellow' is as follows: Pound the roots of *Ti-huang* foxglove *Rehmannia glutinosa* in a motar. Mix with *Lixivium*, and stir thoroughly. Wring out the steeped liquid into another container. Pound the residue to a fine mince, mix with more *Lixivium* to make a thin paste. Pour into a stain-free iron pot to the undyed material. Turn over frequently to insure an even soaking. When there appears saccules with air bubbles within, the fabric is now well-done. Take out, shake off the dregs, sun to dry. Drain a rich syrup (from another batch of roots, without adding *lixivium*) through a piece of silk, place the dried piece into a panful of warm, rich syrup for a second dyeing. Spread quickly to secure an even colouring. Wring out when the dye has cooled down. Sun to dry. The more dyewort used, the better colour will result. Ashes of *Quercus*, *Morus* and *Artemi-*

sia are all good to use."[107]

Other dyestuffs, including *Huang-lu* a type of Sumac *Rhus succedaneum* which contains *Fisetin* were also used for yellow dyes. The barks of *Huang-nieh* yellow berberine, *Berberis thunbergii* is from a tree which the Chinese have used for its yellow dyestuff since the Han dynasty (206 B. C. - 220 A. D.), if not earlier. *Seeth* water is the liquid from which the indigo precipitate settles out at the end of the oxidation process. When *Seeth* water is evaporated, yellow-brown to deep-brown residues are obtained.

Che a tall thorny tree, *Cudranida triloba* was widely used as well as the roots of a plant of the salt marshes called *Huang-chin*. However, these yellows reflect a brownish tone. *Hung-hua* the dried flowers of *Carthamus tinctoria* were also employed. *Hung-hua* contained a *Carthamin* derivitive constituting the active ingredient of safflower dye, which produces vivid yellows and yellow-orange colours. The stigmata of the saffron crocus was used to bring out a vibrant yellow. Both *Hung-hua* and saffron were used only occasionally as they were very expensive. Moreover, although they were fast to washing they tended to fade on exposure to light.

A very popular dyestuff, *Huang-chih* or *Chih-tzu* identified as *Gardenia florida* had been used since ancient times also. The propagation of this plant is fully described in the *Ch'i-min yao-shu*. After preparation, the colours derived are a brilliant and pleasing deep yellow with a hint of reddish hue or yellow-orange. This colour dye has been sometimes referred to as "Lama yellow" or as "Imperial yellow". Besides brilliant colour it also has an aromatic quality.

Black Dyes

The colour black or *Tsao* in T'ang dynasty documents, was obtained by first dyeing the material in a deep blue with a liquid indigo then soaking it in the liquids of boiled *Lu-mu*, Venetian Sumac or *Rhus continus* wood and afterwards in those of boiled *Myricaeceae* bark.

According to another method, the tender indigo leaves are first soaked in water then *Tsao-fan* or green vitrol and *Wu-p'ei-tzŭ* or gallnuts are added, and the material is soaked together in this liquid. Materials dyed in this fashion, however, will deteriorate rapidly. Still another dyestuff was employed which is *Hsiang-wan-tzu* or *Li k'o*, acorn caps or husks, *Quercus chinensis*. Oftentimes, *Lien-tzŭ-k'o* or lotus-seed shells or husks were also used. The material to be dyed is first boiled for a day in a mixture of water and any of these shells or husks and strained off. It is boiled again for one night in a vessel containing the aqueous solution of iron ore and green vitriol. This results in a deep black colour. *Hsiang-wan-tzŭ* was used as dyestuff in Chou times (1122 - 221 B. C.)

Other Colours and Techniques

The colour purple is obtained by using *Su-fang-mu* or Sappanwood as a base and then dyeing with *Tsao-fan* or green vitriol containing ferrous sulfate.

In order to produce intermediate shades and hues and secondary colours, the Chinese dyers combined two or more of the primary or basic dyestuffs. In most cases the material is dyed in different dyestuffs successively and allowed to dry in between.

A Han dynasty (206 B. C. - 220 A. D.) process of obtaining a brown colour followed three stages, although actual ingredients are not given. The first stage was to dye the material into a pale red colour, with a yellowish tinge, called *Ch'üan*. This somewhat orange shade material is given a second dyeing of a deep red called *Ch'êng*. The third stage, called *Hsüan*, is to dye the material in a dark red dye with *Purpurin*. The result is said to have been a brown colour.

From the Ming dynasty work *T'ien-kung k'ai-wu*, we learn that sometimes the same dyestuffs are used except in a more dilute solution, while other times agents are combined to obtain a variety of colours and shades. Various Chinese *Hung* or red colours, such as *Lien-hung* lotus pink; *T'ao-hua hung* peach-bloom pink; *Yin-hung*, silver pink, and *Shui-hung* a clear pale pink, all are obtained from safflower. The different shades resulting from variation in the amount of dye used.

On the other hand, another shade of red, *Mu-hung* or wood red was obtained by boiling *Su-fang-mu* or Sappanwood in water, with *Pei-tzŭ* gallnuts and alum added. Mauve colouring was obtained by first dyeing in a dilute Sappanwood solution, followed by a soaking in dilute liquids of *Lien-tzŭ-k'o* lotus-seed shells, and of *Tan-fan* gall or blue vitriol respectively.

In yellow colouring, it is noted that a *Chin-huang* or golden yellow is achieved by first dyeing with the aqueous solution of boiled *Lu-mu* Venetian sumac wood, followed by shampooing with an alkaline solution of water leached hemp ash. *Ngo-huang* or Goose yellow, a fine yellow, the colour of a gosling and often referred to as "canary yellow" by most Westerners is obtained by first dyeing the material with an aqueous solution of boiled *Huang-nieh* or yellow berberine wood and then soaking in the *Seeth* water of indigo. Earth brown or *T'u-huang* is dyed with the aqueous solution of boiled *Lien-tzŭ-k'o* lotus-seed husks or shells and then rinsed with the aqueous solution of green vitriol. Ivory colour is obtained by dyeing slightly in the liquid *Lu-mu* Venetian sumac, or in an aqueous solution of yellow earth.

Indigo is chiefly used to obtain various blue and green shades. *T'ien-ch'ing* deep sky-blue is a result of first dyeing the material lightly in a vat of indigo and then washing with *Su-fang-mu* or Sappanwood solution. Grape blue or *P'u-t'ou ch'ing* results from having the material deeply dyed in a vat of indigo and then washed with a concentrated *Su-fang-mu* or Sappanwood solution. *Ts'ui-lan* peacock blue and *T'ien-lan* sky blue both are dyed with indigo, the difference being only one of shade. Likewise, pale blue *Yüeh-pai* or *Clair-dê-lune* and light blue *Ts'ao pai* are both achieved by dyeing slightly in an aqueous solution of indigo. Often, the slightly boiled liquid of *Mu-lan* horse indigo species is used for the best results *Tan-ch'ing* egg-shell blue or commonly called "Robin's egg blue" is a colour obtained by first dyeing with *Huang-nieh* yellow berberine solution and then soaking in a vat of indigo.

Dark green or *Mo-lu* is first dyed with the juice of boiled *Huai* flowers or *Sophora japonica* and then it is soaked in an indigo solution. Alum is used as a mordant for both the lighter and draker shades of this colour called *Yu-lu*. To obtain a bright green *Tou-ch'ing*, material is first dyed with the liquid of boiled *Huang-nieh* yellow berberine and then soaked in indigo solution. To get a very brilliant hue, called *Yeh-lu* grass green, the same process is used except that the indigo solution is that of the *Polygonum tinctorium* or *Ma-lan* horse indigo species of indigo plant.

The various colours and shades that have been described were not the entire repetoire of the Chinese dyers but the most typical ones included in various Chinese publications. Many of the water soluble plant pigments which were used as dyestuffs by the Chinese either do not dye directly on the wool or else are not fast. To correct this various agents were used as mordant. In the *Ch'i-min yao-shu*, we find a number of recommendations to collect ashes as provision for dyeing. Ashes from *Tso* or *Quercus*; *Sang* or *Morus*; and *Hao* or *Artemisia* were recommended. Other *Lixivium* are obtained from *Li*, tumbleweeds, *Hu* a species of oak, *Chiao* pigweeds *Chenopodium* and *Chi-li* or *Caltrop tributus*. Sometimes *Shih-liu* or pomegranates were used as the polybasic acids in the unripe fruits were a valuable agent. In lieu of these agents acetic and lactic acids were resorted to which could be found in vinegar and also a liquid called *Ch'ing-fan-chiang* a clear sour rice drink which is slightly fermented rice meal soup. *Ming-fan*, alum, or alum water *Pai-fan-shui* along with the other sulfates chiefly, ferrous sulfate found in *Tsao-fan* or green vitriol, were among the other substances used.

Some of these mordants acted as an agent in fixing the dyestuff to the wool, although at times some of these mordants also may alter the colour of the main dyestuffs. All of the mordants which were utilized were basically native to China.

Up until the mid-nineteenth century the Chinese followed the ancient custom of using natural plant dyes by mixing them either with soda or vinegar according to their properties; in other cases some alum or green vitriol was used as a mordant.

For many centuries natural substances either from plant, animal or mineral had been used as the source of colour and many of them were not only expensive, but required for proper application, a long and complicated technique which was usually guarded as a trade secret. Even so, there were no standards and the various batches of dyes were not always uniform.

Synthetic Dyes

With the beginning of the Industrial Revolution in the West and the development of dye chemistry, a cheaper and more uniform colouring agent was sought. Towards the beginning of the nineteenth century, various experiments were conducted with derivatives of the benzene nucleus. In the 1830's a German chemist, experimenting with coal-tar, obtained a product that gave a bright blue colouration under the influence of bleaching agents. Neglected for more than twenty years, this discovery became of practical value in 1856 when Sir W. H. Perkin, using earlier experimentation, produced the first aniline dye with a structure based on the benzene ring which was the colour mauve. Thereafter the whole gamut of "synthetic dyes" was developed in rapid succession. Synthetic aniline dyestuffs were derived from thick black coal-tar

Plate XXV

A totally geometric design rug with swastika-fret borders and swastika pattern in the field. A large medallion features the character *Shou* "Longevity" and the four corners are decorated with angular stylized dragons. 79x156 cm.

secured by the distillation of bituminous coal in the production of il-
luminating-gas. These synthetic dyes were mainly introduced into China
by returning Chinese students who had been educated abroad and by
Europeans.

The first phase of synthetic dyes or the aniline phase was a short-
lived one as the first aniline dyes were neither fast to light nor to washing. Moreover, synthetic dyes rarely produced the splendid effects
achieved by the use of the best natural dyes. For the most part these
dyes are strongly acid and the effect on the wool fibre was sometimes
quite devastating. However, in the latter part of the nineteenth century
there were two major breakthroughs in artificial dyes. In 1868, Graebe
and Libermann developed an artificial red which had the same chemical
composition as the natural madder dyes. An artificial indigo followed
in 1880 by the discovery of Baeyer. These two major colours brought
about new hope that good dyes could be artificially produced. Still,
there were the traditionalists, who for the most part adhered to the
older ways and refused to change over to the new dyes. The aniline
dyes tend to upset the sober colour schemes so carefully worked out by
the Chinese. The Chinese traditional ways could be maintained, however, since the large scale carpet industry for international commerce
was in its infancy and the clamour and demand for Chinese rugs was
negligible. Also, the new aniline colours on the whole were unsuited to
Chinese tastes and colour preference.

On the other hand, chrome dyes which were synthetics mordanted with potassium bichromate, took a quicker and stronger hold in
China. These newer chrome dyes were marvellous innovations of industrial development as they were fast to water, alkalis, and sunlight and
they seem to cause little or no harm to the wool. They were easier to
use than the natural dyes and a wider variety of colours and shades
could be obtained. At the same time, colouration could be standardized and made uniform. This was a most ideal substance for dyeing in
the carpet industry as it was also more economical in cost and labour.

Chrome dyes were introduced into China during the period of
World War I. The traditionalists in China still held rigidly to natural
dyes and shunned these innovations. However, during this period, due
to the closing of the Middle East because of hostilities, a great demand
for Chinese rugs caused the Chinese manufacturers to look for quicker,
easier and cheaper methods of dyeing. Moreover the bulk of the carpet

firms at this time engaged in exporting were owned and operated by foreigners. These companies, such as Fetté's, Nichols, Shoemaker's and E. A. Punnett's created exotic rugs called "Peking" and "Tientsin" rugs, which used elements of Chinese designs but were basically foreign to the Chinese as they were made to satisfy Western tastes with what were perceived as exotic but conformed to Western colour tastes. These corrupted forms of Chinese rugs used artificial chrome dye-colours very effectively to create their "artificial" Chinese rugs.

The colours produced from chrome dyes tend to be so fast and unyielding that they present a rather stiff appearance. It is questionable if these colours would mellow or age gracefully like the natural dyes to achieve a richness, lustre and softness which is characteristic of the finest Chinese rugs. Since the majority of modern rugs are all synthetically dyed the practice of giving a chemical washing to the finished rug has arisen. This helps to create a soft and mellowed effect.

The main purpose of this washing was to tone down the brightness and harshness of the colours. Various chemical washes were developed, however in all cases the rugs were treated with a bleaching agent to remove excess colour. Chlorine and other substances were used at various times. Inasmuch as a softer hue resulted, nevertheless such harsh chemicals may seriously weaken the fibres having a deleterious effect of their durability.

Frequently, one may notice that a single colour in a rug may vary from one portion of the rug to another. This variation of the same colour, if not an intentional part of the design or the result of a repair, is called "abrash" and results from the practice of dyeing the wool in small batches. Abrash is seldom found in modern rugs while in older rugs it is most common. Some rug collectors consider it an appealing quality while others consider it a defect. It is, in sum, a matter of individual taste.

Among other peculiarities, rugs manufactured in Tibet and Mongolia, including Ch'ing-hai, Pao-tou and Ning-hsia, often have full designs created by the use of undyed wool from black, brown, grey and white sheep. The designs often feature a much sought-after mottled or streaked effect that is produced by the imperfect blending of unbleached and undyed yarn, which the Chinese call *Ts'ang* or *Ts'ang-wei* meaning luxuriant.

How can one tell whether the colours in a carpet result from the use of natural dyestuffs? The answer is that is is not possible to do so with certainty unless chemical tests are performed. One has to rely on clues, experience and one's educated eye for colour.

Natural dyestuffs, properly used are unquestionably the best. They are rarely garish in themselves and usually produce subtle and harmonious combinations. The Chinese utilized these subtle tones to great artistic advantage in various combinations which reflected the intended use of the particular rug. Moreover, preferred colour schemes varied with social class and over various epochs.

One of the most common and well-known colour combinations is the black and white and blue and white rugs of the Ming period. One of the colour combinations which would be rarely if ever used would be yellow and green as such combinations would be termed: *Huang-lu*, which means the harvest of last year will not last until this year's is ripe. An expression used for things failing to come to a successful end, or in other words, bad luck. One should, however, be cautious not to generalize except for such clear cut examples. We should not take simplistic attitudes toward such a rich world of colour without noting other clues to determine tastes of various periods.

On one hand, other applied arts such as pottery and porcelain, fabrics and textiles, along with architectural decoration and colours should be considered. Architectural manuals for the Sung and Ming periods could be studied from the various editions of *Ying-tsao fang-shih*. Textiles and fabrics along with colour and design could be studied from figurines, paintings, various manuals on ceremonies and rites as well as government statutes such as *Ta-Ming-li* and *Ta-Ch'ing-li*.

In evaluating and appreciating Chinese rugs, it is well to bear in mind that from ancient times the Chinese had an acute sensitivity to colour deriving from their five basic colours, *Wu-sê* and both colour and design must be in accordance with a traditional schema.

Plate XXVI

The vase and pomegranate motif covers this entire rug with the repeating leaf design occupying most of the ground. The four central fruits form a sort of medallion. 129x234 cm.

CARPET MATERIALS

Choosing the most appropriate materials for rug-making is most essential. Flimsy or stiff and boardlike, springy or matted and lifeless, the finished textile cannot differ greatly from the yarn that is used to weave it, and the yarn can only possess the qualities of the fiber from which it is spun.

Two basic terms, fiber and filament are used to describe yarns. A filament is a long continuous thread, like those spun by the spider or silkworm or produced synthetically. A fiber is a short length of the basic material, and several are usually spun together to make a yarn. All fibers are either natural or synthetic.

Synthetic fibers are the result of twentieth century technology and were not used in older hand-made rugs. The natural fibers which offer a sumptuous range of tactile qualities, may be divided into the following groupings:

Animal -- Wool and silk (with silk also being the only natural filament.)
Plant or vegetable -- Cotton or linen.
Mineral -- Includes gold and silver.

In traditional rug-weaving cultures, traditional materials have been used with predictable results after a period of trial and error. The most common and abundant materials available were used most.

Although various grasses and raw plant fiber have been used, most have failed because they were inappropriate materials which were unsuitable for use as a floor covering or mattress. A basic knowledge or understanding of the different properties of the fibers used is paramount to the weaver. These properties include staple length, the length distribution of a group of fibers, diameter, texture, lustre, colour, elasticity, tensile strength, resistance to abrasion, wear, affinity for dyes, and several other characteristics which are difficult to quantify.

By tradition the most common materials for Oriental carpets are sheep's wool, goat hair, camel hair, cotton, linen, and silk. Gold and silver threads were also utilized, and in Tibet even Yak hairs are reported to have been used.

Wool

Of these traditional materials, wool is the major material used in rugs, forming the soft pile. Serving as an insulation against cold and repelling dampness, wool fulfills the basic functional requirements of the carpet. Wool has been associated wth the nomadic cultures which has led many people to believe that rugs and woolen products were synonomous with these peoples. This is a rather simplistic view, for aside from the making of felt which needs little or no complicated technology and equipment, woolen products from the loom necessitate a knowledge of spinning and weaving without mentioning the processing of the raw wool.

To support his own collection of Khotanese rugs and to downplay the key role of the Chinese in their development, Bidder maintains that "Chinese proper is no wool producing land, and the Chinese reveal in their literary sources a notable aversion to wool as a material and also to its processing."[108] He further states that the "Chinese dictionaries list under the word *Mao* (wool, hair) the name of thirty foreign woolen materials, which for a painfully obvious lack of more exact terms, are laconically defined as 'rough materials' made of wool."[109]

Bidder offers no supporting evidence for this claim and his condamnation of the word *Mao* is subject to the same criticism in that the term *Mao* is a generic term meaning the hair of any animal, fur, down, feathers, nap, rough and coarse. It can also mean a fuzz like peach fuzz. The word *Mao* usually cannot stand alone, except as a surname, but must be used as a compound term, *Yang-mao*, sheep's wool; *T'o-mao*, camel's hair; etc. However, *Mao* could be used as a comparative term such as *Mao yü ssŭ* literally animal hair, wool and/or silk, but meaning coarse or fine material.

In view of the fact that the Chinese had silk of various weaves and other textiles including cotton and linen, woolen goods would, of course, not rank with silk. However, woolen products were not despised as Bidder suggests.

Instead of the term *Mao*, Bidder should have examined other terms as *Jung*[110] with meaning of flannel, velvet, wool, floss and so forth. Under the *Jung* products, there is the highly favoured *T'ien-ngo jung* literally "wild swan's down velvet" or superior velvet.

Sheep were known and domesticated in ancient times. Sheep's wool fiber were used to make felt or downlike fabrics that were subsequently fashioned into hats, socts and other small articles of clothing. There were two kinds of sheep. The *So-i yang* or woolly sheep was the first native to China. The other variety *Hsi-yü yang* was introduced to China from the "Western Regions" during the Han dynasty (206 B. C. - 220 A. D.). The outer hair of this sheep is not very long, but the inner hair is fine and soft and is separated and woven into pubescence fabrics.

It is related in Chinese history that when Han Wu-ti campaigned against the Hsiung-nu in 121 - 119 B. C., not only did he defeat the enemy but also that he captured a million sheep and they were brought to Lan-chou in Kansu to pasture. Before the introduction of this better breed of sheep, the hair of the woolly sheep was woven into coarse fabric to clothe the poor people. The wool fibers of the 'Western Region' sheep along with the hairs of camel and rabbit were used for making a soft and fine wool cloth which was very fashionable during T'ang times, (618 - 906 A. D.).

During the T'ang dynasty, the *Hsi-yü yang* or "Western Region" sheep was called *Yü-t'iao yang* or "the cashmere goat" by the people in Shensi to distinguish it from the woolly sheep. The high grade wood from this animal was fashioned into various woolen products in Lanchou and called, *Lan-jung*, Lanchou woolen or *Ku-ku-jung*. The finer, inner hair of this animal usually must be obtained by combing, since the animal will not permit shearing or clipping. In combing, many long dark hairs come out, and these must be separated by hand, a long and tedious process.

The seventeenth century work, *T'ien-kung k'ai-wu*, in regard to cashmere, notes the following:

"Cashmere goat hair is classified into two categories. One termed *Ch'ou-jung* or combed wool, is obtained by combing the coat of the goat. The resultant hair fibers are first spun into yarns and then woven into such fabrics as *Ho-tzǔ* or serge or twill, and other woolen goods. The other termed *Pa-jung* or picked wool, is obtained by hand-picking the finest inner hair one by one. This is also made into yarn and then woven. Rubbed against the face, this fabric feels so smooth and silky as silk itself. A spinner working for a whole day can produce only about 0.1 ounce of yarn of picked wool . . . The amount of "combed wool" that can be spun in a day, however, is several times that of picked wool."[111]

No matter how much care is used, some of the long hair remains in the fleece and this is characteristic of cashmere yarn. The natural colour of cashmere varies from pure white to gray or brownish gray. The quantity of white fleece is small, perhaps 20 percent of the total. Cashmere is used to make luxurious woolen goods and has special appeal because of its soft touch, light weight and excellent warmth.

As for the woolly sheep, in the sixth century agricultural encyclopedia *Ch'i-min yao-shu* detailed descriptions for the care, breeding and veterinary treatment of sheep as well as directions for obtaining wool and woolen products are given. There is also a detailed description of wool shearing.

"White sheep: In the third month, when invigorated by good pasturage, the underfur begins to loosen. It is time to shear. After shearing wash the sheep in a stream, so that later pilage will be clean and white.

In the fifth month, underfur is going to be cast, shear again. Wash after shearing as before. In the eighth month, before the ripening of the cocklebur, shear once more. Wash after shearing as before. Those sheep shorn in the later half of that month, however, ought not to be washed. Nocturnal chill is advancing, so washing will do harm. Shearing after the ripening of the cocklebur is undesirable; not only because of the trouble of the burs, but the time is already too late for enough consummation of the hair cover, and the sheep will suffer. Sheep of the Gobi and beyond the Great Wall should not be shorn in the eighth month, for the sheep cannot stand the cold. In Northern China, they must be shorn in the eighth month or the long wool will stick together and induces difficulty in felting.

Black sheep: Shear by the end of the fourth month or early fifth month. They are not so tolerant to the cold, so that if shorn earlier, they may die of cold.[112]

Fiber from the live animals is called fleece. It contains up to 50 percent of its weight in impurities which must be scoured out. The first fleece is sheared from a lamb when it is about six or eight months old, it is called lamb's wool, first clip or fleece wool. The quality of wool varies even on the same animal. The fleece from the shoulders and the sides is the finest, from the lower part of the back is of good quality, while that from the tail and the legs, is called "britch wool" and is stiff, straight and coarse. The fleece from the head is the least desirable of all. Pulled or scraped wool comes from sheep that have either died or been slaughtered. The wool is removed by submersion into a lime solution and is called by the Chinese *Hui-t'ui-mao*. It is regarded as inferior to shorn fleece in every way. Oftentimes dried flesh and follicles are visible as white flaky dots which make the wool look dirty. This wool is always dull and has no lustre.

The fleece is then baled and sent to the mill where it is sorted by experts according to length, diameter, crimp, strength, colour, and a number of criteria. It is then scoured to remove oil, wax, and extraneous vegetable matter before being spun into yarn. Although various alkaline solutions have been employed including goat's urine, the most popular method is a caustic soap solution prepared from a homemade potash solution. Ashes are collected and placed in woven baskets lined with leaves and water is poured over them and allowed to seep through and the liquid is collected. A hen's egg is used as a crude hydrometer and must float to a certain level to determine the desired potency of the solution. This solution is poured over the wool and agitated. The wool is then immediately rinsed and allowed to dry in the sun. Normally the grease or oil that is washed out constitutes 40 to 60 percent of the wool's weight, however since a great loss of oil makes the wool brittle, the Chinese alkali solution is usually not made so concentrated that all of the oils are washed out. The dried fleece is then ready for carding and spinning to make the yarn.

Despite the differences resulting from the various breeds, all types of fleece share similar important qualities. Fleece from all sheep grows in locks or "staples" with a convolution or crimp that gives the fleece its characteristic curly appearance. Unlike the oils that may be scoured out of the fiber the crimp is permanent. Generally speaking, the short fine diameter fibers have many more crimps per inch than the longer ones. When fleece is spun, these crimps maintain air spaces in the yarn; the more of them there are the more the yarn will insulate. Even the most tightly spun yarn, twisted from long staple fibers, is almost 50 percent air.

At the base of the lock, there may be some straight fibers that seem to have little relation to the rest of the fleece. These are called "kemp", a vestige from the days when sheep like other animals, had a double coat of fur close to the body and a longer hairy outer coat for protection against rain and moisture. Kemp was long ago bred out of sheep but does occasionally reappear in breeds that spend much time in rainy climates. In addition to its stiff, hairy appearance, kemp does not spin well or take dye easily. However, kemp fibers may be found in some grades of carpet wool since they are hard-wearing.

A microscopic cross-section of a wool fiber shows it to consist of an inner core surrounded by a thin but extremely tough outer layer. This covering, called the "Cuticle", is formed of minute "epithetical scales" running outward from the root to the tip. It is these scales which allow wool fibers to conjoin so readily in spinning and which enable the material to be felted. The scales breathe much like our own pores, opening in heat and closing in cold, and so may be shocked into cohesion by the application of moisture with temperature extremes. It is the scales also which cause some people to itch upon contact with wool. A fiber has anywhere from 600 to 3000 over-lapping scales per inch. The short, fine wools, which are most spinnable, have many closely spaced scales in contrast to the long fibers whose scales are large and flat and more openly spaced.

Wool has the lowest tensile strength of the natural fibers. It is about one-third as strong as cotton and has only one-fifth the strength of linen, but its strength is more than adequate for rug-weaving. It makes up for this shortcoming by being the most resilient and elastic of all the fibers. The crimp works like a spring to give wool tremendous resilience, as evidence on pile carpets which have been a traditional vehicle for wool for centuries. Additionally, the crimp imparts so much elasticity that a wool fiber can be extended to almost 35 percent of its length and immediately resume its original dimension when released. Since prolonged tension will cause the fiber's molecules to realign in the extended position, loom tension must be released when weaving is not in progress.

Wool fiber is both absorbant and extremely dye-receptive. It can absorb up to one-third of its weight in water and still feel dry. It accepts colour readily and dyes to deep, rich hues. Wool is known for its

Plate XXVII
Two diamond shaped medallions each with a stylized floral centre fill
the long central panel of this highly geometric design. Equally intricate
geometric forms fill the narrow and wide borders. 407x192 cm.

insulating capacity.   In actuality, it is not the wool itself which provides the greatest insulating capacity, but the "dead air" which it entraps within the woven fabric.   Thus Chinese rugs, with their thicker wool yarns and their somewhat looser pile, provide greater insulation than Near Eastern rugs which have thinner yarn and a denser concentration of knots per unit area. Rugs have functioned as barriers against the cold on floors, on the *K'ang* and on walls since ancient times. The thicker a wool rug is, the warmer it is, so that plush rugs could significantly increase comfort when used on furniture.

Overall, wool is very durable. Its resilience allows it to yield to pressure rather than to resist it. Its elasticity enables it to absorb the strain of wear and tear. A wool fiber can be bent 20,000 times without breaking, enough folding to last many lifetimes. Its resistance to acids is high. Many synthetic dyes used to colour wool are in an acid base to which the fiber readily responds. In fact, after cleaning a stain with a mild soap it is wise to add a drop or two of vinegar to the rinse water since wool is extremely sensitive to alkalis even in their mild form. Wool is able to withstand temperature to 400° F, before scorching and will smolder before it actually ignites. The fiber, which burns slowly, will extinguish itself if the flame is removed. This makes wool an ideal wall, *K'ang* and floor covering. Also burning wool is easily noticed because of its sulfurous odour, so it can generally be caught before the damage is irreparable. Wool's only drawback is that it is susceptible to moth attack. The Chinese remedy this by storing woolen rugs in large camphor wood chests.

Wool may be blended with other animal fibers with camel hair for softness, with silk for lustre and a soft hand and with other fibers such as horse hair for strength and durability. In the *T'ien-kung k'ai-wu* it is noted that "the coarsest kind of blankets and rugs are made with horsehair and shoddy mixed with sheep's wool."[113]

Wool will generally remain dominant in appearance, although the hand and the quality of quality of such blends will change somewhat according to the fiber with which the wool is mixed. Wool is also the traditional fiber for the weft in hand rug-weaving. The scaly structure of its fibers allows these weft yarns to interlock in a subtle way which actually increases the strength of the rug many times over.

Other Animal Fibers

Sheep are the only animals that produce fleece. Other animals have a double coat: hair, the sleek water repellant outer covering, and fur, the insulating underlayer. Fleece, hair and fur are all fundamentally the same chemical composition, the protein *Keratin*, but the physical appearances of the three are vastly different. Hair is generally coarse, hard and stiff; fur is shorter, softer and finer in diameter. Neither has the crimp of wool fleece and both are devoid, for the most part, of epithetical scales, so they are smoother and somewhat more lustrous.

Although there are many animal fibers incorporated into yarns and fabrics, the Chinese used basically camel hairs, goat hair, and in Tibet, reportedly Yak hairs.

Camel hairs come from the two-humped Bactrian camel native to Asia. Fibers are obtained by brushing or plucking rather than by shearing. Hairs are also obtained by collecting the hair that falls off during the shedding period. The coarse outer hair may reach a length of 15 inches while the fur, or down remains one inch to five inches in length. Warp yarns spun from the hair and weft yarns from the fur may be found in many Oriental carpets and rugs. Distinguished by its tan or reddish-brown colour, camel hair is never dyed.

Goats[114] are related to sheep and while there are many different kinds of goats, the long-haired variety are the ones whose hair is used for weaving. Goat hair is stiff and coarse and ranges in colour from black to brown and even gray. It is not possible to dye it, so it must be used in its natural colour. Although it does not have the elasticity of wool, goat hair is resilient because it is so wiry.

The yarns made from horse hair are very high in tensile strength owing to the extreme staple length of the fiber which usually comes from the manes and tails. Used in their natural state, lustruous horsehair yarns are coarse, wiry, resilient, resistant to abrasion and exceptionally durable.

Through experience or empirical observation, the Chinese knew enough of the characteristics of the various fibers so that not only could they devise combinations or blends but they also knew to isolate certain fibers to give the best results in luxurious goods that wore well and were pleasing to the touch.

Processing into Yarn

From their raw cleaned state, staple fibers must undergo numerous operations before being made into yarn. Essentially the entire process is one of making fibers parallel so that they can be drawn out and spun into yarns of uniform diameter. Short, fine fibers which are merely carded -- drawn between wire brushes passing in opposite directions -- make a soft, bulky yarn. In order to have greater strength, they must be highly twisted. The hard longer fibers undergo more straightening but do not need to be twisted as much because their length makes them inherently stronger. In general, the more a yarn is twisted the harder it will become; thus strength and softness are fairly incompatible properties.

All yarn spun from staple fibers is first produced as a single continuous length with a uni-directional twist. A right-handed (left to right) orientation is known as a Z-twist, the left-handed (right to left) as an S-twist. Plied yarns consist of two or more single yarns twisted together. The direction of the ply is commonly opposite to the twist of the single yarns so that the resulting strand will remain intertwined. Thus, two S-twisted singles will be made into a Z-twist two-ply. The Chinese call this two-ply twisting *Tzŭ-mu* and it was used as early as the Shang dynasty, (1766 - 1122 B. C.).

A cord is made by twisting together two or more plied yarns in the opposite direction of the ply. The yarns of this type are very strong. As technology developed or as more understanding of the behavior of materials was gathered, the techniques and requirements of spinning changed: the exception to this is that some isolated areas did not benefit from advances. From the Han dynasty (206 B. C. - 220 A. D.) to the T'ang dynasty (618 - 906 A. D.) the spinning of yarn progressed from the two-ply to the three-ply called *Chiu* to the four-ply or *Shuang tzu-mu*. In fact four-ply or *Shuang tzŭ-mu* and five-ply was used during the Yuan dynasty and even in part of the Ming dynasty. The technique of spinning the yarns remained relatively constant between the T'ang and Sung periods, up to the seventeenth century. From the seventeenth century onwards, due to the introduction of various spinning machines, the techniques, as well as yarn-ply, varied with multi-ply yarns. These variations in the spinning of the yarn may be a key to dating Chinese rugs, however more research is needed in order to fully understand their changes over time and formulate tables to give more reliable dates.

Silk

The invention or discovery of *Ssŭ* or silk in ancient times is accorded to the Emperess Lei Tsu, the daughter of the feudal chief of Hsiling and the wife of Huang-ti, the third of the Five Emperors. As the patroness of silkworms she was worshipped in China by an annual sacrifice by the reigning empress at a special altar, *Hsien-tsan-t'an*, in the palace grounds. While Lei Tsu may have discovered silk, it seems that it did not come into much use until the Chou dynasty, (1122 - 211 B. C.). In the *Mémories concernant l'histoire . . . des chinois*[115] we find the statement:

"All the ancient writers agree in saying that Yao, Shun and Yü were clothed in simple cloth in summer and in skin in winter. The silk which the wife of Huang-ti has discovered had disappeared. The celebrated and learned author of the *Shuo-wên* has proved that all the characters into the formation of which the ideograph for silk enters, do not go back before the Chou dynasty and that all those that refer to the clothes of the ancients are only composed of the ideographs for hair and hemp."

Many works have been written about silk including the early treatise such as *Tsan-ching* written by Liu An during the Han dynasty and *Tsan-shu* by Ch'in Kuang of the Sung dynasty. The earliest surviving silk textiles of the pre-Han period were found in the Pazyryk burial mounds and more Han period fragments were found along the Silk Route.

The species of silkworm or catepillar cultivated by the Chinese was, and remains to modern times, the *Bombyx mori*. The silkworms were bred and tended to constantly and fed freshly cut mulberry leaves every four hours each day for thirty-two days. At the end of this period, the silkworms had grown considerably in size. When ready to spin their cocoons, the silkworms stopped eating, raised their heads, and evinced a desire to climb. They were then transferred to a spinning trellis constructed of bamboo and rushes, with branches of rice straw to hold the cocoons. When the silkworm was placed on the trellis for spinning it discharged two silk filaments in the form of a gummy liquid from which it is fastened itself to a number of straws.

The silkworm has two glands which secrete the silk or *Fibroin* and another two that secrete a soluble gummy substance called *Sericin* that binds the two silk *Fibroins* and cements together the cocoon. The ducts of these four glands connect at the spinncret, an opening just under the catepillar's mouth. Spinning lasts three days and is completed when the catepillar has completely enclosed itself in a hard, pecan-sized capsule that contains anywhere from 300 to 1,800 yards of continuous filament.

Silk is composed chiefly of the animal protein *Fibroin* with traces of wax, fat, and salts. Under magnification, a lengthwise filament appears as a smooth, translucent rod, while a cross-section reveals it to be triangular in shape rther than round. Silk has the finest diameter of any natural fiber, measuring .008 mm or smaller. No other natural fiber compares to the lustre of silk.

Silk has the highest tensile strength of the natural fibers. A filament of steel of equal diameter will snap before silk does. Like wool, silk is highly resilient. However the fiber does not respond well to extension. Nevertheless, it is highly absorbant and dye-receptive. Silk can insulate somewhat, but not to the degree that wool can.

Overall, silk has only moderate durability. It is not particularly abrasion resistant and is affected by all but the weakest acids. It is able to withstand temperatures of nearly 325° F. without scorching. Silk burns, slowly and gives off a mild odour of burning hair, and leaves a lumpy ash. It is unlikely to be attacked by moths or mildew. Silk is very versatile and can easily be blended with wool, linen, cotton and other fibers.

Before silk can be used it must first be reeled. The ancient Chinese method of reeling required the utmost patience and was inexpressibly tedious. A little furnace was built of bricks and clay, and heated with charcoal. The cocoons were placed in a pan of hot water on the furnace. If the water was too hot the cocoons rose to the surface, if it was too cold, they sank to the bottom.

The reeler then stirred the cocoons and searched for the loose ends that had been fastened to the spinning trellis. When these were found, he jerked off the coarse threads on the outside of the cocoons disclosing the fine silk below. This was the part he sought for reeling.

The filament of one cocoon was much too fine to reel. It was discovered that several filaments from many cocoons could be joined together and reeled at the same time. This not only gave a much stronger thread, but reduced the labour in proportion to the number of filaments that were handled at once.

In unwinding several cocoons at a time, the filaments were joined

Plate XXVIII
An all-over floral diaper pattern fills the centre of this rug. The outer
border is decorated with symbols of gentlemanly pursuits. Ten different floral and geometric patterns complete the outer border. The inner
borders consist of flowers and the running-T. 133x201 cm.

together by being drawn through small holes or eyes, their natural gum-miness when they first came out of the water caused the filaments to adhere as soon as they come in contact. The thread was then drawn over the spools and wound upon the reel. The crude apparatus used resembles a skein winder, which lightly twists the several filaments into a yarn, known as a "single" since the filament of only one cocoon is too fine to be reeled alone. This was at first turned by hand but later by foot power. The thread had to be kept a regular thickness by adding a new filament for each one that was exhausted. This was indicated by the chrysalis being drawn to the surface of the water. If the filament broke, another was added to take its place. During the reeling the hot water for the cocoons was frequently changed, a third at a time. Each cocoon would furnish from 300 to 1,800 yards of filament, aside from the coarse threads discarded in the beginning and a portion at the end too fine to pay for reeling.

The process of reeling not only demanded the greatest care but was very inefficient. Working all day the ancient Chinese reeler could only reel from twenty to thirty ounces of thread a day. This reeled single thread was called "raw silk" and it undergoes a subsequent operation known as throwing in which singles from one or more bobbins are twisted into a sturdier yarn.

The unreelable ends were spun like cotton or wool into "tow silk", a yarn whose texture, rather than brilliance or strength, is the chief characteristic. Spinning was probably the original method of utilizing the filaments, though it fell into comparative disuse after reeling was perfected. The distinction between spinning and reeling is absolute. Reeling is simply the unwinding of the silk from the cocoons which the silkworms have already spun.

In making spun silk, the shorter fibers, combed out from the tangled or broken pieces made in reeling the pierced cocoons, other silk which couldn't be reeled or would otherwise be wasted, was twisted and spun into thread just as cotton or wool is spun with the S-twist or Z-twist. To prepare either the reeled or spun silk thread for weaving, it was twisted, doubled, and then twisted again as many times as necessary to give the desired weight and strength to the yarn. The same ply-count as in wool applies to silk. All silk must finally undergo a de-gumming process to remove the silk glue, *Sericin*.

The Chinese prized silk very highly. They derived, wove and

fashioned various textiles, such as *K'o-ssu*, *Chin*, *Ling* and damask, etc. throughout history. The single-ply yarns were used for the ground warp of *Lo* or net, the two-ply yarns for *Chuan* or Pongee, and the five-ply yarns for *Ling* or damask.[116] For rugs the four- and five- or more-ply yarn would be used. Although silk is not an easy material to work with in knotted pile rugs due to the fine nature of the material, nevertheless, silk rugs were made as we learn from T'ang dynasty poetry. The practice continues into modern times, as silk rugs are still being made.

Cotton

In ancient Chinese literature cotton was called *Hsi-ma*, which is nettle-hemp, and was widely grown in China. There was also *Mu-mien*, the tree cotton plant or *Ceiba pentandra*, which was cultivated by the Chinese. This led to some confusion of terms as *Ts'ao-mien* or *Gossypium indicum*, which is the true cotton plant, was believed to have been introduced into China from India in the early Han dynasty, ca. 138 - 176 B. C. and it was not until the Southern Sung dynasty, (1127 - 1279 A. D.), that it was cultivated widely as a fiber.

The use of cotton in both the Old and the New world did not reach peak proportions until after the invention of the cotton gin in 1793 by Eli Whitney. Cotton then came to surpass linen in worldwide use. One of the chief reasons for this late development is that cotton seeds embedded in the fiber are difficult to separate and the processing of the short fibers is cumbersome.

Cotton is a warm climate crop and it requires almost two-hundred frost free days to come to muturity. In China, cotton is planted in the spring and the seeds sprout two weeks after planting and leaves develop two or three months after that, followed closely by buds. Blossoms appear about three weeks later. The petals wither and drop off in a matter of days, leaving a flattened green pod, or "Boll" about half the size of a thumb. The bolls are picked selectively day by day as they mature and split open; therefore not all the cotton can be harvested at the same time.

Inside each boll are from three to five compartments, depending on the variety of cotton, each containing seven to ten seeds. Each seed sprouts about 10,000 fibers from special cells in its outer wall, for the cotton is essentially a cushion to protect the seed. These many fibers become twisted and cramped as they vie for growing space within the restricted area. Nevertheless each grows to its complete length between one-half inch to two inches.

As the fibers grow, they ever expand the boll. After about a month and a half, the ripened boll bursts open to reveal the fluffy mass within. Exposure to sunlight causes the moist fibers to dry and collapse into flat, ribbon-like shapes.

After harvesting, the cotton is ginned to separate the fibers from the seeds and then packed into bales. The cotton gin used and described by the Chinese in the seventeenth century work *T'ien-lung k'ai-wu* is very similar to the one invented by Eli Whitney in the United States in 1793. The baled cotton is then carded, combed and spun into yarn. Under the microscope, cotton is clearly shown to spiral along its length. The number of twists varies from 150 to 300. These twists provide the friction by which cotton fibers can be spun. The average diameter of a cotton fiber is .003 mm.

Cotton is netiehr as elastic nor as resilient as wool, but it has a greater tensile strength. In relation to linen it is more resilient and elastic but not as strong. Interestingly, cotton is stronger when wet. It is so flexible that a fiber can be bent 20,000 times without breaking.

Cotton can absorb up to 27 times its weight in water and has good receptivity to dyes. Cotton is washable, able to withstand boiling water, and is not weakened by dilute acids and alkalis as long as they are rinsed from the fiber before they dry. The fiber can be bleached with regular chlorine bleach. Cotton is subject to mildew, so fiber, yarn and fabric must be kept dry.

Although the longest cotton fibers are frequently shorter than the shortest wool fibers, they are processed and spun in the same manner as wool. A plain cotton yarn is merely carded and spun. Combed cotton, which undergoes extra straightening operations, is stronger and smoother.

Cotton yarn or finished cotton products are frequently mercerized -- a process of immersion in a caustic-soda solution -- which makes the fiber stronger, more lustrous, and more receptive to dyes.

Inasmuch as Chinese cotton pile rugs are considered rare today, a specimen can be seen in the Vienna Museum. Another, excavated in Sinkiang in 1959[117] belongs to the Pei-ch'ao period, fourth century A. D. and a more recent Sung dynasty cotton-pile rug was found in 1975 in

Plate XXIX
Two five clawed dragons with a flaming pearl decorate this chair back rug. The plain borders of the sides, shoulders and top compliment the simple lines of the Chinese chair. The lower border provides both simple decoration and symbolic elements associated with dragons -- mountain and waves or the *Fu-hai shou-shun* motif. 61x65 cm.

Lan-ch'i in Chekiang province.[118]

During the reign of Wu-ti of the Liang dynasty, (502 - 549 A. D.) there is a popular quote "People wore cotton clothes, black tents."[119] By the period of the Five dynasties (907 - 959 A. D.) the *Tz'ŭ-chih t'ung chien*, an historical treatise notes that "Cotton pile rugs were used as floor coverings during the autumn and winter periods."[120]

In more recent times, cotton pile rugs are rare in China as elsewhere and cotton is primarily used as a warp because of its reasonable price, easy workability and moderate strength. In some Tibetan rugs it is used in the weft.

With mechanization of the processing of cotton during the nineteenth century, it is remarkable to see that machine-spun cotton had replaced the hand-spun cotton warps in many rug-weaving centres. Great Britain had flooded these centres with cotton yarns from her cotton mills and the spread of cotton was similar to the spread of aniline dyes. However, in China, machine-spun cotton yarns pre-date those of Great Britain and Eli Whitney's cotton gin.

Both the use of water power applied to textile manufacturing and a machine similar to the cotton gin had already been in existence in China in the late thirteenth and early fourteenth centuries, as illustrated in the *Nung-shu*.[121] Murry L. Eiland, who has made great contributions to the state of our knowledge of the rugs of many localities, may not have been aware of this fact when he wrote, "A Chinese rug with machine spun warps obviously cannot date from the Ch'ien-lung period; yet this kind of inconsistency is frequent in books on Chinese rugs which do not seem to take account of this."[122] The presence of machine-spun yarn in a rug should be considered in dating the rug but it must be considered in the context of the state of Chinese technology during the period under consideration, not dated from the state of Western technology at the same time.

The first edition of *Nung-shu* published in 1313, mentions a primitive version of the cotton gin. As early as 1637, when the first edition of the *T'ien-kung k'ai-wu* was published, the Chinese were using a cotton gin called *Mien-kan*, a machine to separate the cotton fibers from the seeds. A foot-operated and a water-powered spinning machine called *Fang-lu* which spun yarns into threads was also described.

Since the use of cotton was very popular during the tenth century, it is presumed that a high technology in processing cotton was in existence to meet the demand. The early Ch'ing emperors were very much interested in cotton. Fan Kuan-ch'eng, 1698 - 1768, an official, supervised the drawing of sixteen illustrations on cotton culture and weaving, with explanations he wrote himself, which he submitted to Emperor Ch'ien lung in 1765 under the title *Mien-hua t'u*. In the same year Emperor Ch'ien-lung, so highly pleased with this work, added one poem in his own handwriting to each painting. Soon thereafter, Fang had the whole work carved in stone, and rubbings of this work appeared in two sets of albums, prefaced with an earlier written long prose poem by Emperor K'ang-hsi entitled *Mu-mien fu*. In 1808, Emperor Chia-ch'ing ordered an official reprint of this work which appeared early in the following year in rearranged form and with additional documents, under the title *Shou-i kuang-hsun* in 2 *chüan*. This great interest by the early Ch'ing emperors prompted many officials to encourage the cultivation of cotton and the establishment of cotton mills. In 1836, Ho Ch'ang-ling, while governor of Kweichow province, established a special bureau to improve cotton fabrics, which had not hitherto been developed in that remote province.

After the Mohammedan Rebellion, which lasted from 1862 to 1877, devastated most of Shensi and Kansu provinces, Tso Tsung-t'ang, (1812 - 1885) encouraged the establishment of a cotton industry in these areas and throughout Chinese Turkestan. He outlined the proper methods in his booklets which he had published earlier in Foochow under the publishing house he had established, the *Cheng-i-t'ang shu-chu*. Tso had had a great deal of experience with the cotton industry after having established that industry earlier in Foochow when he was the governor. Other high officials in the nineteenth century such as Chang Chih-tung also encouraged and established cotton mills in China during this time and had full governmental support.

Therefore quite early in the nineteenth century, if not even earlier, China had used a machine-spun cotton. It is not a great surprise to discover nineteenth century Chinese rugs with machine-spun cotton. From the period of 1860 onwards as a result of China being defeated by the several Opium Wars, and having to pay huge indemnities to foreign governments, these governments moved to assure that payments would be exacted. Great Britain seized the Internal Revenue system of China. The task of collecting maritime custom duties was placed in the hands of a Briton named Sir Robert Hart. With a large foreign staff the diligent task of keeping records of imports and exports began and there is a mass of data relating to the trade in machine-spun cotton thread. From these and other records, we may further increase our knowledge of the rapid expansion of the Chinese cotton textile industry and their suppliers of raw materials. From these records we can also gather information regarding the varieties of cotton threads.

Another useful work for tracing the status of cotton trade is the *Chinese Commercial Guide: containing treaties, tariffs, regulations, tables etc.* by Samuel Wells Williams.

To use cotton for dating, we should follow the same system as that of wool. The process of machine spinning tends to alter all the cotton fibers in the parallel directions so that under microscopic examination we find that there are fewer aberrant fibers protruding from the sides. The practice of twisting threads in the various plied-thread follows that of wool, such as two-ply, four-ply, five-ply, and so forth.

Linen

Ma or linen is the name for the fabric made from the fibers of the flax plant. It is the most well-known member of the bast fiber family which also includes jute, hemp and ramie. Bast fibers are the long, strong fibers contained in the wood stems of these plants which have been used in the making of textiles since pre-historic times. It is amazing that the use of the fibers dates so far back in time for unlike the readily visible and available wool and cotton or the filament of the silk cocoon which can be unwound with a little practice, the bast fibers are concealed within the plant stalk and must undergo numerous operations before they can be used. The Chinese called these textiles *Ma-pu* or *Ko-pu* which were coarse materials worn during the summer and often associated with the poor.

Although the Chinese made great advances in the spinning of flax and ramie, their physical properties make them suitable only for the bottom of rugs. Such a common material as flax has been so highly developed that Chinese today wear clothing made of flax called *Ma-sha* which rivals the finest pima cotton of the West.

These materials, although they were used in rugs, nevertheless are more common as woven mats and covers. The material is spun like cotton and the overall durability is average. The lack of resilience and elasticity in linen yarns makes them susceptible to breaking. At the same time, the brittle threads are hard and smooth so dirt particles cannot easily work their way into the fibers. Linen is susceptible to the detri-

Plate XXX
Eighteen Lama priests with the eight precious Buddhist symbols. The number of priests most likely is intended to represent the eighteen arhats of Buddhism. 136x305 cm.

mental action of strong acids and alkalis and is weakened by mild acid solution even if they are quickly washed out. Linen may also mildew if allowed to remain damp over an extended period of time. It is not a good material for a knotted pile. Linen's primary use in rug weaving is as a warp and ground weft.

SYMBOLISM

From ancient times, the Chinese viewed themselves as being surrounded and influenced by the cosmos. They were primarily concerned with the sturcture and form of the world in which they lived and the mysterious forces that operated within the geometric framework of that world. Earth was viewed and symbolized as a flat, square plane covered over by a round circle or dome of Heaven. It was commonly believed that the stars and planets that punctuated the canopy of Heaven controlled the destiny of each man. Heaven and Earth were pierced with invisible criss-cross lines that conducted vitalizing, life-giving energy and surging power throughout the system.

The view of the universe was re-created in a human scale by symbol and design. Rooms, palaces, gardens, temples and even entire cities evidence an attempt to incorporate the Chinese view of the cosmos -- seeking to portray the harmony of the universe in a microcosm. Entrances and paths within man-made structures were designed to harmonize with the natural forces. The ancient Chinese studied the secret geometry of the universe; tried to comprehend it, to diagram it, and to imitate it in their designs and structures.

In the third century B. C., when the walled city of Ch'ang-an,(the capitol of the Han dynasty) was built, the distinguished historian Pan Ku praised the cosmic design of the city and its great palaces:

Their frame and image were matched with Heaven and Earth,
Their warp-lines and weft-lines were matched with yin and yang.

Yin and *yang* were the two most important and fundamental energies that permeated all things. The basic meanings of these words are "shady" for *yin* and "sunny" for *yang*. They may be viewed as comparable to the negative and positive forces. The principle of *yang* is conceived to be the rule of the Heavens. It corresponds to light, fire, life, masculinity, and movement. The principle of *yin* is realized in the earth. It corresponds to darkness, water, death, feminity and stillness.

The two principles, *yin* and *yang*, divide to form the points of the compass. Winter correlates to the north, when *yin* is at its zenith and *yang* is reborn. The winter solstice celebrates this event. Spring corresponds to the east and the colour green when the world of nature is reborn. Summer matches with the south; *yang* is at its zenith and *yin* is reborn. Finally, autumn and the west correspond to the setting sun, when nature has finished producing its crops for mankind and begins the long rest of winter.

The Chinese were not concerned with creation or protogenesis, but with the needs of the common man, the changes of the seasons, planting, harvesting, and the rest. The winter solstice celebrates the rebirth of the *yang* principle, symbolized by the sun which begins to grow in strength. Its firery life is reborn, causing nature to awaken. Man, on the other hand, passes from life to death and is not reborn; only through his progeny does he continue his line and assure that he will be fed by his descendants' offerings when he dwells in the unknown life of the nether world. It was perhaps from such a knowledge that the ancient Chinese formed the idea of rebirth. If one could imitate nature and hold in his grasp the principle of life and *yang* then the process from life to death could be reversed. *Yang* instead of being replaced by *yin*, could be restored; man might perhaps be able to return to his roots and restore the origin or as the Chinese say, *Fan kên hui pên*.

One method to achieve this was to find a way to communicate with the spirit world and influence the workings of the invisible forces of nature for one's own benefit. Symbols were developed which could be utilized and geared to man's daily needs. Besides the changes of season and weather, essential for planting, harvesting and building; these symbols were to aid in the cure of sickness, bless marriages, ease childbirth, protect the household from fire, drive off pestilence and misfortune, and guard against calamities. In short they were to make the daily life of the people easier.

The Chinese cultural personality attached great importance to stability and harmony. Primarily a people of this-world, the early Chinese strove to attain harmony and stability in their immediate world, not in distant paradises or in remote future times. It seems very natural that the Chinese wished to prolong their lives in order to enjoy the pleasures of their worldly existence. Thus, a very common element of decoration were symbols for longevity.

To the Chinese, the concept of decoration is an extension of language and a means to create harmony with the cosmos and to communicate with the influencing forces. Decoration is most frequently symbolic. It is a vehicle to convey a clear non-verbal expression or prayer. The importance of a non-verbal expression is to influence and reverse the *yin* and *yang* principles. This followed the Chinese axiom, *Yen yu chin, i wu-ch'iung* or "words have limitations but an idea is boundless".

Symbols, however, were not arbitrarily assigned or adopted but logically and methodically developed in a manner similar to the formation of the written language with its pictograms, ideograms, phonograms, etc. Furthermore, a symbol not only depicts an object, but must embody a deeper or inner meaning. In a symbolic context a picture of a book evokes the idea of learning or literary accomplishments.

Of course, it must first be understood that decoration, at its outset millenia ago, began with ornamental designs freely invented and unencumbered by the necessity to imitate nature. The zig-zag lines, wavy patterns and cross-marks had mysterious meanings to harmonize with the cosmos. In later developments, even with an abstract design, we could read their meanings more readily. We find archaic jade talismans decorated with dots to signify grain and curved lines or S-lines termed *lei-wen* or thunder patterns. These designs, combined as symbols, served to ask for rain and a plentiful harvest. As time progressed, designs and symbols became more uniform and graphic and were thus more easily interpreted and understood.

To mark the four points of the compass, *ssu-chi* and the four seasons, four supernatural animals called *ssu-ling* were depicted. They are the dragon, phoenix, tortoise and the *ch'i-lin*, popularly called the unicorn. Of these four animals, the dragon and the phoenix are the most recognizable and most popular. They are usually depicted as a pictogram.

The Chinese dragon is not the gruesome and destructive monster of medieval western imagination, but a symbol of strength and goodness. The dragon is the spirit of change, the *yang* element and therefore symbolizes life and the productive force. Of the three major species of dragons,[1][2][3] the *lung* is the most revered and is described as having nine resemblances: the head of a camel, the horns of a deer, eyes of a rabbit, ears of a cow, neck of a snake, belly of a frog, scales of a carp, claws of

Figure 4
Five examples of disguised dragon motifs. The symbols of the Four Joys of the Literati are depicted on the bottom row.

a hawk, and palm of the tiger. There is a ridge of scales along its back, eighty-one in number, nine times nine, nine being the *yang* number. On each side of its mouth are whiskers, and a beard hangs under its chin. It desires to mount upwards to the Heavens and it rises till it challenges the clouds.

A primitive form of the dragon is known as *k'uei* or hydra as it is sometimes called by Westerners. It is a beneficient creature, said to exert a restraining influence against the sin of greed. This primitive form of the dragon generally is found on ancient Chinese bronzes and archaic jades and is also used in rug decoration, especially for the corners of rugs. This conforms to the idea of the *lung-wang* or dragon-kings which identifies with the *Nagas* of Hinduism; each ruling over one of the four seas which form the border of the habitable earth.

The dragon became the emblem of vigilance and protection. Consecrated by early religious belief, the dragon was the minister of the will of heaven and the guardian of the temples and shrines. Therefore it is not surprising that pillar rugs should most commonly incorporate the coiling dragon design.

From the time of the reign of Emperor Kao-tsu of the Han dynasty, 206 - 194 B. C., the five-clawed dragon was the symbol of Imperial power and rule, and was restricted only to the Emperor's use. Princes of the third and fourth rank were allowed to use the four-clawed dragon, called, *mang*. Princes of lesser grades were only entitled to employ a serpent-like creature as their emblem. In late Ch'ing times the right to use and wear the *mang* on one's robes could be purchased, although it carried no rights or privileges and was not used in governmental ceremonies. However, dragons in various forms, such as the foliated dragon, *ta'ao-lung*, the geometric hidden dragon, *k'uei-lung*, were used by the upper classes as the embodiment of the *yang* and the generating element.

The phoenix is the kind of birds and a legendary creature described by the Chinese as the composite of various animals. The male is called *fêng* and the female called *huang*. It resembles a wild swan and has the throat of a swallow, the bill of a fowl, the neck of a snake, the tail of a fish, twelve feathers, the forehead of a crane, the crown of a mandarin drake, the stripes of a dragon, the vaulted back of a tortoise and scales of a unicorn. The feathers have five colours, which represent the five cardinal virtues. It is benevolent and does not injure living insects, nor tread upon living herbs. It feeds only on the seeds of the bamboo, *chu-shih*. The phoenix is not only an emblem of beauty but also a symbol for peace and prosperity. This bird would only alight on the *wu-t'ung* or dryandra tree, which is a beautiful flowering ornamental tree which grows to great height very rapidly.

The phoenix presides and rules over the southern quadrant of the heavens and is associated with the sun and warmth of summer to guarantee a bountiful harvest. Since the sun is the *yang* symbol, the phoenix is the complimentary influence in the begetting of children. Therefore a common decoration for a wedding is the dragon and phoenix together gazing at the sun or a ball of fire, the generative power. The phoenix is also commonly depicted alone as by tradition, two are never seen at once, although they are so used in later Ch'ing art. The phoenix was also adopted as the symbol of the Empress and Chinese brides to this day adorn their wedding robes with the phoenix. The dragon-phoenix motif is synonomous with Chinese culture and is not used in the West. However this dragon-phoenix motif had been adopted and incorporated in an Anatolian rug of the fifteenth century. It is without a doubt that this design came directly from China.

The unicorn is another mythical animal that symbolizes goodwill gentleness and benevolence. The *Shih-ching* or Book of Songs describes the unicorn as having the body of a deer, the tail of an ox, the hoofs of a horse, one horn, the scales of a fish, etc. The male is called *ch'i* and the female, *lin*. The unicorn butts with his forehead, so the horn is covered with flesh to show that while able for war, it wills to have peace. It is supposed to appear during the inauguration of a golden age. Later Ch'ing depictions of the *ch'i-lin* have two horns instead of one as a means to distinguish it from the *hsieh-chai* used as a rank symbol for censors. However the pictogram of the unicorn was not used until later times. That is not to say that this important animal of the four quadrants was not used in early rug designs. It was represented in abstract form in the diaper-patterns or *hua-wên* or *chin-wên* as scale designs. This most sacred creature, which was present when Confucius was born, could not be used so presumptuously, therefore the lion or lion-dog, popularly called the fo-dog was frequently substituted, along with the deer or stag, *lu* and pomegranate, *shih-liu* to signify many sons. Nevertheless, the great reverence that the Chinese had for the unicorn could

Plate XXXI

The tortoise back pattern dominates the design of this all-over geometric rug. Stylized flowers and small diaper patterns fill the interstices enhancing the tile-like appearance. The inner border has the running-T design and the outer border has floral diaper patterns with the four joys of the literati and other auspicious symbols. 132x195 cm.

Figure 5
Three forms of the various tortoise diaper patterns.

not be averted, therefore, only the scales of the unicorn's body were used. A poem from the *Shih-ching* or Book of Songs celebrated the sons, grandsons and parents of a prince comparing them respectively to the feet, the forehead, and the horns of this benevolent animal:

> The feet of the Lin
>> The noble sons of our prince,
> Ah, they are the lin
>> The forehead of the lin
> The nobel grandsons of our prince,
>> Ah, they are the lin
> The horn of the lin
>> The noble kindred of our prince,
> Ah, they are the lin.[124]

The unicorn therefore was also seen as the begetter of sons and noble descendants which fulfilled one of the 'Three abundances' or *san-to* that every Chinese prayed for and sought: the abundances of blessings, of years to enjoy life and of male offspring. The unicorn was the symbol of posterity.

The fourth of the sacred animals, the tortoise of *kuei* is the emblem of longevity, strength and endurance. It is also believed to preside over the northern quadrant of heaven and symbolizes winter when *yin* is at its height and *yang* is generated. The divine tortoise is described as having a snake's head and a dragon's neck, the bones are on the outside of the body and the flesh within, and the intestines are joined to the head. On its shell are markings which were believed to have influenced Fu-hsi to devise the sacred symbols of the *pa-kua* or the eight trigrams. The tortoise is associated with the constellations of the sky, more particularly with the Great Dipper. In sculpture the tortoise is usually depicted with a huge tablet on its back or with a snake coiled around it. In rug designs however, it is abstractly depicted in the diaper patterns as hexagonal or octagonal shapes similar to the patterns on the tortoise shell and is frequently used. This is contrary to Murray Eiland's statement that "the tortoise was rare on rugs".[125] Additionally it is also represented as zig-zag marks on the borders. This design called *hsing-chen* traditionally consists of the seven stars of the Great Dipper. However, it is also represented with only three stars depicted as three dots connected by thin lines similar to the inverted V. The desire for longevity among the Chinese was extended in scope to include the idea of physical immortality. This desire was so acute that many symbols for longevity were developed. These included a geometric, circular design for the word *Shou* or longevity. The roundness of this design was most frequently used as a medallion symbolizing the fulfillment of one's life. Added to this were usually five flying bats representing the five happinesses. In a more pictorial representation, longevity was also symbolized with the peaches, the *Shou-lao*, the human depiction of the Great Dipper and the crane or *hsien-hao*.

Being a this-worldly people the desire for longevity and other earthly blessings and pleasures gradually was extended and embellished in scope to include the five happinesses of *wu-fu*. Of these blessings the first is longevity, *shou*; the second is wealth and riches, *fu*; the third is soundness of body and serenity of mind, *k'ang-ning*; the fourth is the love of virtue, *tê*; and the fifth is an end crowning of life, *k'ao chung ming*.

Instead of representing each desire singularly, this was symbolized collectively by five bats. The bat is called a *pien-fu* and so is a homonym for happiness, *fu*. Thus the use of a phonogram as a symbol is incorporated. Furthermore, the bats are usually red, *hung*, in colour which would be termed *hung-fu* a homonym for an abundance of the five happinesses. Yet the design of the bat is often so abstract that it no longer posesses more than a distant resemblance to reality. Using phonograms in symbols, the Chinese have been able to expand their vocabulary of good wishes. The citron, *fo-shou* or *citrus medica* was popularly used not only because its shape was like hands grasping money but because of its name was a homonym of *fu-shou* meaning happiness and longevity. Similarly butterflies called *hu-tieh* were another homonym for the word *tieh* meaning seventy or eighty years of age and the cat called *mao* also means a man aged eighty.

This method of expressing one's wishes by indicating words or sounds using symbols and images lends itself to a truly unique feature of Chinese decoration -- the device of the rebus.

There are several methods of forming a rebus, or an expression conveyed by use of images, which are phonograms. One example, out of the numerous possibilities, might be useful. A halbert, called a *chi*, is the homophone that could mean good luck or auspiciousness. A sonorous stone or a chime, *ch'ing*, is equivalent to another word of the same pronounciation meaning "good luck or blessings". An ingot of gold, *ting*, is the phonetic equivalent for the words meaning "surely or assured", and a Chinese brush, *pi*, is the phonetic equivalent of 'mostly'. Therefore these four symbols of a writing brush, a gold ingot, *ting*, a halberd, *chi*, and a sonorous stone, *ch'ing*, appearing together form the rebus, *Pi-ting chi-ch'ing*, meaning "May you be most assured of having good luck and good fortune." If an elephant, *hsiang*, is substituted for the sonorous stone or chime, another rebus would be formed, *Pi-ting chi-hsiang*, or "May good luck and happiness be assured to you".

Quite often we see depictions of some lotus seeds, peanuts and a small fruit called *long-ngan* or *lung-yen*. The subject matter and the combination of objects would be baffling unless we read it as a rebus. Lotus seeds are called *lien-tzu*, peanuts, *hua-sheng* and the dried *lung-yen* fruit is called *kuei-yuan*. Together they form the rebus, *Lien-shêng kuei-tzŭ* meaning "May you continue to have honourable sons."

Another form of symbolism consists of the representation of various flowers, fruits and plants which for one reason or another evoke certain ideas or concepts.

Fruits

The peach or *t'ao* is also called *hsien-kuo* or the immortal fruit and it holds an important place in Chinese culture as it is the symbol of longevity and immortality. In legend it is supposed to have been grown in the Imperial gardens of Hsi-wang-mu and it was believed that it blossomed once in 3,000 years and required another 3,000 years for the fruit to form and still another 3,000 years for the fruit to ripen. Both the fruits and the flowers of the peach have become auspicious symbols.

The citron with its finger-like protrusions is commonly called *Fo-shou* or Buddha's hands. It is very fragrant and is frequently used as a religious offering. Due to its shape, like hands grasping money, it is seen as a symbol of wealth. Also because its name is a homonym for happiness and longevity, it has also acquired these attributes.

The pomegranate or *shih-liu* is believed to have been introduced to China by Chang Ch'ien from Afganistan in the second century B. C. and was first called *an shih-liu*. The brilliant red fruit is thought to have medicinal qualities. Since the ripened fruit bursts open revealing numerous seeds, it resembles a grinning mouth of teeth and is thus seen as a sign of joy. As it has many seeds, *tzŭ*, which is a homonym for off-

Figure 6
The top three are examples of the pomegranate design while the lower
three are examples of the persimmon patterns.

spring, it came to symbolize prosperity and an abundance of sons. The flowers which are both single and double, range in colours from white to pink and have also been used to denote the same symbolism as the fruit. It blossoms in the fifth lunar month which is called *liu-yueh* or pomegranate month.

The persimmon or *shih*, owing to its bright and festive colour, symbolizes joy. It is also used in decoration because *shih* is a homonym for 'business' or 'market' so that together with a pear of *li* it forms the rebus *li-shih* meaning 'prosperous or profitable business'. *Shih* can also denote time, with *shih-shih* meaning 'always' or 'constantly'. The persimmon is most frequently used as a geometric design similar to an elongated four-petal flower in the diaper patterns in the central field of a rug.

The pear of *li*, besides being a homophone for profitable, (which it shares with the prunus which is also called *li*) is one of the emblems for longevity since the pear tree is very long-lived. Oftentimes three fruits are depicted together to signify the three abundances or *san-to*: longevity, happiness, and posterity.

Flowers

The peony or *mou-tan* is frequently referred to as *fu-kuei-hua* or the flower of honour and riches. This later term was coined by a Sung dynasty scholar, Chou Lien-ch'i in his famous poem *Ai-lien shuo* or the 'Love for the Lotus'. Besides being a symbol of wealth it is also an emblem of love, good fortune, affection and feminine beauty. The peony is looked upon as exemplifying the *yang* principle and the tree-peony is used as the sign of spring.

The lotus, *lien* or *ho* was dubbed the 'flower of the superior man or gentleman' by Chou Lien-ch'i. It grows straight up out of the muck and blossoms over the water remaining pure and delicate without being stained by the mud from which it grew. It is the most serviceable plant as every part of it is used, even the lotus roots and seeds, which are edible. The lotus is a symbol of purity, truth and perfection and the emblem of summer and fruitfulness. The sixth lunar month is called *Ho-yüeh*, Lotus month. The lotus is also the emblem of Ho Hsien-ku, one of the taoist Eight Immortals and a sacred symbol to the Buddhists as well. In fact most Buddhas sit upon a lotus seat or throne. Because of the number of seeds in a lotus pod, it is also the symbol for posterity and many offspring. Oftentimes, the lotus is so highly conventionalized as a design that it is mistaken for a peony or even a chrysanthemum. A lotus is often, but not always, depicted with a lotus pod in the centre which should help distinguish it.

The chrysanthemum of *chü-hua* is the symbol of autumn and the ninth lunar month is called *chü-yüeh* or chrysanthemum month. The fresh flowers are used in cooking and the dried blossoms used as a tea and a medicinal herb. The chrysanthemum is generally associated with a life of ease and retirement. The poet T'ao Ch'ien, 365 - 427 A. D., had a great love for the chrysanthemum and inspite of poverty, refused to take a government rank, preferring to devote his life to poetry, music, wine and retirement. Chou Lien-ch'i called the chrysanthemum, 'the flower of the hermit'.

The peach flower or *t'ao-hua* blossoms in the third lunar month and this month is called the peach-blossom month, *t'ao-yueh*. The peach blossom is the sign of spring and the felicitous time for marriages. An ancient poem from the *Shih-ching* or Book of Songs reads:

> *The peach tree is young and elegant*
> > *Brilliant are its flowers.*
> *This young lady is going to her future home,*
> > *And will order well her chamber and house.*
>
> *The peach tree is young and elegant*
> > *Abundant will be its fruit.*
> *This young lady is going to her future home,*
> > *And will order well her house and chamber.*
>
> *The peach tree is young and elegant;*
> > *Luxuriant are its leaves.*
> *This young lady is going to her future home,*
> > *And will order well her family.*

Being a flower of felicitous time, it is also an important adornment for the celebration of the Lunar New Year. Sprays or branches of the blossoms are placed at the doors of houses at New Year's to magically prevent all malevolence from entering thus insuring peace of mind.

The prunus, or plum flower, called *mei-hua* by the Chinese blossoms during the tenth lunar month, *mei-yüeh* or prunus month. It is the emblem of winter and is commonly regarded as a symbol of longevity. The blossoms appear on the leafless and apparently lifeless branches.

Plate XXXII

The brush, incenser, peony, vase and persimmon flower form the rebus:
Ssŭ-shih p'ing-an -- Pi-ting fu-kuei or "May you most assuredly be blessed with happiness and wealth. May you enjoy peace of mind at all
times". 72x131 cm.

Figure 7
Examples of peonies shown as single blossoms and with foliage as border designs.

It is often confused with the peach blossom, however, the peach branches have leaves along with flowers while the prumus is always depicted as blossoms on a branch without leaves. The genus *prunus* is also called *li* and the written character is made up of three parts, *shih* (ten), *pa* (eight) and *tzŭ* (sons) or 'eighteen sons'. Therefore, it has also become a symbol for posterity. The prunus and the peach depicted together, *t'ao-li*, mean disciples or students, being unripened fruits receiving their development from the teacher or master. The prunus also signifies perseverance as the prunus blooms in the coldes months.

The orchid *lan* is the emblem of love and beauty, reflecting refinement and exquisite yet simple taste. It is also a symbol of numerous progeny. Confucius remarked on its exquisite characteristics as being the embodiment of a perfect or superior man.

The pomegranate flower *liu-hua* which appears as either handsome single or double blossoms in the fifth lunar month, symbolizes posterity who would be virtuous, filial and attain high rank in officialdom. The pomegranate flowers are usually used as geometric patterns in the fields of older rugs and are quite often mistaken for another flower as pomegranate flowers are not commonly seen in the West.

The depiction of the peony, peach and pomegranate blossoms together forms a rebus of ideograms: *Fu-lu-shou*, 'Happiness or wealth, longevity and posterity'. Another rebus could be formed partly by using the symbol of the lotus as a phonogram and the peony and peach as ideograms forming the phrase *Lien fu-shou* or "May you continue to enjoy happiness and longevity".

Plants

The *ling-chih* or the divine fungus, (probably the *Polyporus lusidus*) if picked at the beginning of winter becomes very durable and will be preserved without change. This fungus is believed to be the elixir of life and ensures long life. It is not surprising that it is the symbol for longevity and immortality. It is believed that this plant grows on the islands in the Eastern Sea called *San-hsien-shan* where immortals lived. In Chinese popular belief this was the elixir that the first Chinese Emperor, Ch'in-shih Huang-ti, 221 B. C., sought after and his expeditions into the Eastern Seas led to the populating of the island of Japan. The sceptre or *ju-i* is a refined shape of the *ling-chih*.

The pine or fir tree, *sung*, is believed by the Chinese to have eter-

Figure 8
A variety of lotus forms used as border patterns and central motifs.

nal youth because it remains green. It has thus become the symbol of longevity. Also, since it winters without dropping its needles and remains a constant green, it symbolizes true friendship; always remaining constant in adversity. The bark always looks ancient and is viewed metaphorically as an old man.

The bamboo or *chu* is another evergreen that flourishes throughout the year and has come to symbolize longevity. The bamboo plant is very useful and every part of it is used by all classes of people. As an evergreen, it is called *lu* which is the homonym for *lu* meaning 'happiness or prosperity'. The bamboo bends before the storm and springs back so that it is an emblem of uprighteousness and a person with high principles. The bamboo *chu* is often used as a homophone meaning "Wishing you" or "congratulations".

The *wu-t'ung* tree or *Dryandra cordifolia* is an ornamental species which grows to a great height very rapidly. The seventh lunar month is called *t'ung-yüeh* or *wu-t'ung* month, as this is when the tree blossoms forth producing a bell-shaped flower that is white with a reddish-brown centre. As mentioned previously, according to folk belief, this is the only tree on which the phoenix will alight. Therefore, it is also a complimentary symbol of the phoenix and is the emblem of rapid rising or promotion. It is also frequently used as a homophone since the term *t'ung* also means 'together' and since the large green leaves open up very early in the spring or *ch'un* it forms the rebus, *t'ung ch'un* or 'together enjoying youth and good health' or 'being joyful'.

A depiction of the bamboo, pine and prunus tree together forms the ideogram, *Han-sui san-yu* or 'the three friends of winter' which implies endurance, harmony and lasting friendship.

Animals

Besides fruits, flowers and plants and trees, birds, animals and even insects are used as symbols of well-wishes. Aside from the mythical dragon, phoenix and unicorn, the deer or the stag is most frequently depicted.

The deer or stag, *lu*, is first of all a homonym for happiness and prosperity. The Chinese believe that deer live to a very great age and therefore represent longevity. Moreover it is said that the deer is the only animal which is able to find the *ling-chih* or divine fungus of immortality. It is therefore common to find the deer pictured with a *ling-*

chih in its mouth which is usually mis-identified as a *ju-i*. Sometimes the spots on the deer, similar to plum blossoms, are used in geometric shapes as diaper patterns in the borders or in the field of a rug.

The lion, *shih* or *shih-tzu*, although not native to China is commonly used as a symbol. Westerners frequently refer to the lion in Chinese art at the 'Fo-dog'. This misnomer stems from the stone sculptures of lions in front of official buildings and temples. Usually in pairs. the female fondles a young cub, while the male plays with a ball. This portrays the dual powers of nature. The lion is most commonly connected with Buddhism and more specifically with Manjusri who is depicted riding a lion. He is worshipped in China as a God of Wisdom, and by the Manchus and Mongolians as their patron saint. The lion therefore is the emblem of valour, courage, energy and wisdom. The Chinese consider the lion to be a peaceful creature unlike the fierce tiger with which they are so familiar. The lion is also used as a homonym as *shih-tzu* has the same sound as the words for male offspring with each generation. Oftentimes two lions are depicted, one large and one small forming the rebus, *t'ai-shih shao-shih* or "May you gain the rank of Grand Tutor or Junior Tutor". On Tibetan and Mongolian rugs the lion is used as the symbol of Lamaism. Quite often the round spiral curls of the lion's mane are used as geometric shapes in diaper patterns either on the field or as meanders on the borders of a rug.

The horse, *ma*, is the emblem of speed and perseverance and loyalty. It has the uncanny ability to sense danger. The *Pa-chin-ma* or the Eight steeds of Mu-wang, 1001 - 746 B. C. (the fifth sovereign of the Chou dynasty) are popularly depicted in Chinese art. Furthermore the horse is used as a homonym meaning quickly or speedily.

Birds

The crane, *hao* or *ho* is second in importance only to the phoenix, as it is reputed to be endowed with numerous powers. It is the symbol of longevity and the messenger of the Gods. The two readings of *hao* and *ho* are homonyms meaning 'goodness' and 'harmony'. Oftentimes it is used as a round medallion forming the idiomatic phrase *yuan-hao* or "May you enjoy a life of fulfillment".

The wild goose or *yên* or *t'ien-ngo* reflects the *yang* element and is an emblem of marriage, enduring relationship and high honour. The first quality reflects the fact that wild geese always fly in pairs and mate

Plate XXXIII

A typical Pao-t'ou rug with a stag and crane with lush growth and flowing water, together denoting: *Fu-lu ch'ang-ch'un* "May you enjoy everlasting happiness and longevity". 152x148 cm.

once for life. Since they fly very high and follow the sun, obeying instinct as to route and time of migration, they become a symbol of the *yang* principle and high attainment. Therefore the phrase *Yen-t'a t'i-ming* or 'to have one's name inscribed on the temple of the wild goose', becomes the idiomatic expression of being honoured to have attained the degree of *chin-shih* which is equivalent to the doctoral degree in the West.

The peacock of *k'ung-ch'iao* is the emblem of beauty and dignity. The handsome feathers with a circular eye marking have been used since Ming times as a designation of being distinguished. The phrase, *K'ung-ch'iao k'ai-p'ing*, "the peacock spreading or displaying its tail feathers" has come to mean "good luck smiles on you" as all eyes are looking at you. Oftentimes only the peacock feather is depicted.

Most often the crane and the deer are depicted together as meaning longevity, prosperity and happiness. However, in Chinese rules of decoration, a particular bird is almost invariably associated with a particular flower. Therefore long tailed birds such as the phoenix, peacock, fowl and pheasant are drawn with the peony; the duck is shown with the lotus; the swallow with the willow; quails and partridges with millet; cranes with the pine and the phoenix with the *wu-t'ung* tree.

Flowers are also used to denote time. Each of the twelve months of the year there are associated with a particular flower: prunus, peach, peony, cherry, magnolia, pomegranate, lotus, pear, mallow, chrysanthemum, gardenia and poppy. Flowers are also used to denote the four seasons: the tree-peony for spring, the lotus for summer, the chrysanthemum for autumn, and the prunus for winter.

Bats and butterflies are also used as signs of happiness and longevity as their names are phonetically identical. The bat or *pien-fu* is a homonym for 'happiness'. It is often depicted as red in colour forming the rebus *hung-fu* or 'bountiful happiness'. Bats are usually depicted five in number as to represent *wu-fu* or the five happiness or blessings, which are longevity, wealth, soundness of body and serenity of mind, the love of virtue and an end crowning of life. Later designs also depict four bats surrounding the character *shou* or longevity to give the same meaning. The stylized wings resemble the *ju-i* shape. Bats are often so stylized that they bear a strong resemblance to butterflies, and are often mistaken for butterflies by Westerners.

Figure 9
Six varieties of the disguised butterfly motif. The two lower examples
are the bat motif.

The butterfly or *hu-tieh* is used as an emblem of joy and happiness in reference to an incident from the life of the philosopher Chuang-tzu called *Hu-tieh mêng*, the Butterfly Dream. Chüang-tzu reported dreaming that he had been transformed into a butterfly and found great happiness with the freedom of flight and movement. In the regional, Shao-hsing opera *Liang Shan-po yü Chu Ying-t'ai*, the lovers were changed into butterflies signifying eternal love. However a more suitable interpretation is that the word *tieh* is a homonym meaning a person aged seventy or eighty. Thus it reflects a full life span that, as a symbol of longevity, is most appropriate. Hans Lorentz suggests that "the bat (fu) is a symbol for luck . . . the character *hu* in butterfly . . . There is not much difference in southern China between the pronounciation of *hu* and *fu*. The Japanese, too, cannot distinquish between h and f."[126] In Chinese, the Hunanese seems to be one of the few, if not the only, dialect that pronounces the word *hu* in the term *hu-tieh* as *fu*. Therefore it may be entertained that to persons from Hunan province the butterfly could be a rebus for 'joy and happiness with old age'. However, the *hu* in *hu-tieh* is usually used as a compound. *Tieh* alone could mean butterfly but not the word *hu* alone. Lorentz's pronounciation *hu-tiao* is incorrect. It is pronounced as *hu-tieh* or *hu-t'ieh* but not as *hu-tiao*. Futhermore Lorentz's statement on Japanese is also in error. In the Japanese syllabary, there is only one sound *fu*. The *hu* sound is non-existant in the Japanese language and the syllabary in *kana* reads: *ha, hi, fu, he, hō*. Also the Japanese word for butterfly is *chōchō*.

The use of the symbol of the fish *yu* or more particularly the carp, *li-yu* is quite popular as an emblem of wealth or abundance. Basically this significance is derived from the fact that the word *yu* is the same pronounciation as 'abundance' and the carp, *li-yü* is similar in sound to 'an excess of profit.' Owing to its reproductive powers, it is also a symbol of fertility and regeneration, and as it is happy in its own element, it is an emblem of harmony and connubial bliss. Hence, it is a must as a betrothal gift to the bride's family on account of its auspicious significance. Fish are reputed to swim in pairs and so become the emblematic of the joys of union, especially of a sexual nature. As a pair, fish are included as one of the Eight Buddhist symbols of happy augury and as a Taoist symbol, it is a *yin* element having thirty-six scales, six times six, six being a *yin* number. However, the carp in Taoist tradition swims upstream and jumps over the rapids of Lung-men and changes into a dragon and ascends to Heaven. There is also a symbol of literary eminence or attainment.

The carp with its scaley armour represents martial attributes and is admired because it struggles against the current, and it has therefore become the emblem of perseverance. As designs, the fish scales and the fish roe, represented by little dots, are used in the diaper patterns in the field or borders of rugs.

To symbolize various other attainments and qualities of accomplishment, symbols as ideograms are utilized. The four attributes of the literati or scholar are frequently depicted with four objects: the book, *shu*, a painting *hua*, the lute *ch'in*, and the game of chess *ch'i*. These four objects are popularly interpreted as the book for learning and literary knowledge, the painting and the lute for art and music, and the game of chess for thinking of strategy. These have been described by Westerners as objects denoting the pursuits of the gentleman and the cultured man and rugs with these symbols have often been called scholar's rugs. However this is but an absurdity and an over-simplification as Murray Eiland so aptly suggested.

In the *Lun-yü* or the Analects by Confucius, here is a passage that reads: "Yên Yüan asked about virtue. The master said to subdue oneself and return to propriety, is perfect virtue. If a man can for one day subdue himself and return to propriety, all under Heaven will ascribe perfect virtue to him. Is the practice of perfect virtue from a man himself or is it from others? Yên Yüan said, 'I beg to ask the steps of that process'. 'Look not at what is contrary to propriety, listen not to what is contrary to propriety; speak not to what is contrary to propriety.' Yên Yüan then said, 'Though I am deficent in intelligence and vigour, I will make it my business to practice this lesson'."

The Japanese have tried to depict this statement by Confucius in the decoration of the Tokugawa Shrine in Nikko, Japan by carving the famous three monkeys with one monkey covering his mouth with his paws, another covering his ears and the third covering his eyes. This is known in the West as 'Speak no evil, hear no evil, see no evil'. However the fourth attribute, "make no evil moves" could not be successfully depicted so it was omitted.

The Chinese artist on the other hand, had used the four objects, a lute, painting, book and chess to symbolize this same teaching of Confucius. The lute is to hear good tones and the painting is to see good depictions. Since the Chinese read their books aloud, the book is to recite good verses and the game of chess, is to make good, sound moves to win the game. This meaning is more in accord with Chinese culture as it contains a clear statement but also embodies an indepth meaning. Confucianism urges the development and the cultivation of virtue, or *te* so as to choose right from wrong, to set a good example. It is also an intellectual system which declares that one errs only through ignorance, and that if one is sufficiently learned to discern that which is good, one will, of necessity, do that which is good. This is the knowledge of human nature which is in harmony with the cosmos.

Elements of Nature

Symbolizing elements of nature, pictograms such as clouds, water, mountains are readily used by the Chinese. The clouds, *yun* not only denote loftiness but are also a homonym for luck, fortune or fate. The Chinese use the phrase *Yün ch'ung lung* or "clouds come with the dragon', to indicate the eminence of the *yang* or positive element in nature, heralding awakening, growth and good fortune. From the *I-ching* or Book of Changes there is a statement, *Yün hsing yü shih* -- the clouds move and the rains fall -- the rain of benevolence. *Wu-sê yün* or the five coloured clouds denote the glory of nature with peace and harmony. The expression 'clouds of five colours' is a very ancient one in Chinese folklore. Reports of this occurance in nature appear repeatedly among the auspicious events listed in the Chinese annals. The *Sung-shih* or History of the Sung dynasty, 960 - 1280, noted that the 'five coloured clouds' are omens of great peace and are called *ch'ing-yün* or 'auspicious clouds'. In Ch'ing dynasty laws, it is decreed that the background of the robes for the Emperor, Empress, Imperial Consorts and the Heir Apparent must have five coloured clouds. The literary phrase, *Ch'ing yün chih shang* or 'auspicious clouds rising straight up' gives the meaning of rapid promotion of one's position or great wealth abounding. Oftentimes, the cloud patterns are linked together as a chain of clouds, this is to form the rebus *lien-yün* or "May you continue to receive good fortune".

The stylized symbol basically is directly borrowed from the early written form of the word. In the *Shuo-wên* dictionary we find that this word was symbolized as a spiral with a tail similar to a question mark without the period. The *Shuo-wên* is an ancient dictionary compiled by Hsü Shên in 100 A. d. containing 10,000 characters, analyzed with a view to prove the hieroglyphic origin of the Chinese language. This would seem to refute the claims of Hans Bidder that it is an "old Turkish motif".[127] Surely this motif is considerably older than Bidder thought. Gröte-Hasenbalg, Dimand, Lorentz and other authors have accurately shown that it is of Chinese origin. In the famous eighth century Chinese rug in the Shosoin, the cloud pattern is already utilized in the decoration and is quite fully developed.

The motifs of the mountain and water of *shan-shui* likewise could be seen in the Shosoin rug. The mountain, usually three stylized peaks shaped like the ancient pictogram for the word *shan*, emerges from the water and is often referred to in Western rug literature as *Pao-shan hai-shui* which only means 'precious or sacred mountain and waves of the sea". This offers no clues to its understanding whatsoever. The Chinese thought of this mountain as Mount K'un which is believed to be the traditional centre of the Universe in ancient Chinese cosmology. This concept was recorded in the *Shên-i ching*, a work ascribed to Tung-fang Shuo of the second century B. C. This ancient motif is traditionally described as consisting of five parts -- four lesser ranges grouped around the central mass. In Chinese cosmology the numbers five and three are *yang* elements so later depictions are not totally incorrect as the three peaks may have represented the three islands of P'êng-lai or the *San-hsien-shan*, the three islands of the Immortals. The mountains, sea, *li-shui* or 'rising waters' are the basic cosmic symbolism for Earth and Sea with its cloud-filled sky -- the cosmic universe in a microcosm. This depiction also suggests the phrase, *Shan-ho wu-yang*, 'the mountains and the rivers (water) are quite well' -- territorial integrity is maintained. Such symbolism is very appropriate to use for decoration on Imperial or Religious objects.

However, in later development of this design, we usually find a highly eroded, weather-beaten crag jutting from the waves or sea. This motif is commonly termed *shou-shan fu-hai* or 'the mountain of longevity and the sea of happiness.' The felicitious statement is derived from the poem *Shou-shan fu-hai t'u-ko* by Liu Chi, 1311 - 1375, who aided the founding of the Ming dynasty. It is also a contraction of the ever-popular couplet, *Fu ju Tung-hai, Shou pi Nan-shan.*[128] "May you enjoy happiness as vast as the Eastern Seas and be as long-lived as the Southern Mountains." This ever-popular couplet has led many to interpret that the sea and the mountains symbolize happiness and longevity while ignoring the cosmic meaning.

Official and Religious Symbols

Of the various designs and symbols used, there are those which were restricted exclusively for official use. One set of twelve symbols called *shih-êrh chang* were set forth in the *Shu-ching* of the Book of History.

"I (Yü) wish to see the emblematic figures of the ancients -- the sun, the moon, the stars, the mountains, the dragon, the flaming fowl, depicted on the upper garment; the temple cup, the aquatic grass, the flames, the grains of rice, the hatchet, and the symbol of distinction, which are embroidered on the lower garment -- I wish to see all these displayed with the five colours, so as to form the official robe."[129]

These twelve symbols were described and interpreted in a memorial by the seventh century scholar, Yang Ch'iung and preserved in the *Chiu-T'ang shu* or History of the T'ang dynasty, 618 - 960 A. D.

The sun, a red disk, the moon, a greenish-white disc the stars or constellation, usually represented by three dots connected with lines in an inverted V, symbolize the light of the good and wise ruler shining upon the world.

The mountain amidst the cloud and water symbolize the beneficence of the good and wise ruler to his people.

The dragon, a symbol of change, represents the adaptability of the good and wise ruler according to the needs of the time.

The flaming fowl, represented as a pheasant with five colours on its body symbolizes the cultured accomplishment of the good and wise ruler.

The temple cups with representations of the tiger and the monkey symbolize the ability of the good and wise ruler to pacify rebellions with supernatural force of the tiger and the cleverness of the monkey.

The aquatic grass, which rises and falls with the water, symbolizes the good and wise ruler responding to the needs of the time.

The flames which fire pottery, melt metals and cook food, symbolizes the good and wise ruler's supreme virtue which is renewed daily.

The grains of rice upon which the life of human beings depends, symbolizes the good and the wise ruler as the mainstay of all things.

Plate XXXIV
A Lama figure standing above foaming waves and calling the monks to prayer by blowing on a conch. Clouds and sacred symbols surround the figure. 206x78 cm.

The hatchet which is used to cut and sever, symbolizes the decisiveness of the good and wise ruler when confronted with situations.

The symbol of distinction consisting of two 'chi' characters, back to back, symbolizes the harmony of the ruler and his ministers.

Whether in its pure form, altered or disguised, all twelve symbols have been used in rug decorations although the original intent was for robes. In addition to the twelve symbols, the only other set of symbols prescribed by law were the Eight Precious Objects or *Pa-pao*.

According to the *T'ang-lu* or the Statutes of the T'ang dynasty, 618 - 960 A. D., the eight symbols were to be as follows:

One object to symbolize the perpetuation of rule. Another object is to symbolize the Mandate of Heaven to rule over the country. Three objects to represent the Emperor and another three objects to signify that he is the Son of Heaven. Although these symbols were to represent sacred power, their descriptions were rather vague so that it gave great latitude for its selection so long as they were eight different objects. Without hesitation, symbols were selected to represent wealth and achievement. Having no standard prescription, three sets of symbols existed, the Eight Ordinary Symbols, *Su Pa-pao*, the Eight Sacred Taoist Symbols, *Pa-pao* or *Pa-hsien pao*, and the Eight Sacred Buddhist Symbols, *Pa-chi-hsiang*.

The first set of symbols or the Eight Ordinary Symbols include the following:

1. The pearl which symbolized purity and preciousness and grants every wish.
2. The coil or cash to symbolize wealth or riches.
3. The Rhombus or lozenge to symbolize victory and a prosperous condition in the state.
4. A pair of Books to symbolize knowledge and learning and in early times as sacred writings.
5. A scroll or painting which in early times were rolls of silk to symbolize tribute to the Emperor.
6. A pair of rhinoceros horns to symbolize sacrificial cups and the power of judgement.
7. The sonorous stone or chime to symbolize ritual, ceremony and blessings.

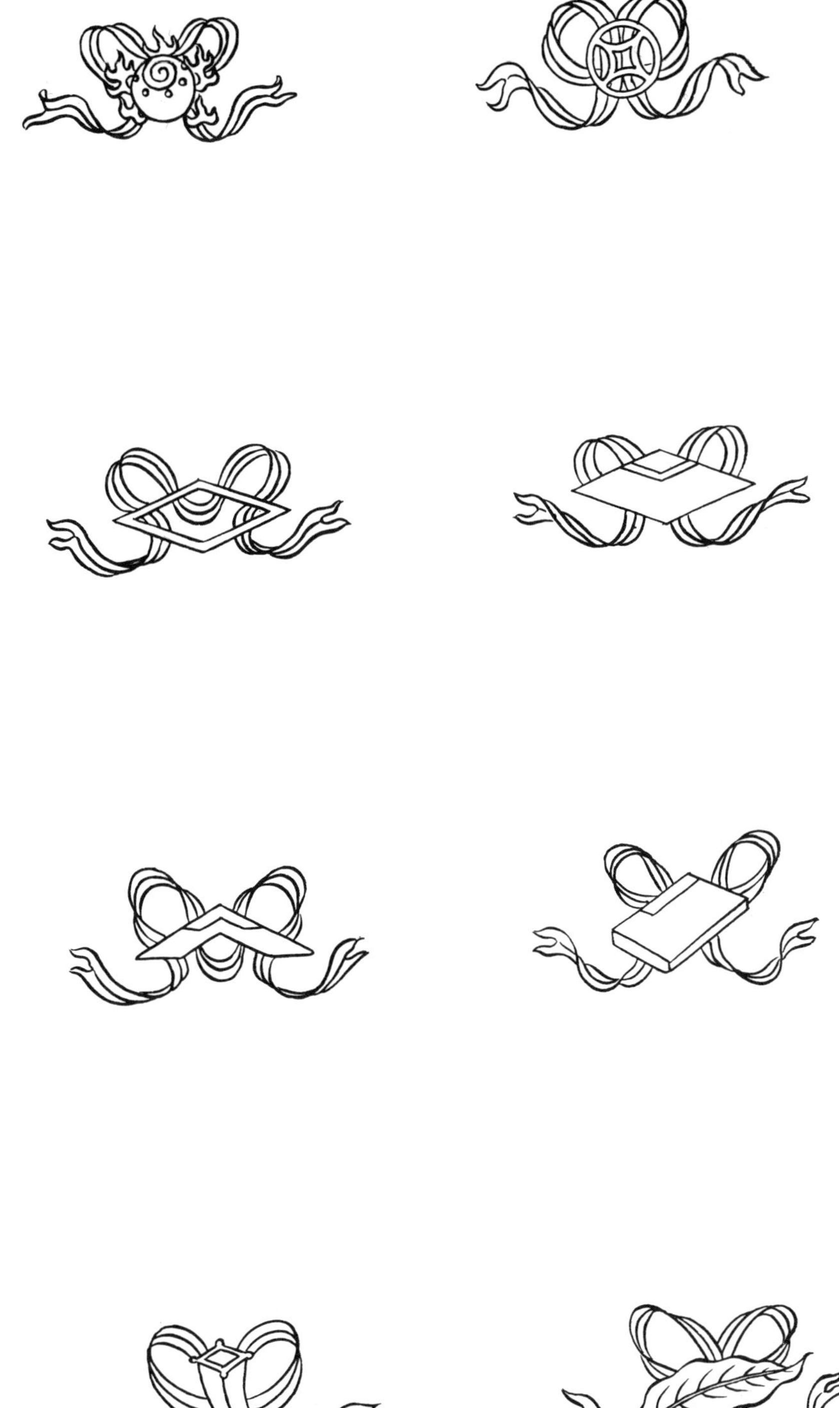

Figure 10
The Eight Ordinary Symbols or *Pa-pao*.

Figure 11
The Eight Sacred Buddhist Symbols.

8. The artemisia leaf, similar to the water weed, is to symbolize the responding to the needs of the time. The artemisia, a fragrant plant represents a good omen and a prevention of disease.

The Eight Sacred Buddhist Symbols also called *Pa-pao* but more often termed *Pa-chi-hsiang* include:

1. The parasol, or umbrella of state is a symbol of majesty and dignity.
2. The conch shell, a symbol of holy victory, used to call the faithful to prayer. It is the symbol of the blessedness of turning to the right.
3. The lotus, the symbol of divine purity. It is the pledge of salvation or Nirvana.
4. The vase which contains the heavenly elixir called *kan-lu* or sweet dew by the Chinese. It is the 'treasury of all the desires.'
5. The wheel symbolized the law and doctrine of Buddhism which leads to perfection.
6. The standard symbols victory and is the standard erected on the summit of the Palace of Salvation.
7. The endless knot or mystic diagram is the symbol of the thread which guides to happiness. It is variously interpreted but is most probably derived from the mystic mark on the belly of Vishnu.
8. The pair of fish joined together symbolize the union of happiness and utility, and were originally the emblem of Vishnu and Kama.

Frequently these symbols are generally shown in or above the waves. Their association with water reflects the Lamaistic belief that the sea is the source of wealth.

The Eight Sacred Taoist Symbols the *Pa-pao* or *Pa-hsien pao* include the following:

1. The fan of Chung-li Ch'uan, also called Han Chung-li.
2. The sword of Lü Tung-pin.
3. The pilgrim's gourd of T'ieh-kuai Li also called Li T'ieh-kuai.
4. The castanets of Ts'ao Kuo-chiu.

5. The flower basket of Lan Ts'ai-ho.
6. The bamboo tube and rods of Chao Kuo-lao.
7. The flute of Han Hsiang-tzŭ.
8. The lotus of Ho Hsien-ku.

The Eight Immortals

The Eight Immortals are usually collectively represented as symbols of longevity and happiness. Although various Western writers have read into each particular object, giving them fanciful meanings without any basis in fact. The term *pa-hsien* or Eight Immortals may be represented either singly or in a group and is always associated with joy and happiness. The number 'eight' has become lucky in association with this tradition, and things eight in number are graced accordingly. To the Chinese, whether singular or as a complete group they represent happiness and protection against any infringement upon this happiness. Of the eight immortals, three of them, Chung-li Ch'uan, Chang Kuo and Lü Yen or Lu Tung-pin were historical personages; the others are mentioned only in fables and romances.

The legend of the *Pa-hsien* or Eight Immortals is certainly not older than the Sung dynasty, 960 - 1280 A. D., and is probably more realistically assigned to the Yüan dynasty, 1280 - 1368 A. D. This late date is suggested by the famous Ming dynasty scholar and bibliophile, Hu Ying-lin, 1551 - 1602. There is no reliable evidence of this legend before the Sung period and the Yüan Emperors had shown a preference for Taoism, which made rapid progress during their reigns. Some if not all of these eight immortals seem to have been previously celebrated in the earlier Taoist legends. In 1115 A. D. the Emperor Hui-tsung of the Sung dynasty conferred on Lu Yen the title "Hero of Marvellous Wisdom" and later proclaimed him as "Strong Protector". The Emperors of the Yuan dynasty bestowed the title of "Pure Active Principle" to Lu Yen and "True Masculine Principle" on Chung-li Ch'üan. It was during this time that the eight immortals were introduced into *tsa-chu* or Yüan drama and the Offering of Blessings *Pa-hsien ho-shou* at the beginning of a theatrical performance began. This practice is still followed today.

The eight immortals are extremely popular in China as they represent all ages and classes of people, Chang Kuo-lao represents the old and Han Hsiang-tzŭ, the young, Chung-li Ch'üan the military, Lu Tung-

Plate XXXV
A boldly coloured pillar rug with fruits, flowers, grain as symbolic offerings symmetrically arranged against a richly toned ground. The lower border is decorated with the waves and mountain design. The upper border has repeating devil's masks. 83x213 cm.

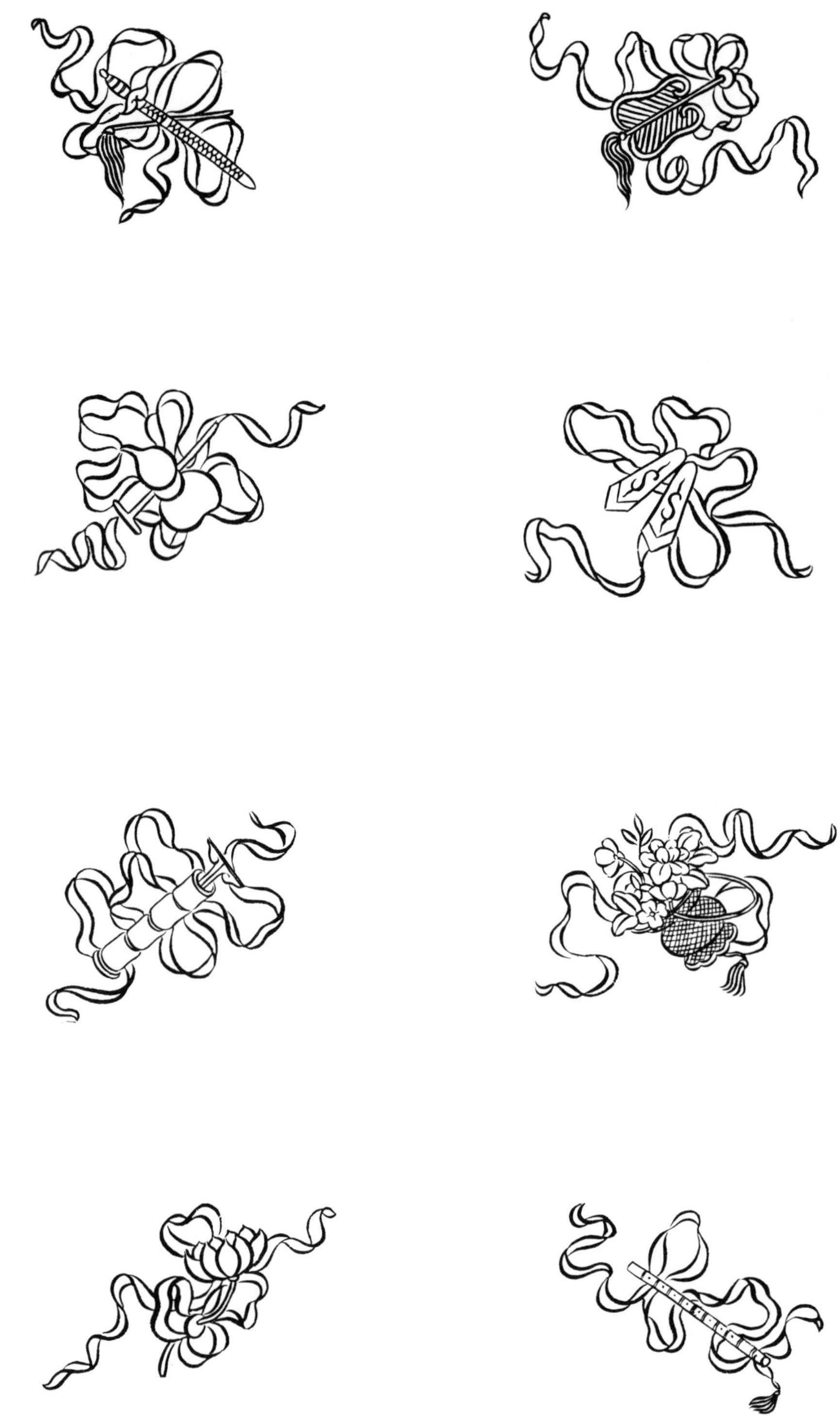

Figure 12
The Eight Sacred Taoist Symbols.

pin the literati and wealthy; Ts'ao Kuo-chiu, the nobility; Lan Ts'ai-ho, the needy; Li T'ieh-kuai, the infirm and lame; and Ho Hsien-ku, the female. These representations therefore, cross all social and age barriers.

According to the popular novel *Pa-hsien tung-yu chi* or the Account of the Eight Immortals' Mission to the East, a modified set of eight precious or magical objects is suggested. This expedition was made to behold the wonderous things of the sea which are not to be found in the celestial sphere,very similar to the present-day outer space and deep sea explorations.

To cross the sea the Eight Immortals utilized their magical treasures and many adventures ensued. Li T'ieh-kuai used his iron crutch, Chung-li Ch'uan his feather fan, Chang Kuo-lao his paper mule, Lü Tung-pin his magical sword, Han Hsiang-tzu his magical bamboo flute, Ho Hsien-ku her lotus blossom, Lan Ts'ai-ho his flower basket and Ts'ao Kuo-chiu his court sceptre or tablet of admission to court.

The *Kai-yu ts'ung-k'ao* by the scholar Chao I, 1727, gives detailed descriptions and biographies of the individual immortals. These bits of information are important as the immortals are frequently pictured individually and the viewer of art is illiterate without some familiarity of meaning beyond the surface.

Li T'ieh-kuai is depicted with an iron crutch and a pilgrim's gourd containing magic remedies. He is identified with several persons one of whom is Li Ning-yang to whom Lao-tzu was believed to have appeared to give him instructions in the various mysteries. Having been initiated, his soul left his body and soarded to Mount Hua to perfect the elixir or *tan*. He left his body in the care of his disciple Lang Ling with the instructions that if he did not return in seven days his body should be cremated. After seven days had passed he returned to find his body gone. He discovered the body of a lame beggar who had recently died of hunger and his soul entered it. Lao-tzu gave him a gold band to keep the disheveled hairs in order and an iron crutch. Thus he became known as T'ieh-kuai Li or Li with the iron crutch. He is reported to have cured a number of people with the medicines from his gourd which he hung on his crutch along with a scroll with mystic writings. He is the patron saint of pharmacists.

Chung-li Ch'üan is depicted as a fat man with his belly exposed carrying a peach and holding a feathered fan, which is believed to revive the dead. Some accounts claim that he lived during the Han dynasty so he is also called Han Chung-li. He is reported to have been a military man in the service of the Duke of Chou Hsiao and having been defeated in battle, he escaped to the Chung-nan mountains where he met some immortals who gave him instructions in the Doctrine of Immortality. At a later time, he is reported to have taught the same mysteries to Lü Tung-pin.

An interesting story about his fan is related. He once met a young woman recently widowed fanning the grave of her husband as it was his wish that she wait until his grave dried before she would remarry. Having found another man she was impatient and was fanning the grave to make it dry quickly. Chung-li Ch'üan aided her with his magical powers and she gaily thanked him leaving her fan behind. He took the fan home and related the story to his wife who swore that she would never commit such infidelity. To test her, Chung-li Ch'üan using his magic, pretended to be dead while assuming the image of a handsome young man and flirted with her promising to marry her if she would acquire the brains of her deceased husband. Following her new lover's request she opened the coffin and was horrified when her husband suddenly came to life while her lover disappeared into thin air. Shame overcame her and she hung herself while Chung-li Ch'üan set the house on fire, saving only a sacred book and the feathered fan.

Chang Kuo-lao is depicted as an old man riding on a white mule and carrying a musical instrument called *yu-ku* in the shape of a bamboo tube or drum with two rods to beat it. His name is Chang Kuo, the suffix *lao* merely mean 'old' or 'old person'. He is believed to be the reincarnated spirit of a white spiritual bat which came out of primeval chaos. He had magical powers and lived as a hermit travelling about on his white mule. Whenever the mule was not required he folded it up like a piece of paper and put it away in his wallet. When he needed his mule he had only to squirt water from his mouth upon the packet and the animal once again assumed its proper shape. He could perform wonderful feats of necromancy and several Emperors tried to attach him to their court but he would not give up his wandering life and disappeared and entered immortality. The depiction of Chang Kuo on a mule offering a descendant to the newly wed couple is often found in the nuptial chambers. It seems somewhat incongruous that an old ascetic should be associated with matrimonial happiness and the granting of offspring, but the explanation may possibly be connected with his performance of wonderful feats of necromancy. In Chinese households, he is affectionately called "Chang-hsien".

Ts'ao Kuo-chiu is depicted as a refined gentleman wearing official robes and holding a pair of castanets which were derived from the court tablet or sceptre giving him free access to the court. He was connected with the Imperial family of the Sung dynasty and legend relates that he was the younger brother of Empress Ts'ao, wife of Emperor Jen-tsung, 1023 - 1064 A. D. Ts'ao is his surname and *Kuo-chiu* merely means 'Imperial Brother-in-law'. His real name is purported to be Ts'ao Ching-hsiu. It is believed that he was ashamed and hid in the mountains after his brother was found guilty of homocide and was condemned to death. Chung-li Ch'uan and Lü Tung-pin found him in his mountain retreat and gave instructions to him for perfecting himself for immortality. Thus he joined them as one of the Eight Immortals. He is the patron saint of the theatrical profession.

Han Hsiang-tzŭ is depicted as a young man playing the traverse flute. His personal name is Ch'ing-fu and he claims to be a grand nephew of the famous T'ang philosopher and statesman Han Yü, 768 - 824 A. D. As a child he was entrusted to his uncle to be educated and prepared for the public examinations. He excelled his teacher in intelligence and became an ardent votary of transcendental study. He was able to foretell events and perform wonderful feats. It is believed that he became the disciple of Lü Tung-pin and entered the ranks of immortality. He is the patron saint of musicans.

Ho Hsien-ku is depicted as a beautiful young woman holding in her hand the bloom of the magic lotus, the flower of open heartedness, or the peach of immortality given her by Lü Tung-pin. Less frequently she is depicted playing the *sheng*, a reed organ. She is reported to have lived during the T'ang dynasty in the time of Empress Wu, 684 - 705 A. D., and was the daughter of Ho T'ai of Kwangtung province. Her personal name is unknown and the term *hsien-ku* merely means 'fairy'. She elected to live on the mountain range called Yün-mu. On that mountain was found a stone called *yün-mu shih* or 'mother of pearl'. In a dream the mountain spirit ordered her to pound the stone and consume it which should give her agility and immortality. Her days were henceforth passed in floating from one peak to another, bringing home at night to her month the fruits she collected on the mountains. Lu Tung-pin met her and gave her a peach which she ate and she was then possessed with the gift of foretelling the future. She became his disciple and entered the ranks of the immortals. She is the patroness of housewives.

Lan Ts'ai-ho is depicted as a youngster carrying either a basket of peaches of immortality or a bouquet of flowers. The origin of this person is unknown. His name is believed to be Yang-su but his surname is unknown. The term *Lan Ts'ai-ho* merely means 'a person carrying a basket and singing.' He is therefore believed to be a strolling singer, begging for his living in the streets. He would chant strange verses which led people to think of him as a fool. One of the songs he would sing is:

> *Ta-ta-ho!*
> *Lan-ts'ai-ho.*
> *May one on earth his equal find!*
> *Youth is a plant that tastes of spring,*
> *The years like weaver's shuttles fly,*
> *The generations pass not to come again,*
> *Yet ever men are born more and more.*

If he were given money, he would thread them on a string and drag them along after him or throw them away in the road. Because he sang this constant refrain:

> *Who will dare say that man cannot be pregnant,*
> *So! I have been so these ten months!*

many thought him to be a hermaphrodite. He is the patron saint of florists and flower growers.

Lü Tung-pin is depicted as a Taoist armed with his magical sword to drive away the demons called *Chan-yao-kuai* and he carries a kind of fly-wisk in the shape of a horse's tail. His family name is Lü and his personal name is Yên, also Tung-pin. He lived in the eighth century and came from an official's family. He was a scholar who had held office but he became a recluse who learned the secrets of immortality from Chung-li Ch'üan. He was exposed to a series of temptations. These being successfully overcome, he was invested with supernatural powers and magic weapons, with which he traversed the Empire, slaying demons and ridding the earth of diverse kinds of evils. He was so successful that several Emperors conferred upon him glorious titles. He was very skillful in fencing with his sword and with his fly-wisk was able to fly at will through the air and to walk on the clouds. By tradition, the authorship of the well-known *Kung-kuo-ko*, a Table of Merits and Demerits, is attributed to him. This had an enormous influence on the people's morality. He is the patron saint of barbers and is worshipped by martial artists and the sick.

The Eight Immortals are extremely popular in folk religion and their symbols are used as decorations for many things. Earlier rugs merely used their symbols or *pa-pao* and later Ch'ing rugs used their depictions. The depiction of the human form on rugs in China could be traced back to the fifth century A. D., when a certain magician named Liu Ling-ch'u fashioned cut-out human figures out of felt for magical purposes. This idea was doubtlessly borrowed from the nomads of the Steppes. Felt dieties are a characteristic feature of Mongolian household worship.

Plano Carpini, who in the year 1246 went as an ambassador to the Great Khan of the Mongols, informs us:

They have certain idols made of felt in the image of man, and these they place on either side of the door of their dwelling . . . whenever they begin to eat and drink, they first offer these idols a portion of their food and drink.

Friar Rubruk, who also made the wearisome journey to Mongolia, records the following:

And over the head of the master is always an image of felt, like a doll or statuette . . . who is, as it were, the guardian of the whole dwelling.

Marco Polo, with reference to the god of the Tartars wrote:

They have a certain god of their called 'Natigay' and they say he is the God of the Earth, who watches over their children, cattle and crops. They show him great worship and honour, and every man has a figure of him in his house, made of felt and cloth.

In Mongolian and Tibetan rugs, we find representations of Lamas and other priests. However, in China, aside from the recorded fifth dynasty incident, human depictions on textiles are quite rare up until the Ch'ing times. The representations of the Eight Immortals as humans are usually very late. The Eight Immortals are oftentimes depicted with another figure *Shou-lao* or the God of Longevity, an old man with a huge forehead holding a peach, the fruit of immortality. Theese depictions are commonly early twentieth century.

The Hundred Antiques

Due to the confusion created by the vagueness of which objects constituted the *Pa-pao* or 'Eight Precious Symbols', a group of various objects were incorporated and termed the *pai-ku* or *po-ku* or the 'Hundred Antiques'. This is a miscellaneous or general collection of emblematic forms comprising the three sets of *pao-pao*, the four symbols of the literati, musical instruments, together with numerous representations of sacrificial vessels, flowers, animals or any small decorative motifs. In essence this is the *potpourri* of design and a later development.

The Ju-i

The *ju-i* symbol has become a ceremonial emblem used by the secular Chinese as well as the Buddhists and Taoists. However, at the outset, according to the *Chung-wên ta-tzŭ-tien*, the Encyclopedic Dictionary of the Chinese Language, the *ju-i* had been a back scratcher which accorded comfort to the user, thus the phrase, *K'o-ju jên-i* 'to give as much comfort or satisfaction as one's heart desires'. A contraction of this phrase became *ju-i*.

The early *ju-i* then took on the shape of the *ling-chih* or plant of immortality and a somewhat cloud-shaped form with four lobed panels set at right angles to each other, each one terminating in a point. Having this auspicious form, it became a fitting gift to present with the rebus *Ju-i chi-hsiang* meaning 'everything according to your desires or as you wish'. These were then made of jade or other precious stone and measured one to two foot long. This later development is recorded in the biography of Shih Ch'ung found in the *Chin-shu* or History of the Chin dynasty, 265 - 420 A. D.

The Taoist version of this S-shaped sceptre has three panels, a large one jutting out on the top, a middle panel as the centre and a smaller one on the bottom. Combined, these became symbolic of the three blessings, longevity, prosperity and posterity. Originally they were cast in iron and called *huan-tan* or the restorer of the decoction that confers immortality. This is discussed at length in the work *Yun-chi ch'i-ch'ien*.

The Buddhist *ju-i* had originally been a short sword that was asso-

Plate XXXVI

The earliest known *ju-i* pattern with the characters worked into the design so that no mistake would be made. Including the name of the pattern in the design may indicate that it was not very familiar at this time. This piece was discovered in the desert near Min-fêng in Sinkiang in 1959 and was dated as Eastern Han, 25 220 A. D.

Figure 13
Various forms of the *Ju-i* motif including border patterns.

ciated with Manoratha, successor of Vasubandha as the twenty-second patriarch and of Maharddhiprapta, a king of garudas. This short sword then merged with another symbol, the *cintamani*, a fabulous gem, or a talisman pearl said to have been obtained from the dragon-king of the sea or the head of the great fish, *Makara*. It has become an important decorative device variously referred to as *ju-i* or *ju-i-chu* and is carried in Buddhist ceremonies at the head of the procession. The *ju-i* has also been associated with Mañjuṣri, the God of Wisdom, who holds it in his hand when debating with Vimalakirti.

Chao Hsi-ku, an archaeologist of the thirteenth century, tells us that the *ju-i* was used 'for pointing the way' and also for 'guarding against the unexpected'.

Still others believe that the *ju-i* is derived from the *kuei* a symbol of 'phallic worship' and male superiority. In all the *ju-i* combines all of the above qualities and 'everything as one wishes'.

On rugs, the *ju-i* motif is commonly used as border patterns in later times. However, in the Han dynasty, 221 B. C. - 220 A. D., it was used as a pattern in the field. Moreover, a piece of Eastern Han textile found in the desert north of Min-fêng in Sinkang indicates from the design that the *ju-i* pattern was not a commonly recognizable motif. In this early first century A. D. textile, besides the *ju-i* pattern, the Chinese characters for *ju-i* are included to name this early design. This gives rise to speculation that it was during this time that the *ju-i* as a decorative motif was first introduced.

What Hans Bidder terms 'cloudhead' which is known to the Chinese as 'yün-tsai t'ou'," is really a *ju-i* border pattern. *Yün-tsai-t'ou* is not a common Chinese term as it only means 'cloud patterns on the top.' Cloudhead would simply be *yün-t'ou*. As stated before the Chinese would have a more poetic and auspicious term for cloud patterns such as: *lien-yün* and *ch'ing-yün chih shang* or *wu-ts'ai yün*.

The *ju-i* is more commonly found as a sculpture in the shape of an S-curved sceptre which is properly used as gifts on auspicious occasions. Lord Macartney described in his journals *An Embassy to China, 1793-1794,*[130] an incident that took place in the Chinese court. After Lord Macartney presented gifts from King George III of England, the Emperor Ch'ien-lung in response presented, amongst other gifts, a *ju-i* sceptre to Lord Macartney, one to his deputy, Sir George Staunton and

Figure 14
Various cloud patterns. The top examples although commonly referred
to as cloud patterns, in essence, clearly show the *ju-i* motif.

a third to be given to King George III.

The Vase

The vase, *p'ing* or *tsun*, is an emblematic device used in decoration in Chinese art to signify perpetual harmony. The Chinese used the vase as either a flower or wine container while other cultures, including the Persians and Turks have lost this practical sense and arbitrarily used them as nothing more than the starting point for an *espalier* tree which embodies the idea of the "Tree-of-Life". The Chinese utilization of the vase in ceremony is very important. In the five sacrificial vessels, *wu-kung*, a pair of the vessels are vases which in modern use contain a stylized *espalier* form of flowers shaped like an elongated triangle or shaped like a fir tree. Oftentimes tree branches such as a bunch of Artemisia or leaves of the *Chung-k'uei*, a kind of mallow are placed in these vases as a sign of everlasting purity, and to ward off evil. Also the term *p'ing* is the homonym for tranquility and peace and *tsun* is the same as 'to honour'. Therefore they are quite important as objects serving as sounds for a rebus.

Hans Bidder calls attention to a pair of wood carved panels that were found in Niya by Sir Aurel Stein with a pair of guardian monsters and a central motif of a vase holding curving stems which end alternately in broad leaves and fruits. Bidder attributes this early motif to the vase pomegranate pattern. It is most interesting that the shape of the vase is a Chinese *tsun* shape found in early bronzes. Bidder may be correct in this case, however, he failed to mention that as well as being a Near Eastern practice, placing certain trees and plants over doors of houses to disperse evil influence was also a Chinese practice. On the fifth day of the fifth lunar month this very practice is observed to commemorate the day when Huang Ch'ao, who captured Ch'ang-an in 880 A. D., gave orders to slay all households except for those with branches of leaves over their doors. To this day, it is not unusual to see a pair of evergreens either in pots or planted in the ground in front of Chinese houses. However, certain trees are avoided such as the mulberry as its name, *sang*, is a homonym for death and sorrow.

Diapers and Borders

A somewhat unique factor of Chinese textiles and crafts is the development of numerous intricate and diversified designs used as either background or the main decoration on the central field, which have become known as diaper patterns or in Chinese, *hua-wên* or *chin-ti*. These beautiful geometric ground motifs are generally used between the main designs to enhance the appearance. They sometime remind one more of a fretwork or lattice designs. Chinese diaper patterns may occur in linear, rectilinear or curvilinear types and may appear as geometric forms, hooks and lattices or as graceful, naturalistic floral ornamentations. The device of repeating or alternating and even facing designs is quite common. One of the simplest and most frequently seen ornaments, found in both early and modern rugs, is commonly known as the meander or key pattern called *lei-wên* or 'thunder pattern' by the Chinese. In the work, *Po-ku-t'u* or Illustrations of Antiquities, this design is noted as having evolved from early pictorial representations of clouds and thunder. A primitive rendition of this pattern in the form of S-curves is found on early bronzes of the Shang and Chou periods. Later the separate elements of this design became grouped and joined together into lozenge-shaped spaces. The lozenge, called *fang-shêng* is a symbol of victory and used extensively in Chinese crafts especially in lacquer work. It is sometimes referred to as 'cloud and thunder pattern'. As border, this meander was merely called *hui-wên*.

From this basic key pattern meander, an array of variations have developed. The *Wo-ts'an* or resting silkworn pattern or a single curl, somewhat like an elongated C is one of the variations. This pattern was looked on as an emblem of wealth. A bit more involved, is the heads of the *ju-i* pattern. This is more frequently found as a border decoration. The *ju-i* motif, like a pointed spade is often referred to as a trefoil and called a *chung-k'uei* by the Chinese. It appears like a palmette or palm leaf, a symbol to ward off evil. A somewhat similiar *ju-i* head pattern, is an elongated four-lobed shape often called a 'cloud' motif by Westerners. The Chinese call it *shih-ti* or the peduncle of the persimmon. It is more commonly used as a repeating design as a diaper pattern arranged in rows. The persimmon was an emblem of joy and its bright festive colour denotes an auspicious event.

Another derivative or variation, is the T-pattern and the swastika motif worked into a composite pattern as a fretwork or lattice. This most popular pattern is an ingenious device of interconnecting the two patterns to form geometric angles resulting in a most pleasing and interesting design that is used not only in rugs and textile designs but also in lacquer work and even in furniture and architecture.

Figure 15
A variety of commonly used border patterns.

Figure 16
Additional border designs from Chinese carpets.

Plate XXXVII
A pleasing geometric floral rosette-forming a diaper pattern with two inner borders of running-T design and a wide outer border of eight floral patterns. The corners feature stylized floral designs. 213x180 cm.

Figure 17
The coin motif used as diaper pattern. Used singularly it is most frequently combined with *ju-i* or butterfly patterns. The lower example although very similar is in reality a snowflake diaper.

Figure 18
Diaper patterns. Top: Cloud patterns. Middle: Swastika fret. Lower:
Star patterns.

The swastika is an ancient design which the Chinese had borrowed and both adopted and developed incorporating it into their own taste and design. It was originally the sign of Vishnu and Siva in India and is said to be one of the sixty-five auspicious signs on the footprint of Buddha and it also appeared on the breast of the *Ju-lai* Buddha and Shakyamuni Buddha. It appears as an ornament on the crowns of the Bonpa and Lama dieties of Tibet. It has its crampons directed towards the right but another form called *Sauvastika* is directed to the left. To be more precise, the former was the symbol used by Nazi Germany during World War II, while the *Sauvastika*, with the crampons directed toward the left was the one adopted by the Chinese. It is recorded that in the second year of Ch'ang-shou, 694 A. D., which was one of the reigning titles of Empress Wu, this mystic Buddhist emblem was given a Chinese reading as *wan* with the same sound as the word meaning ten-thousand. The reason given was that all good fortune and virtue was embodied in it, and the fret or meander was given the general name *wan-tzu pu-tao-t'ou*. The same pattern used on lacquer, textiles and rugs was given the more specific term *wan-tzŭ-chin*. The use of the *wan-tzŭ* design is extremely popular and many variations exist including its use as the centers of lozenges. This motif was also used in connection with the mystic knot which was considered as nothing but another variation. The mystic knot is found as scattered motifs in the field of a rug but more often in corners and as border patterns. The swastika design is also depicted as a round curling design with all its angular lines changed to curves. This has been often referred to by Anglo-American rug literature as a 'revolving cloud' pattern. However, to the Chinese it is considered as a variation of the *wan-tzŭ* motif.

As discussed earlier the carp, unicorn and tortoise were also used as diaper patterns. The carp and the unicorn are similarly represented as a 'fish scale' pattern with very little difference between them, although each is termed separately as *yŭ-wên* for the carp and *lin-wên* for the unicorn. However in earlier times small circles or 'fish roe' were used to symbolize the carp to emphasize the aspect of abundance. Scales were exclusively used for the unicorn while on occasion, a Y-shaped scale was used to make a greater distinction. The Y-shaped motif is usually referred to by the Chinese as *huo-pu* or the spade-shaped money design. As for representations of the tortoise, there is little difficulty distinguishing it as it is either a pentagon or octagon shaped

Figure 19
A variety of frequently used central medallions, floral, geometric and symbolic.

symbol.

Amongst the diaper patterns, mention should be made of the trellis work design which sometimes appears as a band used for the borders, but more often as the central field. Honeycomb designs are called by various terms being distinguished by what it is in their centres. For example, designs with crosses or with the character *mi*, in the centre are called *hsing-wên* or *hsing-shêng*; and a small flower in the centre is termed *hua-wên* or *hua-shêng*. Aside from geometric patterns, floral and vine patterns are also very popular and represent the concept of one of the twelve ornaments, the water weed.

Peculiar to the Chinese concept in design, the diaper patterns serve as a background and may or may not have any relationship to the central motif or design. That is not to say that a diaper or repeating pattern could not also be the main design of a rug. Furthermore, this concept is also extended likewise for border designs. Unlike Near Eastern rugs, where the border was significant in complimenting the central design and became an integral part of the whole design, Chinese borders serve basically as an enclosing frame. Earlier rugs have several borders while many later creations have no borders at all. The Chinese borders could be very decorative or merely solid-coloured stripes either wide or narrow, extending around the four sides. Early rugs often have several borders with varying geometric and floral patterns. Solely geometric borders are usually of a later period. Frequently, a narrow border of 'pearls' acts as a divider between the various bands, but most often it is employed to separate the border from the central field.

The sea and mountain motif, *fu-hai shou-shan*, is seen in rugs designs as early as the eighth century rug in the Shosoin. Generally they are placed on the top and bottom of the rug. In pillar rugs, they are only used on the bottom. However in later Ch'ing rugs, we find that oftentimes only the wave patterns are used as borders on the four sides of the rug. Murray Eiland suggests that some of the rugs exhibited at the University of Pittsburgh as Imperial Carpets from Peking may be of late nineteenth century manufacture. This suggestion is plausible as we see in several of the rugs exhibited the *fu-hai shou-shan* motif on all four borders. Both the technique of the borders and their variations seem to be a matter of fashion as there are no prescribed rules governing their use or execution.

On later nineteenth century rugs, the borders are more floral and elaborate and oftentimes are likely to represent foliage. It is interesting that the foliated dragon, *ts'ao-lung*, is also utilized. However, they were in greater popularity in the 1920's. Moreover simple key-patterns and purely geometric designs were basically restricted to later productions.

Figure 20
A Chinese brush, a bar of silver and a *ju-i* scepter forming the rebus: *Pi-ting ju-i*, or "May auspicious blessings be assuredly granted to your desires.

RUG CONSTRUCTION

Looms or *Chih-chi* had been invented and developed very early in Chinese history and by the Han dynasty, 206 B. C. - 220 A. D., we find evidence from stone rubbings that they were already rather complex units. Without a doubt this technological development of the loom also accounted for the advancement of Chinese textiles and textile designs. Chinese literature abounds with references and treatises on weaving and various textiles in historical annals and in titles such as *Kêng-chih t'u-shuo, Ssŭ-ch'ou pi-chi,* etc. Moreover, as mentioned earlier in the eighth century, Chinese looms were exported to the Near East. However, in making knotted pile rugs there is no need for a complex loom as it is the creative vision and technical skill, not necessarily the loom, that is the major requisite. The only requirement is a simple structure whose primary function is to hold the lengthwise *ching* or warp threads under tention so a crosswise *wei* or weft could be easily interwoven with them. As for the loom itself, its only requirement is that it be sturdy enough to withstand great warp tension.

Basically there are two major types of looms, the horizontal and the vertical or upright loom. The horizontal ground loom is the older of the two and is still used by nomads and villagers of the Near East althought this form of loom is rare in China except for the minority areas. The loom is constructed in the size of the rug to be woven. After two strong poles are secured parallel to each other by four stakes driven into the ground, the warp is wound directly around them in a continuous figure-eight motion. In a technically advanced variation the warp is passed between two beams which are tied to the poles, thereby allowing for the possibility of more precise tension adjustment.

Once strung the warp is separated by a shed stick so that the threads alternate over and under it. Loops, called 'heddles' catch every warp lying behind the shed stick. The loops are attached to a heddle rod which is set on stones placed at either side of the warp. The device causes the back warp threads to be raised above the others so that a 'shed' or weaving space is created. A 'countershed'is made by turning the shed stick on end. This arrangement is somewhat unusual in its use of the heddle shed as the primary shed. In virtually all vertical warp weaving, the shed stick forms the primary shed, while the heddles form the alternate shed when they are drawn toward the weaver.

The weaving is never rolled as it is made. Rather the weaver squats on the completed web and continues the operation working progressively toward the end of the warp. The horizontal ground loom is ideal for nomad people as the poles and beams need only to be detached from the pegs and rolled up for travelling, to be restaked at a new encampment. The Tibetan back-strap loom is a variation of this type, and is limited as far as the width of the rug. As a rule this loom is used more for flat-woven rugs or kilims.

With the vertical or upright frame loom, the weaver has the advantage of gravity for beating down the weft into place. A combination of ingenuity, materials, and a rug's size or shape requirements has created countless variations on the design of the vertical loom.

In its most rudimentary form, the vertical loom is set up in a similar manner as the horizontal ground loom with the exception of the shed-making operation noted earlier. Cross-pieces are joined to firmly anchored supports which replace the function of the pegs in the ground. Primitive versions were lashed and pegged together with the cross-pieces even attached to two trees growing at a convenient distance apart. In the Chinese vertical looms, crossbeams are set into holes carved into upright supports. Tension is maintained or adjusted by manipulating wedges lodged between the uppper crossbeams and holes.

As weaving progresses, the weaver sits successively higher. A simple scaffolding is sometimes made by placing a plank between the rungs of two ladders set on either side of the loom. This method, uncomfortable though it may be, has the distinct advantage of allowing full view of the rug as it is being made.

The fixed warp loom remains viable today. However, an ingenious and more sophisticated tensioning has evolved. The top warp beam is attached to an adjustable rod which is in turn laced to the top cross-piece of the support frame. As weaving approaches an uncomfortable working height, the lacing is slackened and the entire warp could be lowercd. The completed weaving is then rolled and brought around a bottom crosspiece and secured at the back of the loom. The lacing can then be used to readjust the tension precisely.

As the design of the upright loom evolved, warp and roller beams were added to enable the weaving of rugs much longer than the loom itself. This is often callled the roller beam upright loom. The warp beam at the top holds the warp to be woven. At the bottom the completed web is wound around the beam. This is of great advantage and economy as approximately thirty inches of warp length is lost to the loom at the beginning and end of weaving. The percentage of waste decreases as the length of warp increases, so that it is more economical to dress the loom with a warp long enough for two or more rugs. Cotton is usually used by the Chinese for both the warp and the weft. When machine spun yarns came into use as warps, the wefts were still often hand-spun. The warp could also be of silk and, in Mongolian and Tibetan rugs, wool is also used.

Whatever material is used for the warp it must be strong, abrasion resistant, moderately flexible and of a diametre large enough to serve as the basis of a sturdy fabric. Since it must sustain considerable tension while on the loom, a warp should be spun and plied from long, hard fibers. The warp should also be resistant to fraying and abrasion. Even though the threads will be entirely covered by the weft in the finished piece, they are nevertheless subject to constant friction while on the loom. The Chinese usually use a tightly spun 3- or 4- or even 5-ply cotton for the warp.

The knotted pile rug consists of one warp and two different wefts, one for the pile, the other for the background. The function of the weft is to hold the knots in parallel lines and to strengthen the fabric of the carpet. In most carpets the weft consists of two threads, one loose and one tight, which are woven across the warp after each row or line of knots. The weft threads are beaten in against each row of knots with a comb beater. The number of wefts usually was two but may vary to as many as three or four interweavings in earlier rugs.

Since the weft covers the warp completely holding the row of knots in parallel lines, it should be a bit softer than the warp yarn with which it is being woven in order to accommodate the firm beating required to pack it down. The Chinese usually utilize a loose 3-ply cotton weft. Unlike warp threads, which should be of uniform size and fiber type, many different kinds of wefts can be combined to make a rug. A weft should also correlate to some degree with the warp in terms of yarn count and fiber type.

The use of a thick weft with a thin warp works well in rug weaving as long as the warp is sufficiently rigid. Normally a thin warp and weft renders a fabric too flimsy. However, in the case of pile rugs the many thin warps sleyed closely together will allow a suitably small diametre yarn to be tied into numerous knots per square inch. In Chinese rugs, a thicker warp with a thinner weft is usually the rule and the warp and weft are mostly made of cotton as it is a more stable material and has a greater tensile strength which better holds the shape, although it does give the rug a rigid appearance. Woolen warps and wefts tend to shrink or stretch unevenly with humidity which distorts the shape of the rug.

The carpet is always begun at the lower edge with the selvage which the Chinese call *So-pien* or sometimes *Chih-êrh* which is the ancient term used. A certain number of weft threads are woven across the vertical warp threads so as to form a stout edging which will keep the carpet intact, preventing fraying and keeping the knots tight as the knots themselves are not structurally adequate. When the selvage, which is interwoven without any knots, is finished, the knotting of the pile yarns on the warp begins. The pile could consist of various materials, however, wool yarn is most common. Each piece of wool is fixed on to two adjoining warp threads in accordance with one of the two main types of knots.

The Chinese use a thicker 3-ply and 4-ply wool yarn for the pile. Later commerical rugs use even thicker 5- or 6-ply wool yarn. Moreover, the pile of the Chinese rugs is cut higher than other Oriental rugs with the pile measuring approximately 5/8 inch in height. The higher, thicker wool yarn accounts for one reason why fewer knots are used. The density of some of the earlier rugs averages about 40 knots to the square inch and the Chinese usually describe their knotting as "lines per foot". A description '90-line' means that there are 90 pairs of warp strings across 12 inches of the back of the carpet, which indicates that

Platc XXXVIII
An all-over vase and pomegranate trellis design with three wide borders.
The two outer borders feature stylized flowers; the inner border is decorated with linked swastikas. The pale ivory ground of the centre contrasts with the deep rich tones of the borders. 260x114 cm.

there are 90 knots tied to a foot. Since the same number of knots is tied vertically as it is horizontally, the total knots per square inch would be approximately 60.

The other reason for having fewer knots in Chinese rugs is that longer cut, multi-ply wool yarn provides not only a thicker and softer pile but also greater insulating capacity. In actuality, it is not the wool itself which provides the greatest insulating capacity, but the 'dead air' which it entraps within the woven fabric. Thus, Chinese rugs with their thicker wool yarns and their somewhat looser pile, provide greater insulation than Near Eastern rugs which have thinner yarn and a denser concentration of knots per unit and area.

Knots

Apart from the rather distinctive and unusual knots used by the Spanish, Swedish, Berber and Tibetan carpet weavers, there are only two types of knots used universally by most weavers of Oriental rugs. The so-called Turkish knot, often called 'Ghiordes' and the Persian knot, also called 'Sennah'. This naming of the knots by the geographic places once thought to be their origins is misleading since Sennah employs exclusively the Turkish knot.

It was a common belief that weavers of Turkish origin used the Ghiordes knot and the Persians and other peoples of Asia used the Sennah knot. However, this simplistic concept does not hold true as there are so many exceptions to this generalistic approach that most scholars in the field tend to favour other more descriptive terms.

The Sennah knot, variably spelled as Sehna or Senna and termed *la-chiao* by the Chinese is probably better referred to as 'asymmetrical' or 'open' knot as these terms describe this type of knot while conveying no geographical implications. In this type of knot, the yarn is passed between two adjoining warps, looped round one, passed back over it and under the second warp so that the ends of the yarn lie on either side of, and are kept open by the second warp. It is usually tied with the ends coming up on either side of the left warp thread, open-on-the-left, but the form open-on-the-right is also used. Chinese carpets employ 'open-on-the-left' asymmetrical knots almost exclusively, although the symmetrical knots are also used. The open or asymmetrical knot, because of the irregular appearance, is considered one of the more ver-

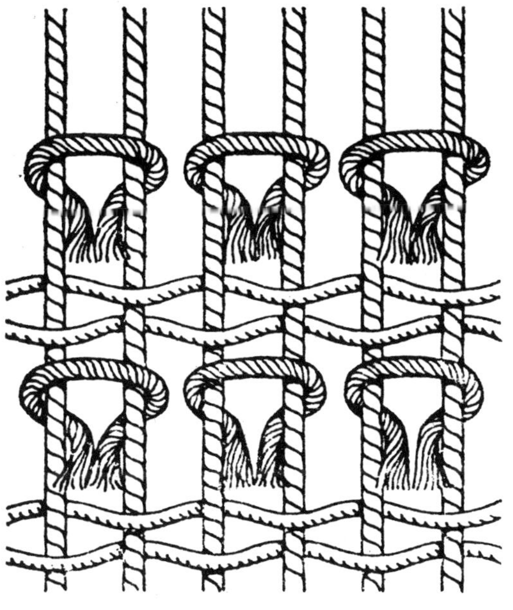

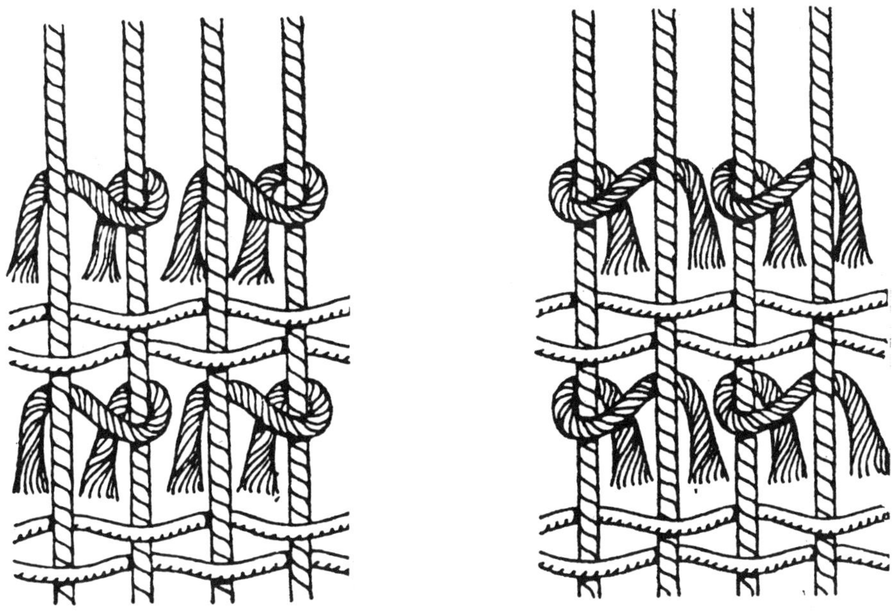

Figure 21
The two principal kinds of knots used. Top: Symmetrical knots; bottom: Asymmetrical knots, open-to-the-left and open-to-the-right.

satile techniques to be employed in more exciting and vibrant curvilinear designs.

The Ghiordes knot called *ch'ou-chiao* by the Chinese, may be better termed as the 'symmetrical' or 'closed' knot. The yarn is passed between two adjoining warps, looped under one, passed back over both and brought to the surface again between the two warps, so that the two ends of the pile yarn lie together enclosed by the collar of the knot. This symmetrical knot has a neater appearance which gives a certain mechanical, over-exactness that lends itself to the creation of more angular and rectilinear designs. This knot was the one used by the weavers of the Pazyryk carpet and is used also by the Chinese with one or more rows along the edge and sometimes at the ends, although the rest of the rug is woven in an asymmetrical knot. The use of the symmetrical knot at the edges gives it a firm edge which serves to help the rug keep its shape. The mixing of the two knots is not a very common practice in rug production although in Chinese rugs only the edges have a symmetrical knot while the main body of the rug uses an asymmetrical knot.

A 'heddle' on the loom creates a 'shed' between alternate warps to allow the weaver to tie the knots which form the pile and to make it easier to pass the wefts between them.

After the knots are made, usually from a skein or ball of yarn, the ends are cut with a knife and the loops that are formed around the warps are pulled down toward the weaver and positioned above the loops in the previous row. Each knot is tied on the same warps as the knot directly below it. The cut ends of this mass of knots in turn create the pile which has a definite direction or nap. After completion of one row of knots, a shot of tabby is thrown and the rod is pulled out. The relation of supplementary wefts to rows of knots depends entirely upon the surface texture desired. A cropped, velvety surface demands only one or two rows of tabby. When two are used, each row of knots is tied with the yarn at the same level and it is possible to hide any trace of the warp by compressing the pile. When a rug has only one tabby, a herringbone effect is created on the back. This is because the yarns are woven on alternate levels at each row, leaving a small portion of the warps showing. In addition to securing the knots, the wefts also give body to the rug and hold their shape as they are not cut off but passed back in the opposite direction. The wefts can either form the selvage edges on the sides of the rug, or be incorporated into them. The density of the pile is determined by the number of tabby picks thrown between the rows of knots. Chinese rugs use fewer knots, but are tied with thicker yarns, with usually two interweavings and the pile is cut at longer lengths. If the weaving is even and tight no warp threads will be visible at all. An important factor is that the knot should be basically square. A properly tied square knot denotes a better rug and will allow for longer wear, even though the knot count is fewer.

The pile is always produced in this manner with a myriad of woollen yarns tied by hand, knotted around a pair of warp threads. There is no short cut to this painstakingly long process aside from cheating with a 'jufti' knot which is never found in Chinese rugs. The jufti knot could be tied in either the symmetrical or the asymmetrical fashion. The difference is that instead of tying the knot on two warps, it is tied around four warps. This not only is an unstable and weak construction, but it is incapable of holding a detailed pattern. Moreover, this practice of using the jufti knot can effectively spoil the rug as it divides in half the density of the pile. This would not only diminish the value of the rug but also cause great blemishes in the design.

Basically there is no difference in the appearance of the pile of rugs that have been woven with either of the two knots, only strands of the yarn are left showing on the face of the rug. However, from the back side of the rug one can see a difference. Usually the symmetrical knot is stacked so that one loop of the knot is lined up directly under the other, so only one loop or bump will be visible. These loops may be on the same level or one on top of the other. In the latter case, the position of the loops is generally dictated by stacking the warps on which the knots are tied. That is to say that in the first case, the warps lie side by side on the same level with little or no ribbing on the back showing clearly the knots tied. This is used in earlier Chinese rugs and in the modern 'antique' rugs. In the second case, when the warps are staggered, or 'double warped' giving the rug a ridged back, the knots are tied so that the loop encircles the lower warp. The ridged back construction could be in two forms, with the tighter called 'close back' and the other 'open back'. In modern Chinese rugs, especially Tientsin rugs the 'close back' construction is used. The warps are staggered so that they lie almost vertically above each other, which enables a very tightly packed

Plate XXXIX
Steps in the rug making process: a & b) spinning the yarn; c) drafting
the cartoon in the exact size to be used; d) weavers knotting a rug; e)
following an outline pattern as a guide to incise the design; f) incising
the pattern; g) the warp threads with the cartoon traced on in ink; h)
team of four weavers seated on a plank at a vertical loom, hand-knot-
ting a large rug; i) finishing touches made to the back of the rug.

and sturdy construction. Since the knot is tied to the bottom warp, it is not visible from the front even when the pile is folded back to expose the base of the knot, there is no visible loop. This effect is only possible with the asymmetrical knot. Technically, this is an advancement unique to modern Chinese rugs alone, and this perfection often leads some people to wonder if these rugs are not machine-made.

As each row of knots is tied and held into place with the weft, the side edges are also formed by the turning of the weft yarn at the end of each row. In Chinese rugs these edges or selvages are called *So-pien* and they are usually quite simple with just a weft overcast.

Murray Eiland points out that, "In the older Ninghsia type of rug, one often finds a two cord weft selvage, with the outer cord consisting of two warps and the inner of only one." At the end of the weaving, a few rows of simple interweaving complete the rug and a small length of the warp threads are cut which become the fringes of the rug. If a second rug is to be woven, a sixteen inch spacing is left between the two weavings.

Patterns and Designs

Patterns and designs are created on the loom by basically four methods:
1. Drawn patterns on the warps.
2. Patterns learned by rote.
3. Oral promptings (instructions)
4. Free design.

In the first method, the cartoons are drawn or drafted in the exact scale as they would appear on the finished rug. The cartoon is then placed in the back of the tightly stretched warp onto which it is then traced with ink. Sometimes various colours are used for the markings.

Since Chinese education and training rely very heavily on learning by rote, with various patterns and designs committed to memory by repeated practice, all that is needed is a small picture or drawing to to guide the weavers to what effect is desired. Oftentimes the weavers follow only written instructions. These instructions might read, for example: "A four feet by six feet woollen rug with a blue ground or field. *Hua-pien* or an outer floral border with *hui-wèn*, a scrolling as an inner border. A central medallion of the five happinesses with a *wan-tzŭ-chin* or diaper." The weaver would then proceed to interpret these instructions. He would prepare to produce a blue rug in the exact or near exact size as requested. However, as for the decorations, he may take some liberties. A floral border may either consist of a floral trellis or any complex design as the Chinese term *hua-pien* not only means a floral border but also a complex geometric design dorder. Moreover, the vague term *hui-wèn* as an inner border may not only mean a scrolling border but any geometric meander. The central medallion with a theme of *wu-fu* or the five happinesses may be executed as five bats surrounding a round geometric symbol of *shou*. The *wan-tzŭ-chin* or swastika diaper would again create a choice of the various forms of the swastika diaper. Since there is to be a geometric inner border and a geometric diaper, the weaver may decide to separate them either by colour or by the use of another added thin border of 'pearls'. The expertise and the technical skill of the weaver, along with his artistic sense and sensitivity, becomes the dominating factor when only written instructions are given. Therefore to be more exacting, a sketch or picture would be more helpful, although again the skills of the weaver determines if an exact duplication could be realized.

The third method, oral promptings is basically related to the second method whereby the various patterns and techniques are memorized. The oral prompting could be made by the leader of the group of weavers who would sit on the extreme left of the raised plank and with each row of knots to be tied, he calls out instructions. In some reported cases, someone overseeing the weaving gives oral instructions. However, in most Chinese shops, there is usually a leader to each group of four persons weaving a large rug. Very much like the musical leader in Chinese opera, he memorizes the entire pattern and merely calls out each row as it is being started.

The fourth method is usually used on plain, single coloured rugs. The person doing the incising or embossing freely executes a traditional pattern with his shears and cuts out the entire design on the rug. This is a more modern technique which has been very unique and most effective, although embossing on rugs to give better definition to a design is an old Chinese technique.

Before the discoveries of pile-loop textiles and velvet in Han tomb No. 1 at Ma-wang-tui in Changsha in 1972, it was believed and advocated by Harold Burnham in his *Chinese Velvets* that velvet was not produced in China until the end of the sixteenth century. This has now been proven to the contrary. Thus it has been shown that embossing and incising was known in China from Han times. This process which cuts a groove partly through the pile around the design, where different colours meet, creates a shadow and enhances and accents the design. In Near Eastern rugs, accents in designs are produced by outlining the design with a single row of knots in a contrasting colour. However, in Chinese embossing and incising methods, the contrasting colours are unnecessary to give definition to the design.

Finishing

After all the stages of weaving and shearing are completed, the rug is taken down from the loom. The loose warp ends are left as is or tied to form a fringe whether braided or knotted. Oftentimes a piece of material, usually red in colour, is sewn around the four sides as on the saddle rugs. The rug itself has a rather raw and crude appearance with loose hairs and clippings at this stage. Before it is brought to the showroom a lustre is added. This is achieved by a process of washing. This washing gives the rug a polished lustre and is very much a necessary part of finishing. Aside from the removing of loose and short staple fibres, removing dirt and dust and washing out of excess dye, it also helps the pile to lie more uniformly in one direction. However, besides mellowing and harmonizing the colours, which adds to the beauty of the rug, sometimes chemicals are used which alter the colours considerably. This is often done as an attempt to 'antique' the rug and give it an older and aged appearance to increase its value artificially. Virtually all rugs sold in the West are washed in one manner or another.

RUG SHAPES and USAGE

An issue of much debate in Western rug literature is the place carpets and rugs play in the daily life of the Chinese. Hans Bidder claims that "carpets were not in demand by the Chinese population except . . . by the ruling class and therefore are mentioned only occasionally."[131] Furthermore he emphasized that "even to the present day China has therefore no form of carpet which has sprung from Chinese soil, and in consequence, no genuine Chinese carpet designs have been created. It is true that the Chinese had floor coverings in the form of mats and felt carpets, and that subsequently they became familiar with the woven and knotted wool carpet. But the carpet has never been an integral element of Chinese civilization, that is, an indispensable necessity in the Chinese household."[132] Bidder concludes the chapter on the foreign element of carpets to the Chinese by stating that, "contemporary usage follows a very sound instinct by characterizing the foreign origin of the pile carpet with the word "Yang T'an-tze" again 'foreign carpet'!"[133]

A more recent publication *Chinese Carpets* by E. Gans-Ruedin echoes the same refrain in the statement that "in China, carpets have never been considered important as they are in Middle Eastern countries where they are indispensable for the decoration of any interior. This is confirmed by M. Beurdeley in his book *Chinese Furniture*, where he quotes the description of the house of a rich merchant of Quangzhou (Canton) in the middle eighteenth century, given by the English architect William Chambers on his return from a journey to China. In Chambers' account, published in 1757, there is no mention at all of carpets. It is because carpets were so little used that production of Chinese carpets was never considerable until this century, when the role of carpets as export goods altered their position."[134]

These statements should not go unchallenged as they are frequently quoted by Western authors. First of all, we agree with Hans Lorentz[135] that Bidder's term *Yang t'an-tzŭ* or 'foreign carpet' is not only a unique term but a term never used in China. Had Bidder used the term *Hu-t'an-tzŭ* it would have had more acceptability, however, even this term is foreign to the Chinese vocabulary. Hans Lorentz's selection of quotes of Du Halde, Gustav Ecke, Marco Polo and Leitch "that rugs were in abundance in the homes of the rich where they found a use as well as being objects of admiration", offers concrete evidence to contradict Bidder's and Gans-Ruedin's assertions.

The poems of Po Chü-i and other poets of the eighth century onwards, along with Ennin's diary notations and the 'marriage songs' which are quoted earlier, offer further evidence that rugs were not only used by the Chinese in their daily lives but also in their rites and ceremonies. Moreover, the Tun-huang murals and the many paintings, by artists such as Chou Fang, Sun Wei, Ch'ên Chu-chung and others give additional illustrative evidence of this fact.

Inasmuch as Gans-Ruedin had quoted Michel Beurdeley's book, he failed to take notice of the many illustrations including plate 84 (which is directly above his quotation) that depict rugs and carpets. Two illustrations, plates 29 and 39 which are paintings by the tenth century artist Chou Wen-chu depict Chinese home-life with carpets in prominent usage. Another depiction of a detail of a dated seventeenth century (1683) coromandel lacquer polychrome screen, not only shows a rug, but also the patterns on it. Furthermore, Gans-Ruedin's citing of William Chambers' account of a mid-18th century Chinese house deserves careful attention and comment.

Chambers as a young man had travelled to China in the service of the East India Company of Sweden. Later in life, he paid a second visit to the Far East, as an architect of the King of England and from this journey, he brought back the ideas which he published in 1772 as *Essay on Oriental Gardening*. This work, like his earlier publication, *Designs of Chinese buildings, furniture, dresses, machines, and utensils*, engraved by the best hands, from the originals drawn in China by Mr. Chambers, were primarily concerned with architecture and gardens.

During Chambers' time, intellectual planners and architects were looking for a means to provide a variety of delights for their varying moods in their gardens, which should embody both nature and art. The function would be to combine, unobtrusively in a manifold but unified

Figure 22
When the bride arrives at the groom's household, a red carpet is unrolled so that the bride may step onto it. This ancient custom is recorded
in the marriage songs found in Tun-huang.

Figure 23

In the traditional marriage ceremony, both the bride and the groom are led onto a red carpet where they perform a ceremony of obedience. The carpet served as a vehicle to announce to Heaven and to one's ancestors the vows of marriage.

plan the varied natural forms as vehicles of the many different emotions. The art theory of the garden had to develop into a kind of metaphysic, by the aid of which the artist might make of the garden an inexhaustible source of varied sentimental reactions. Chambers' essays contained, besides commendation of the Chinese garden, his reasons for rejecting the pure landscape garden such as he found on his return to England.

It is understandable that his descriptions of a Chinese house show his great interest in the architecture, furniture and gardens but little note of decorative items. In his description of the bedroom, he mentions various aspects of the bed with no reference to the matresses, coverlets or pillows. Without a doubt, it is not surprising that there should be no description of rugs or carpets. It may be argued that the house described by Chambers was a merchant's house as he was connected with the East India Company and thus would be categorized by the Chinese as a merchant himself. As such he would have been restricted to visiting only the houses of merchants of the Co-hong, a merchant guild to deal with foreigners. Other may contend that since Canton was a southern-most city that was both humid and hot, there was no place for carpets, however in the portrait of Liu Yung-fu, a famous nineteenth century official from Fukien, carpets and rugs are prominently displayed.

A better description of an eighteenth century household would be that of Jean-Baptiste Du Halde in his *Description geographique, historique, et physique de la Chine . . .* He writes:

"In the Northern Provinces they make places of hollow bricks, in the form of beds, which are larger or smaller according to the number of the family: Besides it is a small stove, of charcoal, whose flame and heat are dispersed to all parts by pipes, terminating in a funnel, which carries the smoak [sic] thro' the roof. In the houses of persons of distinction the stove comes through the wall, and the fire is lighted on the outside, by which means the bed, and even the whole house, is warmed; so that they have no occasion for the feather-beds of Europe. Those who are afraid of lying on the hot bricks, hang a sort of hammock over them, made of cords and rattan, and not unlike the sacking of our beds.

In the morning every thing of this kind is taken away, and carpets or mats ['t'an-tzŭ'] brought out in their room, on which they sit.

As they have no Chimneys nothing can be more convenient; for the whole family work upon them, without feeling the least cold, or being obliged to wear furred garments. The meaner sort dress their victuals, warm their wine and prepare their tea (for the Chinese drink everything hot) over the mouth of the stove. The beds belonging to the Inns are much larger, that there may be room for several travellers at a time."[136]

Gustav Ecke in his *Chinese Domestic Furniture*, describes a "Ming home of the leisured class . . . the floor was laid with black polished flagstones, and the ceiling finished with cloisons in yellow reed-work. Against this sombre background the furniture was disposed, subservient to the discipline of the plan. The amber or purple hues of rose-wood pieces agreed with the subdued tones of the costly rugs, or the chair covers and cushions in tapestry or embroidered silk."[137] These descriptions clearly include the mention of the use of rugs in the houses of both the rich and the humble.

The late seventh century novelette, *Yü-hsien k'u*, by Chang Wen-ch'eng, 657 - 730 A. D., not only contained Chinese classical and literary elements, but also a valuable respository of T'ang colloquial usage and social customs. There is included a description of the reception room of a wealthy person. "The pearls and jade startled my heart, the gold and silver dazzled my eyes. There were pewter colored cushions woven out of dragon's hair, rugs whose borders were silk brocaded, couches made of elephant's tusks and mattresses plainted with purplish silk matting."[138] A description of the bed chamber follows: "The pillows and cushions which were placed about had woven designs. . .There were inseparably attached creatures on a carpet of tenfold thickness and a pair of mandarin ducks on an eightfold coverlet."[139] This last description of a carpet is without a doubt a knotted pile carpet.

Although the Chinese had furniture from early times, it was common for them to sit on the floor, on mats, carpets and rugs up until the end of the tenth century. The change to chairs can be dated with some precision to the two hundred years between the middle of the ninth century and the middle of the eleventh century. The advent of this important social custom is well accepted by most scholars. Nevertheless we should remember that in ancient times the Chinese used low beds both for sleeping and sitting which may be on account of the severity of the winter climate, not only in North China but also as far south as

Plate XL

A large wooden chest for the storage and preservation of rugs. The front is decorated with five bats encircling the character *Shou*.

Figure 24
Male children were greatly desired by the Chinese family. Since infant mortality rates were high, a period of time past after the actual birth, before the child's name was entered in the family records, *chia-p'u*. A carpet was used in the simple ceremony when the father presented his male heirs to his clansmen and ancestors. The child's name was then registered.

the Yangtze valley. On top of these low beds were placed fitted mats and carpets. These low beds are not only seen in the Han tomb pictures but proceed into the T'ang period where we see depictions of them in the Tun-huang murals and paintings.

In Northern China there is another device that is similar to the low beds, which is build-in structure called the *K'ang*. This is the device described by Du Halde in the quote cited previously. The *K'ang* is two feet in height and generally six feet deep, and as wide as the room itself. It is usually covered with thick mats, and then with rugs or flat cushions, so that it is pleasant to either sit or sleep on the *K'ang* without any risk of being burned by the fire below. Throughout the winter months all home life was concentrated around the *K'ang*. Stiff cylindrical cushions or bolsters provide arm rests at the sides and the back to give more comfort in sitting. Small low tables and small cabinets were designed to be used on top of the *K'ang* as it was the only warm place in the house. In effect the *K'ang* is a section of the floor raised up approximately two feet for heating pipes to give warmth, as if it were the floor itself.

The existence of the *K'ang* is known from very early times and the term is included in the ancient *Shuo-wên* dictionary. The Chinese had devised the *K'ang* as a means to counteract the discomfort of cold floors in winter in the north and low beds in the south. Both of which were covered with mats and carpets.

Sizes

Carpets were sized to fit these two devices, the *K'ang* and the low bed. This explains the common 5 x 8 feet and 6 x 9 feet rug sizes. Besides a rug on the *K'ang*, cushions were used which often measured 2 x 2 feet. These cushions influenced the standard sizes for seats when chairs and stools were used. Rugs measuring 2 x 5 feet were used to drape over the backs of the chairs and cover also the bottom front of the chair. In the traditional opera stage a similar chair cover is still used. For larger chairs a 3 x 6 feet rug is often used. However, this size rug is also used on sedan chairs and in front of the low beds of the south. We also find rugs 8 x 10 feet and even 9 x 12 feet but seldom do we find rugs larger. These large rugs are used basically for floor rugs and in T'ang and Sung dynasty paintings, we see them used under the *Hu-ch'uang* or

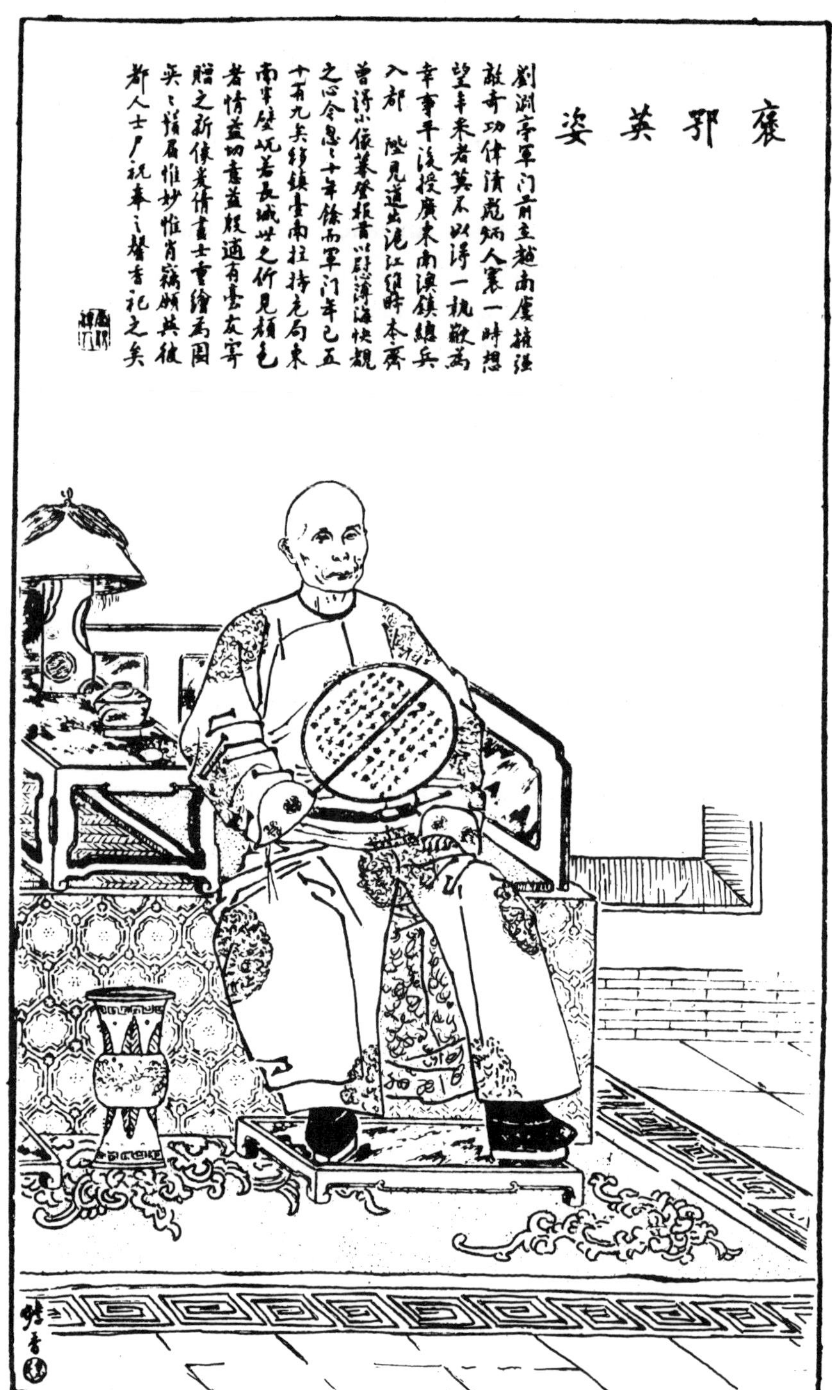

Figure 25

Portrait of the Chinese general Liu Yung-fu, a hero of the Sino-Franco War. Although he was a southerner and a native of Fukien, carpets and rugs are visible both on furniture and the floors.

Plate XLI
A temple meditation rug with the thunder bolt or *vadjra*. This rug is an attractive blend of rich red and blue with quiet shades of golden beige. Four highly stylized butterflies guard the corners and two foliated dragons are arranged in each of the side panels. 127x63 cm.

Figure 26

A woodcut print of children doing gymnastics on a carpet. The number of children, six, and their tumbling and jumping form the rebus: *Lu-mê t'iao-ho* literally meaning, the six pulses are in harmony or to be healthy and sound. The dog and lanterns on the upper right signify *Kao-t'ang ming-ting* or both parents living and having illustrious sons.

barbarian beds and also as dancing rugs or ones on which musicians sat. Such large rugs were and still are used in Peking and other regional operas. In the nineteenth century, Japanese publication on Chinese customs, *Seizoku jimon*, the rug termed *hua-t'an* is listed as an essential item in the Chinese household.[110]

Shapes

Most of the Chinese rugs are rectangular however circular and oval shaped rugs and even oblong rugs with rounded corners are known to have been made. Rugs to cover the seat, or for cushions are basically square in shape and those used to cover the backs of chairs and thrones are either scalloped, stepped or have a rounded top edge. These separate pieces were usually of the Ch'ing period, although the square pieces for seats were used in earlier times. In fact the term for these square shaped rugs, which are used as sitting places, called *Hsi*, survives in the present day language. A chairman or person who presides over a meeting is called *Chu-hsi* or the "head or chief mat or seat" and to be seated is *Tso-hsi*, to "sit on a mat or rug". The twelfth century philosopher Chu Hsi even wrote an essay entitled *Kuei-tso pai-shuo* on the proper way of sitting and kneeling on mats.

Long and narrow rugs although not the most common shape, were made as pillar rugs and seating rugs for monks of the temple and as rugs for use in corridors of palaces of the wealthy. The various uses of rugs and carpets in Chinese daily life, rites and ceremonies determined both the size and shapes of the rugs. Many rugs are brought out only for use on festivals and were kept in large camphor wood storage chests at other times. This accounts for the excellent state of preservation of many antique rugs. They were prized possessions and kept in the same manner which has preserved many of the fine Chinese antiques we see today, like the textiles of Shosoin. Therefore, unlike the rugs of the Near East, antique Chinese rugs and carpets over three hundred years or more have been able to be well-preserved. Many rug scholars, unfamiliar with Chinese culture have overlooked this simple fact and assumed the fine condition of rugs made great age doubtful.

Of the unusual shaped rugs, a four-piece puzzle rug, one piece as a semi-circle, two pieces as quarter circles and one as a narrow rectangular rug was made for Mongolian yurts and military commander's tents. Together they formed a full circular shape. For the Mongolian yurts an unusual T-shaped rug was also used for the entrance which is depicted in the scroll published by the Metropolitan Museum of Art as the "Eighteen Nomadic Flute" painting.

Aside from these unusual shapes, the saddle rugs are the only other odd-shaped rugs. The saddle rug is also quite unique in its weaving as it is constructed in two identical parts. These two pieces are knotted separately starting from the irregular shaped bottom end and proceeding to the centre, with the second piece done in the exact manner. The reason for this procedure is so that the nap of the pile would slant from the centre downwards, thus not only allowing comfort to the rider, but also shedding water and dirt rather than allowing them to be trapped in the pile. After the two identically woven pieces are completed they are sewn together with the two centres joined. In addition, they are lined with cloth, usually cotton, and the edges hemmed with the same material. Four slits, two on each side are cut and reinforced with pieces of leather through which saddle straps are threaded to fasten onto the horse and to tie on the straps for the stirrups. These slits for the stirrups are quite significant as representations of riders in the ancient Middle East, in Greek and Roman art and even in the equestrian reliefs of the Sassanian dynasty in Persia always show the legs dangling free and unsupported.

In Chinese literature the first reference to the stirrup is said to be found in the biography of a military officer who flourished in 477 A. D. The invention and use of the stirrup in China and its spreading influence is evidenced by these saddle rugs with slits to tie them. Therefore, it is not surprising that almost all the saddle rugs have Chinese designs on them. Also their sizes are more or less uniform, usually measuring approximately 2 x 4 feet. Sometimes larger saddle rugs are found which were used on camels, but the varied designs are basically Chinese or Chinese influenced. In T'ang times, there were also large rugs used for elephants as seen in a depiction on a detail from a musical instrument in the Shosoin. In preparing for a military campaign, saddle and saddle rugs were extremely important and they were manufactured in large numbers. In the long ballad *Mu-lan-tz'ŭ*, we read that Mu-lan, a young girl disguised as a male in order to substitute for her father who was called to join the Khan's army, went shopping to equip herself for

Plate XLII
The feet of this twice coiling dragon rest on cloud forms. Sacred Buddhist symbols are arranged around the dragon and the mountain and waves motif associated with dragons forms the lower border of this pillar rug. 70x198 cm.

Figure 27
In high Buddhist rituals, a multi-coloured floral carpet is used as part of
the ceremonial accouterments. In performing the ritual *San-shih ju-lai*,
or the celebration of the Buddha of the past, present and future, the
monks chant on a floral carpet symbolic of traversing time and space.
The five monks performing this ritual portray the five directions of the
Chinese compass.

Figure 28

In Taoist ceremonies, the rug is used as a bridge of communication between the motal world and Heaven. This kneeling or prayer rug is called *kuei* and is one of the objects received by a Taoist monk at the ordination ceremony. This prayer rug when fully open is an expression of the most reverent degree of worship. Half-folded, it is for worship of high-ranking dieties. A similar prayer rug is used by Buddhist monks which is called *chü*.

duty. "At the Eastern market, where she purchased a fine steed and to the Western market where she bought a saddle and saddle-trappings (including a saddle rug)". Also in the Metropolitan Museum of Art's painting of "The Eighteen Songs", we see many examples and designs of saddle rugs.

Pillar rugs are another unique rug form. Their weaving, is not different but their designs involve unusual features. These rugs are long and narrow and usually are made in pairs. They were ceremoniously used on festivals in temples to decorate the tall wooden pillars. The most common motif is a large solitary dragon design. Laid out flat the dragon appears disjointed but when the rug is wrapped around a pillar, as intended, the pieces are transformed into a large dragon curling around the pillar. Therefore the sides are designed without borders as the two sides are meant to be joined together when tied around the pillars. Both the top and the bottom are decorated with various conventional designs to compliment the ascending dragon. These dragons usually have five claws and differ from the Imperial dragon or *lung* as it does not have a *po-shan* shaped lump on its forehead called a *chih-mu* which was reserved for the Emperor's use. Nevertheless since the Lama temples are also the seat of the ruling body, it is not surprising that the five-clawed dragon was adopted. The bottom edge is decorated with the *fu-hai shou-shan* or mountain and sea motif and the top contains a geometric band, sometimes with hanging tassels. On occasion, although not too common, a form of the *t'ao-t'ieh* or devil's mask or even a row of skulls is also placed near the top. It is not unusual for these rugs to have a band with inscriptions, either in Chinese or Mongolian. Tibetan inscriptions would be rare and questionable.

Throughout the central field, around the dragon, are usually cloud patterns along with some sacred Buddhist symbols with flying bats sometimes included. Although the dragon motif is most common, there are pillar rugs with offerings and the sacred Buddhist symbols alone. A more unique motif is with a portrayal of a Lama priest usually blowing a conch, or a retinue of lama priests. These rugs with Lama priests representations are not very common. The pillar rugs are usually made to cover round pillars but there are pillar rugs with four narrow panels to cover a square shaped pillar. Generally the pillar rugs are slightly over six feet tall.

Plate XLIII
Central floral medallion set against a bright, plain background. The remainder of the carpet features scattered floral forms in very bright tones upon subdued backgrounds. 286x146 cm.

Recently a few writers and dealers, who without any understanding of Tibetan or Mongolian practice of Buddhism, have advanced the theory that yellow, amber, ochre, tan or yellow-orange grounds denote earlier rugs while red or reddish browns are of a later date. The two colours, yellow and red denote the main divisions of the *Nying-ma-pa* or the Sect of the Red Caps and the *Ge-lug-pa* or the Sect of the Yellow Caps. Religious wars have created serious strains on Tibetan unity. In central Tibet known as Wu province, the "Yellow Caps" reformists, known more formally as the *Gè-lug-pa* sect of Lamaism, had the upper hand. But in Utsang province the older "Red Caps" sect which enjoyed the patronage of the powerful Sakya monastery near Lhasa was predominant. In 1270, after the Mongol conquest of China, Kublai Khan had placed on Tibet's throne a Lamaist monk of the so-called "Red Caps" sect. This began a dynasty of Sakya priest-kings in Tibet who drew support and protection from the Mongols. The Tibetan kings, who by virtue of their isolation, could escape the usual bonds of vassalage, nevertheless, had a patron-priest relationship which provided the Mongols with a measure of influence which was essential to protect the Southern boundaries of their empire. The "Yellow Caps" sect had long been subjugated by the rival "Red Caps" sect headed by Prime Minister Tsangpa until 1641. In that year the victorious Guori Khan had invaded Tibet proper at the invitation of the Fifth Dalai Lama. After seizing control of Tibet the Mongol commander, for political reasons, deeded supreme religious authority to the Yellow-mitred Dalai Lama with whom he had collaborated. This enabled the Yellow, or *Gè-lug-pa* sect to gain ascendency over the "Red Caps" sect. It also established a "patron-priest" power formula between suzerain and Dalai Lama which was to repeat itself frequently throughout Tibetan history. This domination of the "Yellow Caps" is the basic reason that most Tibetan and Mongolian pillar rugs are predominately yellow, amber, ochre, tan and yellow-orange. These colours have nothing to do with dating as some dealers and writers have proposed.

There are also a few examples of blue pillar rugs which are basically from Ninghsia and Pao-t'ou. Most of these rugs are of a later date and do not represent a religous sect but the laity. Their exact use is unknown. Again since pillar rugs are only brought out on high festival days, and otherwise are stored in large camphor wood chests, these rugs even the older ones, are commonly found to be in a very good state of preservation. Also in the case of pillar rugs they are not subjected to as much wear as rugs on a floor, *K'ang* or seat.

THE BORDER REGIONS

Commonly, in Western rug literature, China is thought of as that large Asian land mass bound by Mongolia and Manchuria in the North; Eastern or Chinese Turkestan in the West; Burma, Laos and Vietnam in the South; and the Pacific Ocean to the East. The common refrain is that China consists of the traditional eighteen provinces within the Great Wall of China. These provinces include: Chihli or Hopeh, Shantung, Shansi, Honan, Kiangsu, Anhwei, Kiangsi, Chekiang, Fukien, Hupeh, Hunan, Kwangtung, Kwangsi, Yunnan, Kweichow, Szechwan, Shensi, and Kansu. Manchuria, Mongolia, Eastern or Chinese Turkestan, and Tibet have been excluded as part of Chinese territory although they have been carved into a number of provinces. The area of Manchuria consists of the provinces of Liaoning, Kirin and Heilungkiang. Mongolia, is also known as Inner and Outer Mongolia, with the former being divided into four provinces of Suiyuan, Ninghsia, Chahar and Jehol. Jehol was later incorporated into Inner Mongolia. Eastern or Chinese Turkestan has been known as Sinkiang province since 1724, and Tibet is known as Ch'ing-hai, Sikang, and Tibet. Moreover, areas under Chinese suzerainty since the eighteenth century include: Dzungaria, Nepal, Burma, Annam, Korea and the Amur region.

It should also be pointed out that during the Yüan dynasty, 1280 - 1368, the Mongol Empire stretched from the Pacific Ocean in the East to the Caspian Sea in the West, practically dominating all of the Asian Continent. This, of course, includes the countries and areas that were influenced by Chinese culture. To better understand the areas of China usually omitted by Western rug literature -- Manchuria, Mongolia, Sinkiang and Tibet -- an examination of the history of these areas should be made as most excavations revealing early rugs have been discovered in these areas and show Chinese influences and domination.

While the nomads of Iranian stock -- Scythians and Sarmatians -- occupied the Western part of the steppe zone in Southern Russia and no doubt, also Turgai and Western Siberia, the Eastern part was under the sway of Turko-Mongol peoples. Of these, the dominant nation of antiquity was known to the Chinese by the name "Hsiung-nu". The Romans and Indians later designated these same peoples the Huns, Hunni and Huna.

According to the *Shih-chi*, the ancient Hsiung-nu were descendants of Chun-wei, a member of the Miao tribe during the reign of the first Hsia emperor in the third millenium B. C. "As early as the time of Emperor Yao and Shun and before, we hear of these people known as Mountain barbarians, *Hsien-yün* or *Hun-chü*, living in the region of the northern barbarians and wandering from place to place pasturing their animals. The animals they raise consist mainly of horses, cows, and sheep, but include such rare beasts as camels, asses, mules, and wild horses known as *t'ao-t'u* and *t'o-chi*. They move about in search of water and pasture and have no walled cities or fixed dwelling nor do they engage in any kind of agriculture. Their lands, however, are divided into regions under the control of various leaders. They have no writing and even promises and agreements are only verbal. . . It is their custom to herd their flocks in times of peace and make their living by hunting. . . from the chiefs of the tribe on down, everyone eats the meat of the domestic animals and wears clothes of hide or wraps made of felt or fur."[141]

The Hsiung-nu were also called *Hu* and in earlier times as *Jung, Ti* and other names. They lived in China Proper until they were pushed to the North. The French Sinologist Henri Maspero supposes that the *Jung* of the North, the *Pei-jung*, established to the west and northwest of present day Peking, were a *Hu* tribe. Other clans were subjugated in the fourth century B. C. by the Chinese of the kingdom of Chao. King Wu-ling of Chao (ca. 325 - 298 B. C.) even captured from them the extreme north of Shansi to the Ta-t'ung region, and indeed the Northern part of the Ordos (So-fang) of today, ca. 300 B. C. Originally, they lived in the territory comprising the area of present-day Kansu, Shensi, and gradually they moved northward to occupy the Tarbagatai-Altai region by the end of the second millennium B. C. By 500 B. C. or during the Chou dynasty, the Hsiung-nu were in Dzungaria and Western Mongolia. Very likely, they acquired the art of horse-riding from their southern neighbours, the Yueh-chih, who had occupied Western Kansu. From these strongholds the mounted horsemen of the steppe zone were capable of causing havoc

Plate XLIV

A view of Ta-ching t'ang or "sutra-chanting hall" of Lu-sha-êrh in Ch'ing-hai province. This temple is a sacred place of the Gê-lug-pa or Yellow Sect of Lamaism. This hall is a perfect combination of Chinese and Tibetan architecture. The structure is of wood and earth with a flat roof supported by 168 pillars. The pillars, embellished with pillar rugs with coiling dragons on a yellow ground as a distinction of the Yellow Sect. The floor is paved with wooden boards and there are carpeted areas where the lama priests can sit in meditation or chant sutras.

in the Chinese frontier settlements. In Chou times the nomads had possessed horses, but they fought on foot, while the Chinese aristocrats fought from chariots. In the fourth century B. C. the innovation of the stirrup in the Ordos region made it possible for horsemen to shoot straight even while riding and calvary became a formidable military instrument. For a long time this invention gave the northern nomads a tremendous advantage over the calvary of sedentary peoples. The technique of cavalry warfare reached China via the steppe; its obvious effectiveness soon forced the Chinese to adopt it for themselves. The great mobility of mounted warriors and their ability to fight on rough terrain soon put an end to chariot warfare in China. In the West it was known neither to the Greeks nor Romans and its seems that only the Avars of the sixth century brought it into common use there. With the use of the stirrups this brought about the use of saddles to tie them onto.

It was to secure effective defense against the attacks of these nomads that the Chinese of the kingdoms of Ch'in (Shensi) and Chao (Shansi) transformed their heavy wheeled forces into mobile calvary. This was a military innovation which brought about with it a complete alteration in Chinese dress. The robe of archaic times, being replaced by calvary trousers. It was also to defend themselves against the Hsiung-nu that the Chinese of Chao and neighbouring states began to build along their Northern frontier elementary fortifications which when unified and completed by Ch'in Shih-huang-ti at a later date were to become the Great Wall.

The survival of a herding and hunting community beside a farming one presented not only a glaring economic contrast, but a social contrast that was even more cruel. Increasingly prosperous agricultural communities developed within sight and contact of peoples still at the pastoral stage, and thus still suffering the appalling famines inherent in steppe life in times of drought. The problem of human geography became a social one. The farming community that cultivated the good rich yellow soil of Northern China was encircled by a belt of poor grazing land where terrible climatic conditions often prevailed and where one year in every ten, the watering places dried up, grass withered, and livestock perished, and with them the nomad himself.

According to the Chinese historian Ssŭ-ma Ch'ien, ca. 145 - 90 B. C. it was in the second half of the third century B. C. that the Hsiung-nu seem to have become a united and strong nation. They were led by a chief called the "Shan-yu" whose full title transcribed into Chinese as *Ch'eng-li Ku-t'u Shan-yu* which translates as "Majestic Son of Heaven". In this term we find Turko-Mongol derivatives. *Ch'èng-li* is the Turkic and Mongol word *Tangri* or Heaven. Under the Shan-yu were two chieftans. The rest of the organization was divided into left and right wings. This nation of nomads, a people on the march, was organized like an army.

The Hsiung-nu are portrayed by the Chinese with the characteristic traits which we find among Turkic and Mongol successors. The Japanese scholar Kurakichi Shiratori notes that the Hsiung-nu wore a queue, and that form them the custom spread to the succeeding, Turko-Mongol hordes, the Toba, Juan-juan, T'u-chüeh, Khitan and Mongols.[142] It was a Hsiung-nu custom of funerary immolations whereby the throats of the chief's wives and servants were slit and they were buried in the tomb along with the dead chief. The *Ch'ien Han-shu* or History of the Former Han testifies that a custom prevailed of sawing off the enemy's skull at eyebrow level, then covering it with a leather sheath, and applying a gold inlay inside to use as a drinking cup. It was also a point of honour to display among their battle trophies the heads which they had cut from their victims, and the scalps were dangled from their bridles. Among the descendants of the Hsiung-nu, the T'u-chüeh of the sixth century A. D., the number of stones distinguishing a warrior's burial mound was proportionate to the number of men he had slain during his lifetime.[143]

The Hsiung-nu were essentially nomadic, and the rhythm of their existence was regulated by their flock of sheep, their herds of horses, cattle and camels. They moved with their livestock in search of water and pasture. They ate only meat, dressed in skins, slept on furs and camped in felt tents. Their religion was a vague shamanism based on the cult of *Tangri* or Heaven and on the worship of certain sacred mountains. All the Chinese writers present the Hsiung-nu as inveterate plunderers who would appear unexpectedly on the fringes of cultivated land, attack men, flocks and wealth, and flee again with their booty into the Gobi desert before any counterattack could be launched. Some references in Chinese historical chronicles indicate that the Hsiung-nu had preserved certain ancient Chinese customs and beliefs. A passage from the *Shih-chi* on their calvary maneuvers reads: "The Hsiung-nu would surround the enemy on all sides, with white horses on the west side, greenish horses on the east, black horses on the north, and red ones on the south."[144] The Chinese considered these four colours as symbolic of the four directions of the compass. This account suggests that the Hsiung-nu held similar beliefs which they had preserved when they had lived in China proper in the third millenium B. C.

Even when the Chinese learned calvary techniques, the nomads possessed certain clear advantages in mounted warfare. Except in periods of prolonged conflict, they were far greater horsemen than the Chinese. Their mobility permitted them great freedom of attack and maneuver. When hard pressed they could retreat into the steppe. While the cultivated fields and complex irrigation works of China were extremely vulnerable to attack and destruction, the nomads carried all their wealth with them. On the other hand, Chinese civilization exerted an attractive force upon the nomads which tended to modify their lifestyle. The steppe offered few of the amenities available in the settled regions of China. Nomads who conquered agricultural populations soon acquired a taste for the luxuries of civilization. The collection of tribute tied them to the tributary region and thus limited their mobility. Attempts to settle down and rule the subjugated peoples did so even more. Becoming progressively less nomadic, the steppe warriors tended to lose the habits on which their original military advantage was based.

The Great Wall of China was an attempt to prevent the incursions of nomads into the Empire. The line of the Great Wall marked the approximate natural limits of both Chinese and nomad expansion. Beyond that line, Chinese settlements and political control were subject to the law of diminishing returns; within it nomad intruders tended to become assimilated into Chinese society. Whereas in China a dense agricultural population produced high yields per unit of land, the steppe could support only a sparse population with a pastoral or semi-pastoral economy. Chinese and nomadic social forms diverged correspondingly. The characteristic social order of China could not adequately be transported into the steppe, nor the steppe into China. No vital economic interests drew the two regions together. Commerce between them was normally restricted to a few luxury products exchanged between rulers: fine horses, hides, precious stones from the nomads, bolts of silk cloth from the Chinese.

Plate XLV

A T'ang dynasty plectrum guard of a *P'i-p'a* or lute made of leather coated with white pigment over which a design of figures riding on an elephant is executed in black, red, vermilion and green pigments as well as gold leaf. The design shows four figures playing music on the back of an elephant on which a rug with fringes is draped. The rug design consists of a floral pattern with a pearl-like border.

The number of nomads in relation to Chinese was never large nor could it be, given the conditions of the steppe life. During the third century B. C. the Ch'in Emperor sent his general, Mèng T'ien to attack the Hsiung-nu and drive them from the Ordos region. The scattered tribes of nomads then formed a confederation and under their Shan-yü, T'ou-man, began their expansion by attacking the Yüeh-chih, who were a nomad people who apparently spoke an Indo-European language and who until then had been established in Western Kansu. After T'ou-man's death in 209 B. C., his son and successor, Mo-tun, defeated the Tung-hu or the Eastern Barbarians of the Manchurian borders. Between the fall of the Ch'in dynasty and the advent of the Han, he invaded the Chinese province of Shansi and laid siege to the capital, T'ai-yüan. The Emperor Kao-tsu tried to repel their attacks but was entrapped by them on the Pai-têng plateau on the frontiers of Shansi. He negotiated with the Hsiung-nu and a Chinese lady-in-waiting was given in marriage to the Shan-yü.

In 176 B. C., Mo-tun attacked the Yüeh-chih again and pushed them out of Kansu, forcing them to emigrate westward, thus giving rise to the first historically recorded movement of peoples originating in the high plateaus of Asia.[145]

The Yüeh-chih have been identified with the Tokhari, and the Indo-Scythians who were known to Greek historians from their having emigrated in the second century B. C. from Turkestan to Bactria. Accordingly, Tokhari and Indo-Scythians were names applied to a single people at two periods in their existence. This group was regarded as having Scythian affinities, or being of Indo-European stock. This identification is based chiefly on the fact that they lived in the Chinese region of present-day western Kansu, which according to Chinese historical records had been called the country of the Yüeh-chih. Strabo's *Geography* (20 - 10 B. C.) mentions Tokhari among the people who took Bactria from the Greeks exactly at the time when the Chinese annals show the Yüeh-chih arriving at the end of their migration at the frontiers of Ta-hsia or Bactria.[146] So consistent a parallel seems to be a strong agrument that the Tokhari and Indo-Scythians were the Yüeh-chih people. Moreover, as late as the fifth and sixth centuries A. D., Indo-European languages were still spoken in the oases north of the Tarim Basin, the earlier domain of the Yüeh-chih. Thus, a large part of Turkestan has been populated by these early people.

Also when Mo-tun forced the Yueh-chih out of Kansu and to flee to the West across the Gobi, one portion of the people, known to the Chinese as *Hsiao Yüeh-chih* or Lesser Yüeh-chih, settled south of the Nan-shan among the *Chiang* or Tibetans, whose language they adopted. The other Yüeh-chih clans, or Greater Yüeh-chih, attempted to settle in the Ili valley and the Issyk Kul basin, and temporarily vanquished the Wu-sun. The Wu-sun were described by Chinese annalists as blue-eyed and red-bearded people. With the help of the Hsiung-nu, the Wu-sun rebelled against the Yüeh-chih, who then resumed their westward march and reached the upper Syr Darya in Fergana on the borders of Bactria. The *Ch'ien Han-shu* notes their arrival in about 160 B. C.

In 128 B. C., when the Chinese ambassador Chang Ch'ien visited the Yüeh-chih, they had already conquered and occupied Sogdiana, and their capital was the town of Chien-shih. Toru Haneda identifies this name phonetically with Kanda, an abbreviation of Markanda or Samarkand.[147] Not satisfied, the Yüeh-chih crossed the Oxus and occupied and replaced the Saka in Bactria. Their migration was the signal for a general tumult of the peoples and a surge of nomads across eastern Iran. Thrust back in the South by the Yüeh-chih, the Saka occupied Seistan and Kandahar. The occupation was permanent, for from that time those countries became in Iranian nomenclature "the Saka Country", hence the modern Persian Seistan. The Saka people whom the Chinese historians called *Ssê* or *Sêk* in ancient pronunciation, first lived in the regions of Tashkent, Fergana and Kashgar and were pushed westward by the Yüeh-chih. The subsequent destinies of the Saka and the Yüeh-chih of these regions form part of the history of Iran and India. It is enough to point out here that from Seistan and Kandahar the Saka expanded to Kabul and the Punjab, then when these countries were occupied by the Yüeh-chih, the Saka moved to Malvan and Gujarat. The Yüeh-chih of Bactria, in the first century A. D., formed the great dynasty of the Kushans and played a large part in the dissemination of Buddhism into central Asia. The aim here is to show the colossal impact of the Hunnic thrust on the destinies of Asia. In driving the Yüeh-chih from Kansu, the Hsiung-nu had started a sequence of repercussions which were felt as far away as Western Asia and India. Afghanistan was lost to Hellenism, the last vestiges of Alexander's conquest in these regions had been wiped out;

Parthian Iran had been temporarily shaken and the tribes driven away from Kansu had established an Empire in Kabul and northwest India. This direction of the migration of the Yüeh-chih, from China westward is confirmed by historical records and is contrary to what is mentioned in most rug literature which commonly expounds a reverse flow but offers no concrete evidence.

The removal of the Yüeh-chih increased the importance of the Hsiung-nu while the routes taken by the migrating Yüeh-chih seem to coincide with the various areas that have become carpet-weaving centres.

The Hsiung-nu, being the prominant force in the North dominated the Gobi, Upper Mongolia and Inner Mongolia to the foot of the Great Wall. Daring raids into China proper were frequent and the Chinese frontier was being threatened at every point when Emperor Wu-ti, 140 - 87 B.C., ascended the throne.

Wu-ti formed a plan to drive the Hsiung-nu back by allying himself with the Yüeh-chih, now settled in Sogdiana. With this plan, Chang Ch'ien was sent as an ambassador but was unsuccessful in his attempt to gain an alliance with the Yüeh-chih. Therefore, Wu-ti started his war against the Hsiung-nu unaided. Under General Wei Ch'ing and his nephew Ho Ch'iu-ping, the Hsiung-nu were driven out of Kansu, while two minor clans offered their services to the Han and were established as confederates north of Nan-shan. In 120 B. C., a Chinese colony was formed in the Ordos. The Han continued to push the Hsiung-nu northwards into Upper Mongolia. Having pacified the Northern areas, Wu-ti created, in Kansu, between the years 127 B. C. and 111 B. C., a series of commanderies and military prefectures, with the object of preventing the Hsiung-nu from returning to that area. The commanderies of Wu-wei, Chang-yeh, Tzu-ch'uan and Tun-huang stretching from Lanchow to the Yü-men pass, marked out the old Yüeh-chih country and guarded the route of the Silk Road.[148] In 108 B. C., the Chinese general Chao P'o-nu pressed even further to the northwest, as far as the kingdoms of Lou-lan and Lop Nor, and of Chiu-shih, the present day Turfan. The Chinese expanded their commercial relations with Fergana who supplied China with horses of the fine Transoxianian breed. Later when the people of Fergana assassinated the Chinese ambassador, the Chinese attacked and defeated them, demanding three thousand horses in tribute.

Plate XLVI
An all-over geometric tortoise shell design with flowers and diaper patterns. Fret, diapers and stylized flowers fill the outer border which is accented with the four joys of the literati and other auspicious symbols. The inner border features the running-T pattern. 200x128 cm.

During the ensuing period, the Hsiung-nu and China struggled with one another for possession of the Northern Tarim oases and the control of the Silk Road, with the Chinese establishing a number of colonies in that area. The main objective of the Chinese was to drive the Hsiung-nu back into Outer Mongolia, away from the Silk Road from which they derived food and wealth. The Tarim Basin oases settlements were so tied to China that they continued to owe allegiance despite the civil wars raging between the "Three Kingdoms" of China, successors to the Han. In 224 A. d., Shanshan (Lop Nor), Kucha, and Khotan, paid homage to Ts'ao P'ei, the King of Wei. When Wei and the other two Chinese kingdoms, Wu and Shu, were superseded by the Chin or Tsin dynasty which reunited China, the king of Kucha even sent his son to serve at the Imperial court.

According to the *Shih-chi*, "The Hsiung-nu had always had a liking for Han silks and food stuffs. . . the Shan-yü has this fondness for Chinese things and is trying to change the Hsiung-nu customs [to that of the Han]."[149]

Under the Han Emperor Hsüan-ti, 73 - 49 B. C., Chinese expansion in the Tarim Basin made a decisive advance. Not only was Turfan captured, but also Yarkand, Kucha, Wei-lei and Kara Shahr. Thus China controlled the Silk Road and maintained suzerainty over the entire Tarim Basin by pushing out the Hsiung-nu clans occupying those areas. The exodus of the Western Hsiung-nu and the removal of those of the East from the affairs of the Tarim Basin secured to the Chinese the hegemony of Central Asia. China's control of the Silk Road at the time of the Later Han, by ensuring the freedom of transcontinental trade along the double chain of oases north and south of the Tarim Basin, favoured the dissemination of Buddhism in the river basin. In the Ordos and the Tarim Basin areas the various peoples came in contact with Chinese aesthetics and steppe and Chinese art interacted and exerted their influence one upon the other. Ordos art is particularly reminiscent of that of Minusinsk, though richer and more imaginative in its plaques ornamented with fighting horses, horses or deer in combat with tigers, bears and fantastic beasts, and also in the ends of shafts decorated with stags or hinds on a round boss.

Hsiung-nu art of Mongolia and the Ordos, according to archaeological research, appears to be as ancient as that of the Scythians. In 1933, the Swedish archaeologist T. J. Arne dated the Ordos bronzes of Luan-p'ing and Hsüan-hua from the early part of the third century B. C. and even from the second half of the fourth.[150]   In 1935, the Japanese archaeologist Sueiji Umehara, believing that Ordos art had deeply influenced the Chinese style known as that of the Warring States, which had flourished from the fifth century B. C., dated the first Ordos bronze from that period.[151]   More recently a Swedish Sinologist Bernard Karlgren put the style of the Warring States even further back in time, to 650 B. C., thereby proving that steppe art in the shape of Ordos art also existed then, since it had brought about a modification in the Chinese style of decoration known as the Middle Chou. All are agreed that the influence of the Ordos art is one of the factors, which together with the laws of internal evolution, (and apparently working in the same direction as these) caused the transition of archaic Chinese bronzes from the Middle Chou style to that of the Warring States. The principle sites of Hsiung-nu finds range from Lake Baikal to the borders of Hopei, Shansi and Shensi. The same art continued until the Ongut of the Genghiz-Khanite period, in the little Nestorian bronzes -- crosses, doves, and Paracletes -- which were yielded in large numbers in the Ordos and adjacent areas. These plaque designs rememble the *güls* in most Near Eastern rugs.

Similar to Chinese symbolism in art, steppe art also gave magical significance to the ornamental motifs. This subject has been studied by a number of scholars including O. Janse in *Le cheval cornu et la boule magique* and Potapoff in *Conceptions totemiques des Altaiens*.

The area of the Pazyryk kurgans, where the earliest rugs have been discovered is within the vicinity of present-day Mongolia and certainly must have been among the areas occupied by the early Hsiung-nu. Early Hsiung-nu woolen fabrics, very similar to the Pazyryk rug, were excavated in Outer Mongolia, Noin-Ula, where the Kozlov mission found that similar designs were used such as a griffin fighting an elk, and a tiger-cat attacking a yak. Moreover, nearly all of the discoveries of early rugs have come from these areas of East Asia, both within and just outside China's borders. These discoveries provide intriguing grounds for speculation that like the migration of the Turkic peoples and the introduction of the stirrup, the art of rug weaving went from east to west instead of the reverse as is commonly held.

The stylistic influence of Chinese designs could be readily seen in many Persian rugs. The cloud band, floral patterns, the palmette, the phoenix and the dragon, and especially the stylized lotus and peony patterns, are all examples of motifs which were brought to Persia with the Mongols. The palmette was a widely used ornamental motif in Western Asia in ancient times that corresponds to the migration of the Yueh-chih into these areas, but its usage was rather limited until the Mongol invasion.

According to Werner Gröte-Hasenbalg in his *Der Orientteppich seine Geschichte und seine Kulture*, there is an even more important feature of the Chinese influence than the introduction of individual motifs, and that is the impulse for greater freedom of expression and a more flowering or more picturesque style. All available evidence indicates that until the late fifteenth century, the Persian carpet designers knew nothing of curvilinear forms. Western Persia, Gröte-Halsbalg asserts, preserved the strict Islamic style longest, while the new free style of design developed in Herat and Eastern Persia. After the Mongol conquests, the geometric style gave way to the floral in Herat. One of the most striking decorative motifs that had been adopted, which is strictly Chinese in origin, is the dragon and phoenix design seen in an Anatolian rug of the fifteenth century. The Turks and the Mongols brought into the world of the Iranians and other Indo-European peoples a culture which was alien in every respect. In 1419, Timur's son, Shah Rukh, a great patron of the arts, sent one of his best painters of miniatures, Ghiyat ad-Din, with a Persian delegation to China. His return further intensified the already wide use of Chinese ideas in Persia.

In examining some of the Persian miniature paintings, and Chinese paintings of the same period, we see that the Mongol rugs depicted often have a similar abstract style, although they most frequently have a dominant central motif. Other carpet designs consist of repeating panels, stars, octagons, etc. The elaborate medallion, which has been thought by many writers to be similar to Buddhist mandala pattern, could also be compared to the Chinese bronze mirror designs and the Hsiung-nu bronze designs on bosses.

Although Mongolia had been associated with a felt culture, nevertheless, knotted pile rugs were used from ancient times. Evidence of their use come from excavations and, in more recent times, from accounts of Jesuit missionaries. According to these accounts, rugs were

Plate XLVII
A landscape scene executed entirely in shades of blue and beige. A
subtle shadow-box frame effect is achieved by an artful border design.
Chinese see in landscapes a meaning far beyond scenery. The entire natural physical environment teems with demons and spirits and has a
numious quality. 125x174 cm.

produced in T'ai-yuan and Ninghsia. T'ai-yüan had been a rug producing centre since T'ang times as we have discussed earlier. The Ninghsia carpet industry in the nineteenth century is described in detail by William Woodville Rockhill his *Diary of a Journey through Mongolia and Tibet*.

"January 17. . . . Today I examined the carpet factories for which this place has been famous for centuries. The wool is brought from the Mongols and each manufacturer dyes his worsted for himself. I found it difficult to obtain very accurate information about the origin and nature of the dyes used. Brazil wood supplies a red dye, 'huai-tzu', a yellow dye, safflower is also used as is a red dye said to have come from Tibet, and which is possibly the 'tso' of the Tibetans. Another plant called here 'tzu hua-tzu' supplies a light drab, and indigo furnishes them with their blues. Aniline dyes, I am sorry to find, have found their way into the Ninghsia market, but are not much used for dyeing wools for carpets, except for supplying purple. The green colours used come, I was told, from the East, and are therefore, I presume, of foreign origin. The manufacturers only dye their wools in summer. In company with Mr. Horoben, of the China Inland Mission, I visited a number of factories, in most of which we found between six and ten looms at which both men and women worked. The looms of the most primitive description, are vertical and the weft is passed between two threads of the warps without the aid of any instrument, the wool being simply rolled into a ball, and is cut off roughly with a rather blunt knife. When a whole line had thus been put in, it is trimmed with a pair of shears. There is no pattern before the weaver, but he evolves the most intricate tasteful designs without their assistance or a moment's hesitation.

I found that the many manufacturers were copying very common patterns of European ingrain patterns. These were to fill orders given them by various officials who had brought here bits of carpets bought at some of the treaty ports. The usual size of the rugs is that necessary to cover a 'k'ang' say ten by six. Prayer rugs, cushions, saddle blankets, etc., are made in large numbers than any other style of rugs, as nearly all of them are sold to Mongols or go to Tibet."[152]

Ninghsia does not always indicate rugs manufactured in that area alone but is a term used as a generic name for rugs of a certain style and quality. These Ninghsia rugs are also woven in Kansu and Ch'ing-hai and are generally a coarse weave with approximately 30 knots to the square inch with usually a cotton foundation. The fleecy wool often contains a large amount of 'kemp' and animal hair. The predominent colour is yellow, with light fruit-red colour. Less frequently we find a tan colour and rarely blue is the predominent colour. Characteristically Ninghsia rugs have browns and blacks of natural coloured wool.

Since the seventeenth century visit of Emperor K'ang-hsi to this area, most Chinese rug dealers assert that a better quality rug is produced Ninghsia. This allows them to raise their prices.

In contrast, Kansu and Suiyuan rugs are mostly blue and white, and Suiyuan rugs are often in varying shades of blue only. The most popular design of these two areas is a stag or a horse standing under a tree or large peony shrub and flying cranes. The rugs from these areas are usually small in size, two feet by four and have the swastika meander as border designs although central medallions are also encountered in the borders. Another frequent design is the stylized peony pattern with various brocade patterns. Suiyuan and Kansu rugs are very similar, however, the Suiyuan's pile is usually thicker and more velvety to the touch and oftentimes their rugs are larger than those of Kansu.

Pao-t'ou is the capitol of Suiyuan and is also a major rug-producing centre as is the nearby town of Kweihwa. Likewise, most of the rugs are of varying blue shades. Their designs are often large massive shapes of animals, flowers and landscapes, and frequently contain no borders. A rather naturalistic Pao-t'ou design is a large peony blossom aside a stylistic rock. In this design red, green and yellow colours are used and the brilliance of the colours is quite contrary to Chinese tastes. Often the flower designs are slightly embossed and when borders are used, floral motifs as well as geometric designs are used. Most of the Pao-t'ou productions resemble tapestries more than rugs. These rugs not only are distinguishable by design but have a finer and tighter knotting with a shorter pile. A particular hallmark is to have shades of tan in the predominately blue rugs. Earlier Pao-t'ou rugs frequently utilize a small repeating pattern throughout the central field with sometimes a central medallion. Later rugs are rather dark coloured and the even later commercial rugs have thicker piles.

The Tibetans, like the Mongols, love bright colours and this preference is brought to bear in their rug production. The bulk of Tibetan rugs reflect the direct borrowing of Chinese designs, however, the patterns have been characteristically "Tibetanized" with a marked difference. Two major differences distinguish Tibetan rugs from Chinese rugs. One is the use of different materials as dye stuffs. The major departure is that besides madder for their reds, the Tibetans use also *lac*, a cochineal-like dye made from an insect product, *Coccus laccae*, found on several varieties of plants. This red could range from a brilliant crimson to a deep magenta colour. Browns are derived from the husks of walnuts and catechu, obtained from the heartwood of a palm tree along with concentrated tea. All the dyes used by the Tibetans are usually mordanted with alum. Inasmuch as the colours are surprisingly brilliant, the designs show the greatest Chinese influence and are also likely to have a more Chinese colour scheme than any other rugs produced in the regional areas.

The other departure which is the most unusual feature of Tibetan rugs is the method of knotting. Although similar vertical looms are used, a unique method of knotting is employed. The rug is formed by cutting loops that are made by pulling yarn tightly over a rod. After several rows of interweaving are completed as a base, the weaving begins. The first knot resembles the asymmetrical knot and a continuous ball of yarn is guided between the two warp threads down and to the left then brought up over them to the right and in between and carried under a rod, cut to the desired width. When the ball is then inserted between the next group of warp threads, a loop has been formed; it can be cut or left as it is. This method is only desirable, however, when complete rows of the same colour are planned or a more complicated plan must be worked out to change to a different colour of yarn. This planning is more akin to the technique of Kilim or flat weaves. This complex technique used uniquely by the Tibetans has caused much confusion in terminology with some writers describing it as either symmetrical or asymmetrical knotting. Many of the Tibetan rugs, especially the Kampa Dzong rugs have both warp and weft of wool rather than cotton. Messinesi, Denwood and Kuløy have each written full accounts on Tibetan rugs and this unique technique of weaving.

The Tibetan rugs have a comparatively limited range of designs but even so an interesting combination allows for a good variety of patterns. Most of the symbols used are of a religious nature with medallions, swastika, vadjra, lotus, and other geometric and floral patterns.

Plate XLVIII

A pine, deer and *Ling-chih* fungus motif saddle rug with swastika fret
and floral border. This design combination forms the rebus: *Shou-lu
ch'ung-chih* or "May you continue to enjoy happiness and longevity".
The holes for attaching the blanket to the saddle are reinforced with
leather. 125x60 cm.

The dragon plays a rather dominant role in pillar rugs and seat covers as well as various temple rugs.

The Tibetans used various rugs in their daily life and large rugs were woven to sleep on, which measure 3 feet by 6 feet and usually have a three medallion decoration. Some rugs have only one medallion and two medallion rugs are uncommon. Oblong and square rugs are used to sit on but rugs used for floor coverings are basically foreign to their way of life. A local style of rugs with fringes on all four sides are called *tso* rugs. They are usually decorated with floral patterns and although they appear unique, this form of rug could be traced back to China and early Buddhism. In an early eighth century painting attributed to Wu Tao-tzu in the Palace Museum of the Lokapala Vaisrvana portrayed enthroned with a musician and dancer below, we find that a small rug with fringes on all the edges is prominently displayed.

The Tibetans pictorial rugs are often with a dragon or dragons, a dragon and a phoenix or bunches of flowers or a vase with flowers. These motifs clearly reflect the great influence of the Chinese. For borders, a T-pattern meander along with the swastika meander are most common. Medallion rugs usually contain a main border with one or two inner stripes or borders but outer guard stripes are seldom encountered. Almost invariably, the sides, both front and back are sewn or hemmed around with a narrow piece of cloth strip which is usually red. The strip completely hides any fringe or side finish. For door curtains, the back of the rug is usually covered with a piece of cloth, quite often felt, which is sewn on the back.

One of the peculiarities of Tibetan rugs is found in their saddle rugs or *masho*. Most common are the two-piece sets with a small rectangular shaped rug to fit over the top of the saddle and a larger piece to be placed under the saddle. The larger piece is usually made in the customary method with the two parts woven separately and then sewn together in the middle. These resemble Chinese saddle rugs in every manner except that the ends are usually squared off instead of being rounded. The larger pieces frequently have holes cut into them and reinforced with leather for straps, however, a rather unique butterfly shape with rounded corners in the front flaring to a point in the rear is sometimes found. In these rugs holes are unnecessary as the front portion is short enough to allow straps to encircle the rug.

With little doubt, decoration and design of Tibetan rugs reflect the total Chinese influence. In fact, the better quality rugs are termed *Gya-rum* by the Tibetans, with the prefix *Gya* usually referring to China.

Rugs from Eastern or Chinese Turkestan should more accurately be termed rugs from Sinkiang. The oases towns in the Tarim basin were first subjected to Chinese rule from the second century B. C. to the fourth century A. D. and from the seventh to the tenth centuries. Again, in the twelfth to the fourteenth century Chinese dominated these scattered towns and the area was finally annexed by Emperor Ch'ien-lung along with Dzungaria, in the eighteenth century. This area was given a new name 'Sinkiang' meaning "new boundaries", and has been a province of China since then.

The Tarim basin is a geographically remote desert area, accessible from the outside only with great difficulty. In the great central portion of Sinkiang lies the Takla Makan desert, extending 1500 miles from east to west, 250 miles from north to south. This vast area is not only unexplored but virtually uninhabitable. Surrounding this area are formidable mountain ranges with the Pamirs to the west, the T'ien-shan on the north and the K'un-lun mountain range to the south, extending eastward in a northerly direction and cutting off free access to central China. A drainageless basin is thus created with the water runoff from the mountains winding through the wastes of Takla Makan and disappearing in salt marshes. The land is not of a richness to invite settlements or colonization from the outside and this makes possible the habitation only of oases towns fed by rivers. Along both northern and southern edges of the great desert there is a string of small inhabited areas. The oases settlements along this natural corridor allow for an overland trade route between China and the West including India. These petty kingdoms of the Tarim were of great economic importance, because the great caravan route between China and the Indo-Iranian and Greek worlds -- The Silk Road -- passed through these oases.[153] The existence of this road is confirmed by the geographer Ptolemy. The Hsiung-nu and Chinese struggled with one another to gain control over them. In periods when neither Hsiung-nu nor Chinese intervened in their affairs, these kingdoms of the Tarim quarreled among themselves. At other times, they sided either with the Hsiung-nu or the Chinese. During the Han dynasty, under the able leadership of General Pan Ch'ao and later his son Pan Yung, the Hsiung-nu were ousted from this area and the Chinese not only subdued the Tarim basin but also established a number of Chinese settlements in this area.

Not only was the Silk Road important to China as a means for distribution of Chinese goods, the oases settlements of Khotan, Yarkand and Kashgar were also significant as a source of gold and the highly prized black and white jades which had been revered by the Chinese. Moreover, the Chinese exported into these areas sericulture and weaving. This is most significant as it was the only area outside of China proper where sericulture was allowed. Therefore it may be entertained that along with sericulture, Chinese textile patterns were introduced either directly or indirectly with trade.

By the seventh century, the Chinese Buddhist pilgrim Hsuan-tsang noted that both in Khotan and Kashgar, pile carpets were produced along with felt.[154] Hans Bidder has written about the rugs of this area in his *Carpets from Eastern Turkestan*. However, from Bidder's book one could get the certainly unintended impression that there were only Khotan rugs and that the products of Yarkand and Kashgar were rather "peripheral". Khotan may well be considered as the greater rug-production centre but as to both quality and artistic talent, the reverse may be true.

The designs of Sinkiang rugs are generally categorized into four varieties:

1. One or more medallion design.
2. A variety of the vase and pomegranate design.
3. The 'gul' design.
4. Integrated Chinese, Indian, Persian and Turkish designs.

Distinctly Chinese characteristics are plainly seen both in colour and design. The stylized cloud pattern, floral patterns, 'ju-i' motif, palmettes, and the stylized lotus and peony motifs are common, but in general, rather ancient designs are preserved in Sinkiang rugs.

Similarly, there is a great deal of interchange between all the different areas that either bordered the Tarim area or transacted trade with it. So it comes as no great surprise to encounter the Kayseri 'saph' design on rugs from Sinkiang, or the purely Turkish geometric patterns. Many Sinkiang rugs are so much like Turkoman and Persian rugs that

Plate XLIX
An all-over vase and pomegranate design with multiple ornate border
designs. The border designs are executed in many colours which serve
to effectively frame the simple two coloured central panel. 395x179
cm.

they are often marketed as 'Samarkan' rugs. This inaccuracy probably stems from their having been sold in that area. There is some justification that some Sinkiang rugs should look like Turkoman and Persian rugs with Herati patterns as these rugs were marketed in Samarkand which was closer than China.

Sinkiang rugs are usually characterized by shades of vivid reds brighter than the Turkoman rugs and not to Chinese tastes. Yellows, red-orange and yellow-orange as well as a rusty-brown are the most popular colours used. Greens are rare until the synthetic dyes came into use.

Of these rugs, Kashgar rugs appear most sophisticated in colour and design. Apart from the woolen pile rugs, magnificent silk rugs are also woven. In these silk rugs the highly developed designs are suitably finely woven with undyed cotton foundation, and the pile is usually kept low as the density of the warp and weft would allow.

Yarkand rugs, with their limited ornamentation have stronger and more striking designs with bold and vivid colours. The foundation is of cotton with the use of blue-dyed stout weft threads. There are two predominant designs used, the pomegranate design and the three 'guls' vertically arranged.

Khotan rugs are more versatile in the variety of designs but the foundation is differently structured. The warps are made of cotton while the wefts are mostly of brown-wool. The weave is looser, and the pile is usually longer. The large number of rugs woven in Khotan results in poorly dyed wool for the pile. Harsh, discordant colour combinations are frequently encountered as are the faded tuft ends of the pile.

All Sinkiang rugs possessed a similar characteristic which is their size. With few exceptions they are at least twice as long as they are wide. Most rugs are made in the size of the 'aivan', a room with a large opening in the ceiling covered by a raised roof. Around the walls of the 'aivan' is a raised platform about three feet above the floor similar to the Chinese 'K'ang' which serves most functions of daily life.

The dimensions and shapes are, therefore, conditioned by the size of the 'aivan' galleries. Consequently the sizes of rugs are gnerally from 3½ feet by 7 feet up to 6½ feet by 13 feet. Runners and saddle rugs are also made but they are not very common. Specimens of Sinkiang rugs

Plate L
This nearly square rug features a stylized floral central medallion and an all-over floral diaper ground. The inner border with the running-T and pearls is executed in contrasting colours of ivory and deep blue, while the outer border utilizes closely blended shades with accents of deep blue in the corners. A dimensional effect is achieved in this outer border by shading the running-T pattern. 67x69 cm.

considered the earliest appear mostly to be square or nearly square. The dating of these rugs presents a problem, as we have little information on which to base any realistic conclusions.

NOTES

1. W. G. Thomson "Chinese Carpets" *Apollo* Vol. II (1925) P. 159

2. *Ibid.* p. 160.

3. J. Cawthorne. "Essay on Taste" *Poems* London, 1771.

4. J. K. Mumford. "Chinese Rugs" *The Mentor* March 1, 1916.

5. *Ibid.* p. 12.

6. *The Tiffany Studios Collection of Notable Antique Oriental Rugs* New York, 1906; *The Tiffany Studios Collection of Notable Oriental Rugs* New York, 1907; *Antique Chinese Rugs* New York, 1908.

7. *A Catalogue of Very Important Old Chinese Rugs from the Collections of Frederick Moore and J. K. Mumford* New York, 1916

8. *Ssŭ-ch'ou chih lu: Han-T'ang chih wu* Peking, 1973.

9. A. Bichirin. *Collected References to Peoples Inhabiting Central Asia in Antiquity.* Moscow-Leningrad, 1851.

10. *Hou Han-shu -- Wu-huan chüan.*

11. Y. S. Yü. *Trade and Expansion in Han China* Berkeley, 1967 p. 194-195.

12. M. A. Stein. *Innermost Asia: Detailed Report of an Exploration in Central Asia, Kansu and Eastern Iran* Oxford, 1928.

13. M. A. Stein *Serindia: Detailed Report of Explorations in Central Asia and Western-most China* Oxford, 1921.

14. H. Uhlemann. *Geographie des orienttepichs* Leipzig, 1930.

15. K. Erdmann. *Der Orientalische knüpfteppich* Tubingen, 1955.

16. A. von Le Coq. *Buried Treasures of Chinese Turkestan* London, 1928.

17. *Yên-t'ieh lun* translation by E. Gales. *Discourses on Salt and Iron.* p. 14-15.

18. *Hou Han-shu.* Chüan 81:1a.

19.   *Ibid.* Chüan 81:2a.

20.   *Ibid.* Chüan 81:2a.

21.   *Yên-t'ieh lun* by E. Gale. *Discourses on Salt and Iron*, p. 15-16.

22.   *Chiang piao chüan* quoted in *San-kuo chih -- Wu*, 2:10a.

23.   *Ibid*, 2:24a-b.

24.   *Hou Han-shu -- Shu shun-tien.* Chuan 117.

25.   *Shu-ching -- Yü-shu Shun-tien.*

26.   *Kaogu Xuebao*, 1974, No. 1. p. 87.

27.   *Shih-chi.* Chuan 123; *Ta-huan lüeh-chuan.* Chuan 63.

28.   *Shih-chi.* Chuan 110.

29.   O. Franke. *Geschichte des chinesische Reiches.* Vol. II, p. 182.

30.   *Chou-li -- Ti-kuan pien.*

31.   "Documents historiques sur les Tou-kioue" *Journal Asiatique*, 6^e serie. Vol. IV, p. 236.

32.   *Isaiah* 40:22.

33.   *Psalms* 104:2.

34.   B. Laufer. "The Early History of Felt". *American Anthropologist*, n. s. Vol. 32, No. 1 (1930) p. 15.

35.   *Hsu T'ung-chih.* Chüan 118.

36.   *Nan-chou i-wu-chih* quoted in *Yüan-chien lei-han.*

37.   A general term referred to as the Roman Empire; others refer to it as Syria, Constantinople, and other points of the Roman world. In this case it refers to Bactria.

38.   The silk of wild cocoons is also translated as "the threads of the wild cotton plant".

39.   *Kuang-chi.* Chüan 31.

40.   H. Bidder. *Carpets from Eastern Turkestan* New York, 1964 p. 31.

41.   *Chung-kuo ku-chin ta-tzŭ-tien.*

42.   *T'ien-kung k'ai-wu.* Chüan 3.

43.   *Shih-chi -- Mêng Ch'ang-chün chüan.*

44. *San-kuo chih --Wu.* Chuan 2.

45. E. O. Reischauer. *Ennin's Diary: The Record of Pilgrimage to China in Search of the Law.* New York, 1955 p. 180-182.

46. *Ibid.* p. 221.

47. *Ibid.* p. 228.

48. The term 'seven treasures' or *Shippo* refers to the seven precious things, namely, gold, silver, emerald, coral, agate, crystal and pearl.

49. *Ibid.* p. 233.

50. H. Bidder. *Carpets from Eastern Turkestan* New York, 1964. p. 33.

51. *Ibid.* p. 34.

52. *Ibid.* p. 33-34.

53. *Ibid.* p. 33.

54. *Ibid.* p. 34.

55. H. Levy. *Translations from Po Chü-i's Collected Works* New York, 1970. p. 18.

56. *Ch'üan T'ang-shih.* Chüan 454. In the Sung edition the title reads *Hung-hsiu-t'an* instead of *Hung-hsien-t'an* ("red-thread carpet" is a general term designating carpets made of fine threads of many colours).

57. Ten measure is equal to 117½ feet.

58. A length of ten Chinese feet (fixed at 141 inches for tariff purposes) is called one *Chang* or measure.

59. J. B. Du Halde *Description geographique, historique. . .de l'Empire de la Chine* Paris, 1735. Vol. IV p. 468.

60. A figure of speech meaning very lare or over 100 feet.

61. *Ssu-ch'ou chih-lu: Han-T'ang chih-wu* Peking, 1973.

62. A. Waley. *170 Chinese Poems* New York, 1919. p. 228.

63. *Ibid.* p. 223.

64. *Chiu T'ang-shu.* Chüan 64.

65. *Ibid. T'ai-tsung chüan.*

66. A. Waley. *Ballads and Stories from Tun-huang* New York, 1960. p. 176-178.

67. *Fêng-shih wên-chien-chi.* Chuan 5.

68. A. Waley. *Ballads and Stories from Tun-huang* New York, 1960. p. 191.

69. *Ibid.* p. 195.

70. *Ibid.* p. 197.

71. *Ibid.* p. 198.

72. *Ibid.* p. 74-89.

73. *Ibid.* p. 124-144.

74. *Ibid.* p. 130.

75. *Wenwu* 1959, No. 6. p. 35-37.

76. *Sinica Françiscana.* Vol. I, p. 42.

77. *Ibid.* p. 187.

78. H. Yule. *Book of Ser Marco Polo.* Vol. I. p. 252.

79. *Ta-hsüeh yên-i-pu.* Chüan 98.

80. J. C. Chao. *Ku-wan chih nan* Chuan 21.

81. J. B. Du Halde. *The General History of China* 3rd ed. London, 1741 Vol. IV p. 224.

82. *Ibid.* p. 225.

83. M. Eiland. *Chinese and Exotic Rugs* London, 1979. p. 13.

84. *Jih-hsia.* Chüan 76.

85. *Wan-shou shêng-tien.* Chuan 40-49. P. Pelliot in *T'oung Pao,* 1921, p. 221, note 4, p. 228-229 and 272, discusses other copies of this work, and mentions a painting of this same subject dated 1717, which is found in the Bibliotheque National in Paris.

86. Hsiang-fei has been incorrectly referred to as *Ko-fei,* a name which does not exist. The term *Ko-fei* has also been translated as 'guest concubine'. This is most improbable as the act of entering the palace is called *chin-kung* so that there cannot be any person living in the Inner palace as a "guest".

87. C. B. Malone. *History of the Peking Summer Palaces under the*

Ch'ing. Urbana, 1934.

88. *Lettres edifiantes et curieuses écrites des missions étrangeres.* Paris, 1749. Vol. XXVII p. 1-16.

89. C. Combaz. *Les palais imperiaux de la Chine.* Brussels, 1909 p. 57.

90. *Ibid.* p. 149-150.

91. A. E. van Braam. *An Account,* as quoted by H. Danby. *The Garden of Perfect Brightness.* Chicago, 1950. p. 155.

92. C. B. Malone. *History of the Peking Summer Palaces under the Ch'ing dynasty.* Urbana, 1934. p. 171.

93. *Shina kogei zuron* Tokyo, 1933. Vol. II.

94. A. Hackmack. *Chinese Carpets and Rugs* Tientsin, 1924. p. 6.

95. The Chinese refer to the five directions of the compass as they consider the centre as one of the points.

96. This passage in the *T'ien-kung k'ai-wu* is taken from the *Shih-ching -- Yü-shu shun-tien.*

97. *T'ien-kung k'ai-wu.* Chüan 3.

98. H. Lorentz. *A View of Chinese Rugs from the Seventeenth to the Twentieth Century* London, 1972. p. 28.

99. M. H. d'Ardenne de Tizac. "Tapis Chinois" *Art et Decoration* Vol. XXX 1911. p. 378-380.

100. *Wenwu* 1973 No. 10 p. 37-51.

101. *T'ang Liu-tien.* Chüan 22.

102. *Shih-ching -- Ts'ai-lu.* Translation by J. Legge. *The She King* Vol. IV p. 412.

103. *Ch'i-min yao-shu.* Chüan 8.

104. *T'ien-kung k'ai-wu.* Chüan 3.

105. The term *Su-fang-mu* was first incorrectly read by A. Hackmack in 1924 as *Ssŭ-fang-mu* and has been copied thusly by later writers.

106. *T'ien-kung k'ai-wu.* Chüan 3.

107. *Ch'i-min yao-shu.* Chüan 8.

108. H. Bidder. *Carpets from Eastern Turkestan* New York, 1964 p. 29.

109. *Ibid.* p. 30.

110. *Jung* is commonly translated as velvet and it includes fine woolen textiles with a nap. The top variety of *Jung* is called *T'ien-ngo jung*.

111. *T'ien-kung k'ai-wu.* Chüan 2.

112. *Ch'i-min yao-shu.* Chüan 7.

113. *T'ien-kung k'ai-wu.* Chüan 2.

114. The Chinese term *Yang* is used for both sheep and goats. The differentiation is when a compound is used, i. e. *Shan-yang* for goat and *Mien-yang* for sheep.

115. *Memories concernant l'histoire, des sciences, les arts, les moeurs, les usage,&c des Chine.* Paris, 1776-1791.

116. *Ling* is a thin silk damask. It was so thin that Roman writers called it 'transparent cloth'.

117. *Wenwu.* 1975 No. 6. p. 54-56.

118. *Ibid.* p. 55.

119. *Tz'ŭ-chih t'ung-chien.* Chüan 159.

120. *Ibid.* Chüan 283.

121. C. Wang. *Nung-shu* (Treatise on Agriculture) 1313.

122. M. Eiland. *Chinese and Exotic Rugs* London, 1979. p. 19-20.

123. There are a number of varieties of dragons, however, these fall into three main categories, the five-clawed *lung*, the familiar four-clawed *mang* and an undetermined type of hydra called *tou-niu*.

124. *Shih-ching -- Lin chih Chih.* Translation by J. Legge. *The She King* Vol. IV p. 19.

125. M. Eiland. *Chinese and Exotic Rugs* London, 1979. p. 30; also H. A. Lorentz *A View of Chinese Rugs from the Seventeenth to the Twentieth Century* London, 1972 p. 55 "(Gigantic marble tortoises may be seen as tomb stones bearing inscribed steles) However, 'wamba' the Northern Chinese colloquial name for tortoise are taboo in Chinese applied art." The term that Lorentz

refers to as 'wamba' is really *Wang-pa-tan* also abbreviated as *Wang-pa* which is a common term of vulgar abuse, equivalent to cuckold. This term is understood as "spawn of a turtle", i. e. misbegotten; the Chinese believe that the turtle or tortoise does not beget its own offspring. However, there is no taboo in Chinese applied art as stated by Lorentz. In fact, tortoise patterns called *Kuei-chia-wên* are most frequently used as diaper patterns on many applied art objects. Moreover, candlesticks with a stork or crane alighting on a tortoise are extremely popular. The tortoise is always represented with the god Chen-wu or Pei-ti, the patron diety of the Ming dynasty.

126. H. A. Lorentz. *A View of Chinese Rugs from the Seventeenth to the Twentieth century* London, 1972. p. 53.

127. H. Bidder. *Carpets from Eastern Turkestan* New York, 1964. p. 64.

128. This is a popular couplet used for birthday congratulations although Lorentz, p. 45, cites it as a two line poem with each line having seven characters. This is not a conventional Chinese poetic form. Lorentz translates it as "Good luck -- like the waters of the Eastern Sea that are in endless flow. Long life -- as the pine trees of the Southern hills that never aged grow". The last half of the couplet *Shou pi nan-shan* is derived from the *Nan-shih* or Southern History, with the passage "In ancient times there is a saying, 'From the Emperor on downwards, all men desire to have longevity as old as Mount Nan'." *Fu ju tung-hai* is the complementary phrase to complete the couplet as 'happiness' is the reciprocal of 'longevity'.

129. *Shu-ching -- I-chi.* Translation by J. Legge. *The She King* Vol. III p. 79-80.

130. G. Stauton. *An Authentic Account of an Embassy from the King of Great Britain to the Emperor of China* London, 1797; an abridged edition entitled, *An Historical Account of the Embassy to the Emperor of China, undertaken by Order of the King of Great Britain* London, 1797 (principally from the papers of Lord Macartney) and S. Hedin. *Jehol, City of Emperors.* New York, 1933. p. 213.

131. H. Bidder. *Carpets from Eastern Turkestan* New York, 1964 p. 22.

132. *Ibid.* p. 29.

133. *Ibid.* p. 34.

134. E. Gans-Ruedin *Chinese Carpets* Tokyo, 1982. p. 7.

135. H. A. Lorentz. *A View of Chinese Rugs from the Seventeenth to the Twentieth Century* London, 1972. p. 17.

136. J. B. Du Halde. *Description geographique, historique, et physique . . .l'Empire de la Chine.* Paris, 1735 Vol. IV p. 468. The English edition does not contain Father Gerbillon's account of the visit to Ninghsia.

137. G. Ecke. *Chinese Domestic Furniture* Peking, 1944 p. 32-33.

138. *Yü-hsien-k'u.* Translation by H. Levy *The Dwelling of the Playful Goddesses* p. 23.

139. *Ibid.* p. 45-46.

140. *Seizoku jimon* Vol. II p. 36.

141. *Shih-chi.* Chüan 110.

142. K. Shiratori. "The Queue among the Peoples of North Asia" *Memoirs of the Research Department of the Toyo Bunko* Vol. IV 1929.

143. S. Julien. "Documents sur les T'ou-kiue" *Journal Asiatique* 1864 p. 332.

144. *Shih-chi.* Chüan 110.

145. E. Chavannes *Les memoires historiques de Ssŭ-ma Ts'ien* Paris 1895-1905. Vol. I p. lxx.

146. Strabo *Geography* Vol. XI p. 8.

147. *Ch'ien Han-shu.* Translation by T. Haneda. *Bulletin de la maison franço-japonaise.* Vol. IV No. 1 Tokyo, 1933 p. 7-8.

148. E. Chavannes *Les memoires historiques de Ssŭ-ma Ts'ien* Paris, 1895-1905 Vol. I p. lxxxvii.

149. *Shih-chi.* Chüan 110.

150. T. J. Arne. "Die Funde von Luan-p'ing und Hsüan-hua" *Bulletin of the Museum of Far Eastern Antiquities* Stockholm Vol. V

1933. p. 166.

151. S. Umehara. *Shina kodo seikwa* Tokyo, 1935 Vol. III.

152. W. W. Rockhill. *Diary of a Journey through Mongolia and Tibet* Washington, D. C., 1894. p. 41-42.

153. A. Hermann. "Die Altesten chinesischen karten von Zentral--und Westasien" *Festschrift fur Friedrich Hirth* Berlin, 1920. p. 185.

154. *Hsi-yu chi.* Translation by S. Beal. *Hiuen Tsiang: Si-Yu-ki* London, 1906. p. 306-309.

SELECTED BIBLIOGRAPHY

This bibliography, although not exhaustive, lists most of the works used and consulted by the authors. Individual articles and personal communications have been omitted except in a few cases.

Anderson, A. *Narrative of the British Embassy to China in the Years 1792, 1793, and 1794.* London, 1795.

Bamborough, P. *Antique Oriental Rugs and Carpets.* New York, 1980.

Barnett, R. D. "The world's oldest Persian carpet. . .New discoveries from the Scythian tombs of Pazyryk" *Illustrated London News,* July 11, 1953; January 1, 1955.

Barthod, V. V. *Turkestan down to the Mongol Invasion* London, 1958

Beal, S. *Si-yu-ki, Buddhist Records of the Western World.* London, 1884.

Bell, J. *Travels from St. Petersburg in Russia to Various Parts of Asia.* Edinburgh, 1788.

Bennett, I. *Oriental Rugs.* London, 1981.

Beraty, P. *Chefs-d'oeuvre of the Industrial Arts.* New York, 1981.

Beurdeley, M. *Chinese Furniture.* Tokyo, 1979.

Bichurin, N. Y. *Collected References to Peoples Inhabiting Central Asia in Antiquity.* Moscow-Leningrad, 1851.

Bidder, H. *Carpets from Eastern Turkestan.* New York, 1964.

Birdwood, G. *The Termless Antiquity of Integral Identity of the Oriental Manufacture of Sumptuary Carpets.* [n. p.] 1892.

Bode, W. von *Antique Rugs from the Near East.* New York, 1922.

Bosly, C. *Rugs to Riches: An Insider's Guide to Oriental Rugs.* New York, 1981.

Bouillard, G. *Peking et ses environ.* Pcking, 1922-1924.

Bushell, S. W. *Chinese Art*. London, 1914.

Calatchi, R. de *Le Tapis d'Orient: Histoire esthetique, symbolisme*. [n. p.] 1967.

Cammann, S. *Substance and Symbol in Chinese Toggles*. Philadelphia, 1962.

Chambers, W. *A Dissertation on Oriental Gardening*. London, 1772.

Chao, J. C. *Ku-wan chih-nan -- Handbook of Chinese Antiquity*. Hong Kong, 1970.

Chavannes, E. *Five Happinesses: Symbolism in Chinese Popular Art*. Tokyo, 1973.

Ch'ên, Y. L. *Ko-chih ching-yüan* 100 Chüan [n. p.] 1735.

Chia, S. H. *Ch'i-min yao-shu* 92 Chüan. Shanghai, 1936.

Chicago. Art Institute *An exhibition of Antique Oriental Rugs* 1947.

Chin, W. N. "Chou Fang" *Wên-wu ts'an-k'ao tzŭ-liao* 1957 No. 1.

Ch'in-ting ta-Ch'ing hui tien. 100 Chuan [n. p.] 1771.

Ch'in-ting ta-Ch'ing hui tien ts'ê-li. 180 Chuan. [n. p.] 1818.

Chugoku no Monyo. Tokyo, 1981.

Chung-kuo k'o-hsüeh-yuan k'ao-ku yên-chiu-so. *Hsin Chung-kuo ti k'ao ku shou-huo*. Peking, 1962.

Combaz, G. *Les palais imperiaux de la China*. Brussels, 1909.

Cordier, H. *L'Expedition de Chine de 1860*. Paris, 1906.

Couling, S. *The Encyclopedia Sinica*. Shanghai, 1917.

Danby, H. *The Garden of Perfect Brightness: The History of the Yüan Ming Yüan and of the Emperors who lived there*. Chicago, 1950.

David, P. tr. & ed. *Chinese Connoisseurship: The Ko Ku Yao Lun--The Essential Criteria of Antiquities, a translation*. London, 1971.

De Groot, J. J. M. *The Religious System of China*. Leiden, 1892-1910.

De Visser, M. W. *The Dragon in China and Japan*. Amsterdam, 1913.

Denwood, P. *The Tibetan Carpet*. Warminister, 1974.

Dilley, A. U. *Oriental Rugs and Carpets*. New York, 1931.

Dimand, M. S. *A Guide to an Exhibition of Oriental Rugs and Textiles*. New York, 1935.

Dimand, M. S. and J. Mailey *Oriental Rugs in the Metropolitan Museum of Art.* New York, 1973.

Dore, H. *Recherches sur la Superstition en Chine.* Shanghai, 1914-1929

Dubose, J. P. "Contribution a l'etude des tapisseries d'epoque Sung". *Artibus Asiae* Vol. XI 1/2 (1958).

Du Halde, J. B. *Description geographique, historique. . . de l'empire de la Chine.* Paris, 1735.

Dunn, E. *Rugs in Their Native Land.* New York, 1981.

Eastham, B. C. and W. C. C. Hu *Chinese Art Ivory.* Ann Arbor, 1976.

Ecke, G. *Chinese Domestic Furniture.* Peking, 1944.

Edwards, C. *The Persian Carpet.* London, 1967.

Eiland, M. L. *Chinese and Exotic Rugs.* New York, 1979.

Eiland, M. L. *Oriental Rugs: Comprehensive Guide.* Boston, 1976.

Ellis, C. G. *Chinese Rugs: Introduction to the Catalogue of the Exhibit 'East of Turkestan'.* Washington, D. C., 1967.

Erdmann, K. *Oriental Carpets: An Account of Their History.* London, 1976.

Erdmann, K. *Siebenhundert Jahre Orientteppich: zu seiner Geschichte und Erforschung.* Hereford, 1966.

Êrh-shih wu-shih (Twenty-five dynastic histories) Taipei, 1965.

Ford, R. R. J. *The Oriental Carpet: A History and Guide to Traditional Motifs, Patterns, and Symbols.* New York, 1981.

Goette, J. and W. C. C. Hu. *Jade Lore.* Ann Arbor, 1976.

Gould, G. C. *Monograph on Chinese Rugs.* New York, 1921.

Gregorian, A. T. *Oriental Rugs and the Stories They Tell.* New York, 1978.

Gröte-Hasenbalg, W. *Der Orientteppich, seine Geschichte und seine Kultur.* Berlin, 1922.

Gröte-Hasenbalg, W. *Meisterstucke orientalischer Knupfkunst.* Berlin, 1922.

Gröte-Hasenbalg, W. *Teppiche aus dem Orient; ein kurzer Wegweiser.* Leipzig, 1938.

Gump, R. L. *Chinese Rugs: A Monograph.* San Francisco, 1926.

Hackmack, A. *Chinese Carpets and Rugs.* Tientsin, 1924.

Hamburg. Museum für Kunst und Gewerbe. *Orientalische Teppiche aus der vier Jahrhunderten.* Hamburg, 1950.

Harada, J. *English catalogue of Treasures in the Imperial Repository at Shosoin.* Tokyo, 1932.

Haskins, J. F. *Imperial Carpets from Peking.* Pittsburgh, 1973.

Hawley, W. A. *Oriental Rugs, Antique and Modern.* New York, 1913.

Hedin, S. *Asien: Tusen mil på Okända vägar.* Stockholm, 1903.

Herbert, J. *Affordable Oriental Rugs: The Buyer's Guide to Rugs from China, India, Pakistan and Romania.* New York, 1980.

Herbert, J. *Oriental Rugs: The Illustrated Guide.* New York, 1978.

Herisson, Le C. d' *Journal d'un interprete en Chine.* Paris, 1886.

Ho, S. C. *Kung-pu ch'ang-k'u hsü-chih.* [n. p.] 1615.

Holt, R. B. *Rugs, Oriental and Occidental.* Chicago, 1937.

Hopf, A. *Oriental Carpets and Rugs.* New York, 1961.

Hosain, A. *Les tapis d'Orient.* Paris, 1956.

Housego, J. *Tribal Rugs: An Introduction to the Weaving of the Tribes of Iran.* New York, 1978.

Hsia, Y. K. *Shan-ts'an t'u-shuo.* Shanghai, 1906.

Hubel, R. G. *The Book of Carpets.* New York, 1970.

Indiana. Art Association of Indianapolis. *Catalogue of Oriental Rugs in the Collection of James F. Ballard.* Indianapolis, 1924.

Izmidian, G. *Oriental Rugs and Carpets Today.* New York, 1978.

Jacobsen, C. W. *Oriental Rugs: A Complete Guide.* Rutland, 1962. . . .

Jacoby, H. *How to Know Oriental Carpets and Rugs.* London, 1962.

Jerrehian, A. *Oriental Rug Primer.* New York, 1980.

Jettmar, K. *Art of the Steppes.* New York, 1967.

Kao, C. *Shih-wu chi-yüan* 10 Chuan. Ming ed. reprint Taipei, 1969.

Kendrick, A. F. and C. E. C. Tattersall *Handwoven Carpets: Oriental and European.* London, 1922.

Kendrick, A. F. and C. E. C. Tattersall *Fine Carpets in the Victoria and Albert Museum.* London, 1924.

Kosugi, I. *Chugoku monyoshi no kenkyu.* Tokyo, 1959.

Kuløy, H. K. *Tibetan Rugs.* Bangkok, 1982.

Lao, K. "Chien-tu-chung so-chien ti pu-po" (Textiles fabrics as seen in the [Han] Wooden slat lettres) *Hsüeh-shu chi-k'an* Vol. 1 No. 4 1953.

Larson, K. *Rugs and Carpets of the Orient.* New York, 1979.

Le Coq, A. von *Buried Treasures of Chinese Turkestan.* London, 1928.

Lee, Y. K. *Art Rugs from Silk Route and Great Wall Areas.* Tokyo, 1980.

Leitch, G. B. *Chinese Rugs.* New York, 1928.

Lettres edifiantes et curieuses ecrites des missions estrangeres. Paris, 1749.

Lewis, G. G. *The Practical Book of Oriental Rugs.* Philadelphia, 1911.

Li, S. C. *Pên-ts'ao kang-mu* 1596 edition re-issued. Shanghai, 1930.

Liebetrau, P. *Oriental Rugs in Color.* New York, 1963.

Lorentz, H. A. *A View of Chinese Rugs from the Seventeenth to the Twentieth Century.* London, 1972.

Malone, C. B. *History of the Peking Summer Palaces Under the Ch'ing Dynasty.* Urbana, 1934.

Martin, R. F. *A History of Oriental Carpets before 1800.* Vienna, 1908

Mathews, J. M. *The Textile Fibers: Their Physical, Microscopical, and Chemical Properties.* New York, 1916.

Memoires concernant l'histoire, les sciences, les arts, les moeurs, les usages, &c des Chine. Paris, 1776-1791.

Messinesi, A. "Rug weaving in Tibet", *Quarterly Journal of the Guilds of Weavers, Spinners and Dyers,* Jun. - Sep., 1956.

Ming hui-tien. 180 Chüan. [n.p.] 1509.

Mumford, J. K. *Oriental Rugs.* New York, 1900.

Needham, J. *Science and Civilization in China.* Oxford, 1955-

Neff, I and C. Maggs. *Dictionary of Oriental Rugs: with a Monograph on Identification by Weavers.* London, 1977.

Nozaki, S. *Kisho zuan kaitei.* Tientsin, 1928.

Reed, S. *Oriental Rugs and Carpets.* London, 1967.

Reischauer, E. O. *Ennin's Diary: A Record of Pilgrimage to China in Search of the Law.* New York, 1955.

Ripley, M. C. *Antique Chinese Rugs.* New York, 1927.

Ripley, M. C. *The Oriental Rug Book.* New York, 1904.

Rippon, B. *Antique Chinese Carpets: Masterpieces from the Te-chun Wang Collection.* Basel, 1978.

Ropers, H. *Mörgenlandische teppiche.* Munich, 1978.

Rorex R. and W. Fong. *Eighteen Songs of a Nomad Flute, the Story of Lady Wên-chi a fourteenth century handscroll in the Metropolitan Museum of Art.* New York, 1974.

Rostovtzeff, M. *The Animal Style in South Russia and China.* Leipzig, 1929.

Rudenko, S. I. *Frozen Tombs of Siberia the Pazyryk Burials of Iron Age Horseman.* Translated by M. W. Thompson. Berkeley, 1970

Rylander, G. W. *Oriental Rug Lexion.* Pittsburgh, 1938.

St. Louis. City Art Museum. *The Ballard Collection of Oriental Rugs in the City Art Museum of St. Louis.* St. Louis, 1935.

St. Louis. City Art Museum. *Inaugural exhibition of a Collection of Oriental Rugs presented to the Museum by James F. Ballard.* St. Louis, 1929.

Sarre, F. "Ein chinesischer Knupfteppich der Ming Zeit" *Ostasiatische Zeitschrift* n. s. Vol. X 1935.

Schurmann, U. *Central-Asian Rugs.* New York, 1969.

Schurmann, U. *Oriental Carpets.* New York, 1979.

Seizoku jimon. Kyoto, 1800.

Setterwall, A. *The Chinese Pavilion at Drottningholm.* Malmo, 1974.

Shen, T. N. *I-lin hui-k'ao.* 40 Chüan [n.p., n.d.]

Shih, S. H. *Ts'ung Ch'i-min yao-shu k'an Chung-kuo ku-tai ti nung-yeh k'o-hsüeh chih shih.* Peking, 1957.

Siren, O. *Chinese Painting.* London, 1956.

Siren, O. *The Imperial Palaces of Peking.* Paris, 1926.

Staunton, G. *An Authentic Account of an Embassy from the King of Great Britain to the Emperor of China.* London, 1797.

Stein, M. A. *Ancient Khotan.* Oxford, 1907.

Stein, M. A. *Innermost Asia: Detailed Report of Exploration in Central Asia, Kansu and Eastern Iran.* Oxford, 1928.

Stein, M. A. *On Ancient Central Asian Tracks.* New York, 1964.

Stein, M. A. *Serindia:Detailed Report of Explorations in Central Asia and Western-most China.* Oxford, 1921.

Ssu-ch'ou chih lu: Han-T'ang chih wu. Peking, 1972.

Sung, Y. H. *T'ien-kung k'ai-wu.* 1637 ed. re-issued. Shanghai, 1929.

Swallow, R. W. and F. Bleicher *Ancient Chinese Bronze Mirrors.* Ann Arbor, 1977.

Sylwan, V. " Investigation of silk from Edsen Gol and Lop Nor" *The Sino-Swedish Expedition Publication* 32 Vol. VII (6) 1949.

Ta-Ch'ing hui tien. 100 Chüan. Shanghai, 1904.

Ta-Ch'ing lu-li. 47 Chüan. [n.p.] 1829.

T'ang liu tien. 30 Chüan. reprint. Taipei, 1970.

Tapis anciens de la Chine. Paris, 1932.

Tiffany Studios, ed. *Antique Chinese Rugs.* New York, 1908.

Toledo. Museum of Art. *A loan exhibition of Oriental Rugs.* Toledo, 1937.

Treasures of the Shosoin. Tokyo, 1965.

T'u-shu chi ch'êng. 5000 Chüan. Peking, 1726.

Tung, S. C. *Kuang Po-wu chih.* 50 Chüan. [n.p.] 1761.

Uhlemann, H. *Geographie des orientteppichs.* Leipzig, 1930.

Umehara, S. *Shina kodo seikwa.* Tokyo, 1935.

Umehara, S. *Studies of Noin-Ula Finds in North Mongolia.* Tokyo, 1960.

Walker, D. S. *Oriental Rugs of the Hajji Babas.* New York, 1982.

Wang, C. *San-ts'ai t'u-hui*. 106 Chüan. 1609 ed. reprint Taipei, 1969.

Weber, G. W. *The Ornaments of Late Chou Bronzes: A Method of Analysis*. New York, 1973.

Wei, S. *I shih chi-shih* 22 Chüan. [n. p.] 1881.

Werner, E. T. C. *Myths and Legends of China*. London, 1922.

Williams, C. A. S. *Outlines of Chinese Symbolism and Art Motives*. Peiping, 1932.

Yu, M. T. *Jih hsia chiu wên k'ao*. 160 Chüan. [n. p.] 1774.

Zipper, K. *Lexikon des Orientteppichs*. Munich, 1981.

Zipser, J. *Textile Raw Materials and their Conversion into Yarns*. London, 1901.